Praise for *Pioneering the Superstore*

Smitty's selling skills first impacted me when I worked for his main competitor, Fry's Supermarkets, in the late '70s. He was quickly becoming the market leader in Phoenix; we watched him closely and applied lessons he had taught us with success. We always admired the selling skills Clyde taught his associates. Clyde's book shares many of these lessons; he was a trendsetter marketer.

— David Dillon
chairman of the board and CEO of Kroger, the largest supermarket chain in America

Clyde Smith's story is a true, uniquely American story. I have had the pleasure of knowing him for many years, and you will see through this wonderful book why he is so highly regarded. He is a man of strong principles and faith.

— "The Admiral" David Robinson
former San Antonio Spurs basketball star, inducted into the NBA Hall of Fame in 2009

Clyde Smith is a modern day success story. In a day when we need heroes, here is one who qualifies. Mr. Smith has not just been a success in business but in his spiritual life as well; only eternity will reveal how many his life has impacted. This is an encouraging story and one worth sharing.

— Gary Frazier, PhD
speaker, author, founder of Discovery Ministries, Inc.

This is a wonderfully revealing autobiography of a member of the "Greatest Generation" who survived the Depression working in the coal mines of Iowa, fought in World War II, and had a career that spanned over forty years in the supermarket industry. Anyone aspiring to start out in business today would be well served by reading this book and taking its teachings to heart.

— Gary Sojka, PhD
president emeritus Bucknell University, current faculty member, author, cofounder of the Potomac Advocates

I have known Smitty now for more than fifty years, and what a blessing it has been. The example he has set for me, and many others, has enabled us to see our dreams come true, have a successful business career, and most importantly, have the opportunity to learn from the best. If you are looking for an example of a true American — and I mean the "real deal," someone who is living the dream — then this success story of a World War II veteran is the book for you.

— Dave Trottier
retired president and general manager,
Smitty's Supermarkets, Springfield, Missouri eventual owner,
current co-owner of Summer Fresh Supermarkets

Clyde Smith has lived the American dream. He turned native intelligence, people skills, and hard work into an amazing success story. I was privileged to be one of those who shared Christ with Clyde and watched as he turned his heart and life over to the Lord. In this life journey story, the reader can join the others who say, "My life is better because Clyde Smith's story has touched me."

— Richard Jackson
retired senior pastor North Phoenix Baptist Church, founder of
The Jackson Center, Howard Payne University, Brownwood, Texas, and author

Anyone who has ever started a business will identify with the challenges Clyde Smith confronted and overcame during his career spanning fifty years, three states, and two entirely different industries. I was inspired by Smitty's determination, vision, innovations, and entrepreneurial spirit in his memoir. In this incredible story, he shares important life lessons for all of us.

— Dick Evans
chairman and CEO, Frost Bank

Clyde Smith's book is the wonderful, true-life "rags to riches" story showing how a busboy at a small restaurant became owner of a large and very successful grocery store chain. Clyde Smith exemplifies the American spirit of free enterprise and self-determination, and his story will inspire and motivate readers to strive for success in any endeavor, to work hard, and to trust in God for the rewards, which will surely come. I encourage everyone to read Clyde Smith's life story.

— Judge Roy Moore
graduate US Military Academy, West Point, veteran the US Army, Judge of the
Sixteenth Judicial Circuit of Alabama, Former Chief Justice of the Alabama Supreme
Court, President of the Foundation for Moral Law in Alabama, author, and speaker

Pioneering the SUPERSTORE

Pioneering the
SUPERSTORE

A RETAIL REVOLUTION

The Story of
Clyde "Smitty" Smith

John Trice and Helen Hosier

Brown Books Publishing Group
Dallas, Texas

Pioneering the Superstore:
A Retail Revolution

© 2010 Clyde "Smitty" Smith

Manufactured in the United States of America.

Unless otherwise identified, Scripture quotations are from the New King
James Version of the Bible. Copyright c 1982 by Thomas Nelson, Inc.
Used by permission. All rights reserved.

Scripture quotations identified NIV are from the Holy Bible,
New International Version R NIV R Copyright c 1973, 1978, 1984 by
International Bible Society. Used by permission of Zondervan Publishing
House. All rights reserved.

For information please contact:
Brown Books Publishing Group
16200 North Dallas Parkway, Suite 170
Dallas, Texas 75248
www.brownbooks.com
972-381-0009

A New Era in Publishing™

ISBN-13: 978-1-934812-76-1
ISBN-10: 1-934812-76-5

LCCN: 2010931815
1 2 3 4 5 6 7 8 9 10

Author contact information:
www.SmittysStory.com

To my three daughters, Sandy, Linda and Karen;
my grandchildren and their children; my wife, Peggy; and my
three stepchildren, Debbie, Cindy, and Chuck.

I pray my true life story will remain a legacy and a faithful
guideline for each of you and all who read it.

This book will forever be dedicated
to my Lord and Savior Jesus Christ.

Contents

Preface

My given name is Clyde B. Smith, but to most of my friends, former associates, and many in the public, I am simply known as "Smitty." In this book, I want to take you on an exciting retail trip to success.

For the greater part of the 1970s, my supermarket chain, Smitty's, was the largest private employer in the state of Arizona with over 6,000 employees. Despite stiff competition from national concerns such as Kroger, Safeway, Lucky Stores, and local chains, our stores maintained an astounding 35 percent market share of the greater Phoenix Metropolitan Statistical Area (PMSA). This was almost double that of our closest competitor! Not bad for a supermarket chain that was less than twenty years old at the time.

By all life's circumstances, none of my success in the supermarket business should have ever happened. I was raised during the Great Depression in a family that made the term "dirt poor" sound luxurious. I dropped out of high school in my sophomore year to help support my family by working in an Iowa coal mine. When I got my fill of that backbreaking, dangerous, and mind-numbing work, I left home at seventeen years old and hitchhiked a hundred miles to Ames, Iowa, in search of a better way of life. The year was 1936, and after bouncing around at a few jobs in Ames, I talked my way into a job in a small grocery store and apprenticed myself to the owner, a man named Keith Rushing.

I am one of the few fortunate individuals who can identify that pivotal moment when your life changes forever. For me, it was the first time I stepped onto the sales floor at Keith Rushing's grocery store. There was something about the thrill of the money changing hands, the way the merchandise was placed neatly on the shelves, and the way one hustled to please the customers that captivated me, giving me a glimpse of what my future could be. A few years later, there was no doubt that this future would be somehow tied to the retail business.

By God's grace, I celebrated my ninety-first birthday on January 12, 2010. This generous expanse of time has given me a unique perspective on the business world. In my lifetime, I have witnessed the retail world change from using hand-cranked cash registers, to integrated point of sales systems tied to super computers capable of moving huge volumes of data across the globe in just a few moments. It has been my privilege to watch American business navigate such economic diversities as the Great Depression, the boom of the post-World War II years, the rise of corporate America in the 1950s, the hyperinflation years of the 1970s, and the globalization of the world economy.

As a retailer, I have been on the frontlines as American retail has evolved from a bunch of small town merchants to the sophisticated corporate cultures we see in today's retail sectors. In 1962, I helped pioneer the "superstore" concept by building a 132,000-square-foot store in Scottsdale, Arizona. This unique store combined a full-line grocery store with a full-line department store. While this is mundane by today's retail standards, this concept was so different in 1962 that we had people come to see this store from all over America. I am proud to say that our store became the prototype for later "superstore concepts" rolled out by the likes of K-mart, Walmart, and Target.

What is so amazing to me is that I was able to accomplish all of this without an MBA, college degree, or even a high school diploma. While I would never advocate this to today's young Americans, it does remind us that there is a side of business that must be learned in practice, as well as in the classroom. Of course, timing and hard work were a big part of my success, but so was a set of disciplines I developed early in my business career that became the college degree that I never earned. I often joked that the "tuition was expensive" as I tested and refined what was to become the fundamentals of our business model at Smitty's Supermarkets.

In the seventy years I have been a businessman, American business has evolved into a very sophisticated medium. Today we live in a business world that runs on the fuel of leverage, free cash flow, hedging, price arbitrage, and the monetization of just about anything. To succeed in business today, you must have not only a rudimentary understanding of these, but a host of other sophisticated techniques such as LIFO, FIFO, and accelerated depreciation, along with a comprehension of financial statements that are as thick as a phonebook. Toss in a complicated tax structure that changes every few years, and American business is much more complicated than when I was a clerk in Keith Rushing's grocery store in 1936. This "business speak" often confuses the small businessperson.

If you boil down all these fancy techniques to their very basics, you will find that business is still nothing more than the transfer of an asset — physical or intellectual — to another at an agreed upon price. If that price is more than the cost associated with the asset, you make a profit. If not, it costs you money. Everything else is just window dressing.

I worry that we have made the state of business today much more complicated than it really needs to be. This often becomes a barrier to many hardworking Americans who would like to be part of the American business community and know the success of owning their own business. You will see from my story that anyone can be a success today in business if you are willing to work hard enough, understand the need of experience, and embrace a few basic concepts.

What I would like to share with you is a code of business fundamentals that I discovered while building our business from one small store in a tiny Iowa town, to a large corporate chain of thriving retail stores ringing up the equivalent of over $2 billion worth of sales annually in today's dollars. These simple fundamentals worked for us, and I believe that they are still vital to succeeding in business today. Sure, it is more glamorous to talk about your business in terms of EBITDA (earnings before interest, taxes, and debt amortization) when trying to impress your banker. But unless you learn the language of these simple principals I am about to share with you, I doubt you will see enough earnings to sustain your business long term. Just like EBITDA, you can only make a duck look like a goose for so long. At some point, your business has to embrace these basics if it is going to succeed. Remember, all the rest is just window dressing.

In this book, I endeavor to share with you what I've learned on my journey to retail success. I've had a wonderful journey and experienced many things, but there was something more that was needed. The Bible, the Word of God, is the key that opens a map to God's direction for our lives. I discovered that, but what happened to me after meeting my precious wife Peggy is of most importance. She introduced me to the reality of Jesus, whose life story is in the Bible. My life took on new meaning when I asked Him to be my companion through the remaining days of my time here on planet Earth. Now my story is in line with what God wanted it to be all along. That can be everyone's experience. We all need Jesus to be our travel partner on this journey through life. My prayer as I let my story be told is that it will motivate and help you in many ways.

Acknowledgments

I am thankful for everyone who prompted me to write this book and supported me during the process: countless friends and family that space does not permit me to acknowledge. I am grateful to each of you.

My friend John Trice retrieved the information from the archives of my memory and placed it on paper thus letting me know this book was possible. His good work paved the way for Helen Hosier to help write and edit the book. I am indebted to them both.

A special thanks to Milli Brown and her entire talented and professional staff for the final editing and publishing of my book.

Smitty's Basics for Business

"Success is a matter of hard work, daring to be different, and having an unwavering trust in God."

—Clyde B. Smith

There are five people basics involved in acquiring, attracting, working with, and keeping the necessary people to staff a business. These are time-tested, critically important things to learn: (1) provide good leadership, (2) share the wealth, (3) keep the lines of communication open, (4) train, train, and train again, and (5) be selective as you hire.

Then there are three customer basics: (1) focus on the customer, (2) dare to be different, and (3) know what your competition is doing and then do it better.

Moreover, the owner or manager of a business must have four visionary basics: (1) set goals and stay focused, (2) stay ethically pure, (3) make your business a market leader, and (4) recognize that relationships are everything.

These business basics held me in good stead all the years I was in business. They are not complicated; they are good, common sense principles that any ambitious man or woman can take to heart and apply to his or her efforts. These things are discussed in more detail in this and succeeding chapters.

Success is a matter of hard work, daring to be different, and having an unwavering trust in God.

Smitty's People Basics

Provide Good Leadership — I have always believed that it is critical for an owner or manager of a business to set the pace in the workplace. The success of your business is often tied directly to the amount of work you are willing to do. If you want the same commitment from your staff, they must see you in the trenches with them from time to time. For a small business, this is often the difference between a motivated staff and one just waiting to clock out. Your team needs you to set the pace for them. They need you to be a leader!

There was no greater pleasure for me than to be on the frontlines with our staff. I found that my enthusiasm to serve the customer really motivated them. If there was some physical work to be done, I likewise wanted to get shoulder to shoulder and tackle the job. I was the first one at work in the morning and the last one to leave at night. I am confident that this made a difference in the commitment the staff made to our company.

Some people go into business naively thinking that they will get others to do most of the work. After all, they are the boss and should have the privilege of the better hours, days off, and time with their family. Well, nothing could be further from the truth. Most successful business people I know take leadership seriously and want to set the pace for their staff; they are often the hardest worker on the team.

Share the Wealth — If there is one thing that separated my business from the competition, it was that I was willing to share the success of my business with our key people. Early in my business career, I found that if I set sales goals for department managers and they succeeded, paying cash for their extra hard work was a great way to pat them on the back for a job well done. As our company grew larger, I began to sell company stock at book value to my key people as a way to reward them.

I saw that both the cash bonus and stock programs helped keep our team motivated and soon "my" store became "our" store. It was amazing how much more we accomplished when this way of thinking took over. When my competitors were buying themselves a new Cadillac for a good year, I decided to keep driving the same old car, and share the year's monetary success with the team that helped make the year successful. I started this process when I had one small store and it was a key component to our future spectacular growth. No business is too small or too large not to share the wealth with the staff for their special efforts.

From my years in business, I know that most small business people instinctively want to keep all the profits to themselves. Most justify this by rationalizing that they took the risk, capitalized the business, and had the idea. And in the end, they are the bosses.

While keeping the profits to yourself may seem like a good idea, I can tell you without a doubt that if you really want to attract good people who will help your company grow, you must devise a program to let them share in the upside of your business. Doing so will increase their commitment to success and reduce negative feelings, which often leads to shrinkage or theft. Being honest and fair with your team when spreading the profits around is the only way you can sustain long-term growth and keep your best people.

Keep Lines of Communication Open — Promoting good honest communication in your business is the key to a success-ful organization. This starts with communicating the core values of the business to make sure that every staff member understands the foundation of your business philosophies. It does not matter if you have two employees or two thousand; if they do not understand the principals on which your business stands, they cannot communicate these to the public.

Many small business people foolishly keep their staff in the dark. This often creates an artificial environment where the staff operates with just half the picture. If some bit of information surfaces—both good and bad—the staff then loses trust in management for not communicating honestly. The old saying that "knowledge is power" becomes counterproductive when your staff is not fully informed.

Communication in your business should be dynamic. It should be ongoing and be both informal and formal. I have always been a big fan of both. I found that scheduling regular times for staff communication became important for us in getting the word out on corporate direction, staff performance, customer service, and product information. Just as effective, I always liked to pull team members aside and compliment them on a job well done or advise on a need for improvement. In both cases, honesty and professionalism in delivery is important as you convey your thoughts.

A big part of communication is listening to what your people are saying. No business owner can know every detail on a daily basis. You must increase your listening skills because there is real strategic value in what your team can tell you if you will just take the time to listen.

For this to work, I have found that your company must embrace the free flow of communication and it should flow in both directions. The staff should feel equally comfortable in talking to management as management should feel in talking to the staff. I was a big believer that all communication should be in a safe environment where everyone has a say—free of petty backlashes. In the end, it is up to you as the owner to act on what you hear from your people, but I knew that I made better decisions when I listened to our team.

Train, Train, and Train Again! — Unfortunately, most small business people view training as an expense. To me, it is an investment in your business and your team. At Smitty's, we developed a training regimen that started from the first day a new person was on the job. Over the period of a team member's time with us, we added to this training extensively. It was hard for me to see future growth if our people did not continue to improve their skills over time. I always felt that it was our duty to them to provide consistent training, which added value to the skill sets of our team and to our stores.

I learned early in my business career that a well-trained staff is the key to producing good growth. You cannot grow if your staff is constantly struggling with how to execute their jobs or put into action the procedures and policies of your company. Inconsistent performance conveys the wrong message to the customer, sending them down the road to your competitor.

If you plan on growing to multiple locations, a well-trained staff is the way you can get there. Training is critical to im-printing your additional locations with the same consistency and texture as the original store. In a single location, the owner usually sets and reinforces the tone of the business by the sheer fact that he or she is there most of the time. When it comes to multiple locations, the way you will be able to create the same consistent feel is from a well-constructed program that trains your team on an ongoing basis. Remember, when in doubt train, and then train again!

Be Selective as You Hire — Finding and retaining the right people has always been a challenge for small business. When I began my career, I instinctively knew the type of people that I wanted representing my business. I looked for people who were full of desire and ambition—people who wanted to make something of their life and have a career, preferably people with a good outgoing personality. I used this profile for both full- and part-time staff. I would rather work longer hours myself than have the wrong person dealing with the public on our behalf.

In today's business climate, you must be fair and ethical in hiring and firing of a staff member. I was a tough boss, but I tried to be equitable in my hiring by taking the time to look inside the person who was standing in front of me. Spending so many years in the retail business, I can tell you that I have found numerous "diamonds in the rough" by giving every person I interviewed a fair shot at joining our team. I likewise tried to be fair and just when it came to letting a person go. We would often give them ways to earn their way back into good standing by retraining or moving them to another department. However, if they did not show improvement, I quickly moved them out.

What most small business people struggle with is when to let staff go if they turn out to be poor hires. There were times I would hire a person thinking they were one way and they ended up disappointing me. Sometimes this would be after we had invested dollars and time in their training. If we could not rectify the problem within a reasonable period of time with support on our end, I felt obligated to the other staff members to let them go. Yes, this was a painful decision, and it often was inconvenient to our staff, but keeping the wrong person around too long is counterproductive. I had to remind myself that it was a business decision, not a personal one.

Finding the right people to join your company is a discipline that both large and small businesses grapple with every day. It is a critical task that must be given careful thought and not rushed. Remember, when you are out of the customer's sight, the person you hired becomes the company in the eyes of the customer. Make sure your customers see the right profile.

Smitty's Customer Basics

Focus on the Customer — At Smitty's Supermarkets, we totally focused on the customer. Everything we did, every policy we made, every store we designed, and every item we stocked in our stores was done with careful thought about how it impacted the customer. It was my feeling that if we really focused on the customer, and understood the all-powerful role they played in our success, we were always going to be a leader in our business.

My personal mission was to imprint this thought through-out every level of our company. It did not matter to me if you worked the night shift stocking shelves and had no customer contact; I still wanted you to know that with each item displayed, you were affecting the customer. Focusing on the customer was a core value of our company, and we wanted all of our team members to know this concept — even in their sleep.

One of the best things a businessperson can do is to walk into your business and see it through the eyes of your customers. Take a hard look at your physical facility and the people that staff it. If you offer some type of technology for your customers to use, give it a try. Put yourself through the steps they would go through to do business with you. What are the frustration levels or roadblocks they meet? The same goes for your policies and procedures. Are they customer focused or just there to baffle them?

With big box retailers spread across this country, every small business person should make focusing on the customer a number one priority for their business. Most big box retailers have poor staffing, and it is hard to get assistance when you need or want it. This often frustrates the public, leaving them looking for a better way to meet their needs. This is the place I think small business can still make inroads and compete against the price advantage the typical big box retailer offers.

Like listening to your employees, it is very important to listen to your customers. When I was in the supermarket business, I spent extended periods of time on the sales floor chatting with customers and getting to know what they were thinking about our stores. When we got to be a large chain, I insisted that our key people execute this important task. We would then debrief these encounters in a weekly meeting.

You must know what your customers are thinking about your business. You also must know when their demands change if you are going to continue to meet their needs. Unlike when I was building my business, today's businessperson has a world of technology at their disposal to develop questionnaires, mailing lists, and social networking media to understand what their customers are thinking. Of course, you could still do this the old-fashioned way by standing in the middle of the store and simply asking them, as I did. Please keep this very important point in mind: Every business today exists by the permission of the customer, without exception!

Dare to Be Different — If you are going to succeed in today's highly competitive and crowded marketplace, you have to "dare to be different." As I was building my company, I constantly searched for ways to distinguish our business from the pack. When the traditional supermarket was 30,000 square feet in 1961, I doubled the size of ours as a competitive edge. As a young retailer in rural Iowa, for a special promotion I leaned out of a low-flying Piper Cub airplane and tossed out paper plates to the small towns and farms. They looked like flying saucers. These were emblazoned with coupons offering gifts of various items when they were redeemed at our market.

While not every concept we had or promotion we tried was successful, most of the time we succeeded in being different from our competitors. This became a trademark of our company, and our customers loved it. In fact, this is one of the reasons we built such a tremendous market share and amazing customer loyalty. I felt it was our obligation to them to dare to be different.

At Smitty's, we encouraged taking risks in our pursuit of daring to be different. This propelled us to new heights. In 1962, when I combined a full-service supermarket with a full-service department store, it was the ultimate way for our company to be different from the competition. As you will see as you read my story, this provided us with the biggest challenge our company ever faced; we managed to make it work through sheer determination and hard work. In the end, it was the best thing we ever did!

If there is one thing that I would emphasize to small business people today, it is that you should devote as much energy as you can to devise ways to make your business different from the competition. Periodically, business owners must take a hard look at how their business works and think about ways to augment what is currently being done by broadening your base. Today, we call this "out of the box" thinking; it is really taking the pieces of your business apart from time to time and reassembling them in a manner that keeps what is working but adds new dimensions to push growth and capture the imagination of the consumer. I learned early in my business career that you cannot stay the same in the eyes of the public forever. If you don't please and excite them, they will go down the street to shop.

Know What Your Competition Is Doing. Then Do It Better! — Even when our company controlled over 35 percent of the supermarket business in the greater Phoenix Metropolitan Statistical Area (MSA), I still watched our competitors vigilantly. This habit started when I was building our business in Iowa and continued throughout my entire business career. I became so determined to know what my competitors were up to that if I heard of something new or unusual, I would drive or fly halfway around the country just to witness it firsthand. It is vital to a business owner's success to know what competitors are doing. To me, not knowing says that a business owner thinks that the way he is conducting business cannot be improved upon. I was never too proud to acknowledge that one of my competitors had a great idea. Likewise, if it was good enough, I was not too proud to borrow it, putting our own unique twist on the concept.

Going to trade shows, shopping different suppliers, surveying your customer base, and shopping your competition is critical to ongoing success. As a business owner, it is up to you to know as much about your competitors as possible. This includes their market strategy, pricing, current developments, and their successes and failures. Competition is dynamic and ever-changing. You have to stay in the game every day to know your competition. If you do not, you are missing one of the most important ways to build market share—exploiting their weaknesses and defending against their strengths.

Smitty's Visionary Basics

Set Goals. Stay Focused — When my brother Swede and I bought a small butcher shop in Roland, Iowa, in 1946, I am sure that the main goal we had was to not lose our money. We were your typical small business guys that just got in and did it, all the while trying our best to serve our customers.

I soon learned that setting goals was very important to growing our business beyond that first store. I began with writing down some things I wanted to get accomplished and then monitored them. These evolved into a series of both short- and long-term time goals that became part of my business practices throughout my entire career.

To me, having goals for a business is a road map to long-term sustainability. Goals are the strategic objectives that one works for daily, knowing that if they are accomplished, they will lead to greater success and prosperity. Having goals is mutually beneficial for your staff, your stakeholders, and your creditors due to the direction and vision that they provide. Goals for your business say that you care enough about your business to know where you are heading and that you have a plan to get there.

No business is too small or too large not to have a set of goals. Goals should be written down and reviewed on a regular basis. They should also be dynamic, changing as the marketplace and the vision of the business changes. When a goal is achieved, it should be ceremoniously marked off your list with genuine gusto.

Goals work well when they are a collaborative effort with key staff members. While the business owner might design the framework of a series of goals, these goals are best accomplished when there is a joint effort in their creation. There is an old saying, "I support what I create," which is true when building consensus on company goals by all parties.

Over my lengthy business career, I observed that most businesses do a passable job on setting goals, but fall short on staying focused. There are so many distractions today in the workplace that the average small business owner often strays off the path that the goals lay out. To me, this is like only running half of a race. Without staying focused, your goals become nothing more than some lofty thoughts on paper.

It is up to the small business owner, or management team, to keep the company focused daily on their goals. This often requires removing the noise that clutters the business day and developing a ritual for methodically asking the question, "Are we staying focused?" Through answering this question, management can determine if the company is on track and aligned with both long- and short-term goals.

Stay Ethically Pure — If there was ever a wakeup call to American business, it has been the disappointing news concerning the widespread breach of business ethics that we have witnessed over the past few years. In 2008 alone, we saw the likes of Bernie Madoff defraud hardworking Americans out of billions of dollars, well-known public corporations indicted for hiring illegal workers, and billionaire Sir Allen Stanford accused of a Ponzi scheme similar to Bernie Madoff's. While these are the most notable, there have been hundreds of other instances where American business has been disgraced.

If you are a business owner, and you take away one thing from my book, I want you to take away the huge significance of practicing good ethics daily in your business. Practicing good ethics strengthens your company and builds confidence in your customers, trust in your creditors, and loyalty from your staff. Practicing good ethics sets a tone in your business that allows everyone associated with you to keep their heads held high. To me, good ethics should be the bedrock from which all the goals and core values of your business emanate.

As I was building my company, I saw plenty of opportunities to stray off the ethical path. There were times where I could have taken advantage of my staff, our customers, and our suppliers. Maybe it was because I had been raised on an Iowa farm during the Great Depression, but I just could not see the long-term success in doing so. Business is tough enough and keeps you up at night as is, without the added burden of being unethical. Yes, business is a game about winning and losing, but given my seven decades in the business community, I can tell you with absolute certainty that cheaters seldom win, particularly in the end.

The Six Nevers

To make ethics in your business a little simpler, I have developed the Six Nevers:

1. Never cheat your stakeholders: partners, stockholders, or bankers.
2. Never cheat or take advantage of your customers.
3. Never cheat or abuse your suppliers.
4. Never cheat on your taxes.
5. Never cheat or take advantage of your employees.
6. Never forget the Golden Rule: treat others in business how you would like to be treated.

It is my fondest hope that you and all American businesses will incorporate my Six Nevers into your daily business practices. I am convinced that if you do so, you will not only ring up more sales but also experience a personal growth and satisfaction that will allow you to be a better leader to your company, your family, and your country.

Make Your Business a Market Leader — We like to associate with winners. I have always felt that we view businesses in the same context. There is something exciting about doing business with a company that is growing, being successful, and setting the pace for an industry. We Americans have always wanted to be associated with the best and most contemporary goods or services in the marketplace.

Being a leader in the marketplace is not for the faint of heart. It is a goal that requires a tremendous amount of work and study on behalf of a business owner. To be a leader today, you must stay current on not only the specifics of your industry but also of the business world as well. This takes lots of energy and dedication along with a big dose of creativity.

Even when our business was small, I talked to my suppliers about what was new in their product pipeline. My job was to get them to think of me first when a product was ready to break. They knew that they could count on us to dedicate lots of energy and display space if they allowed us to introduce the product. In my early business years, I could not outspend my competitors, but I could put tons of energy into a product launch and ultimately be the first to expose the consumer to it.

If your business is going to experience sustained success, you must never quit trying to be a leader in the market. This was our biggest priority at Smitty's Supermarkets, so we worked daily to be number one. Everything we did—from our product purchases, to our marketing, to the training of our staff, to the design of our stores—was done with the single objective of being a better leader in all areas of our market. It became the rallying cry for our team.

Setting your sights on being a leader in your market is an exciting undertaking. It may take years to get there, but the real value I see in the exercise, besides the perks that come with it, is that it challenges you and your team constantly to strive to rise above the competition and be better at what you do. This will consistently improve your business and the services it provides to your customers. To me, that is the real reward in striving to be number one or a market leader. It is what makes American business great.

Recognize That Relationships Are Everything — I can tell you without a doubt that in business, relationships are everything. Relationships are all-encompassing. This includes relationships with your suppliers, bankers, staff, the media, and a host of "centers of influence" that touch your business every day. Build successful relationships, and you ultimately build a successful business.

As a retailer, I concentrated on building a strong relationship with our suppliers. This was vital to us because I wanted to be the grocer that they thought of when they wanted to introduce a new product. I also wanted to be on the top of their list when they needed to move an overstocked item at a good price. Not only was this profitable for us, but it also strengthened our relationship with our customers.

I built strong relationships with our suppliers by paying our bills on time and never beating them down so much that they could not make a profit on a sale. I also tried to include them where I could in our media promotions, which included a golf tournament now and then. Most importantly, I treated them like a part of our family with the set of ethics that we lived by each day at Smitty's. In return, I made a series of friendships that I treasure to this day.

As a businessperson, I encourage you to take stock of those significant relationships in the day to day life of your business and work hard to strengthen them. Often this can be as simple as a handshake, a pat on the back, or a handwritten note for a job well done. This just might be the difference between you or your competitor having the advantage.

As I said at the outset of this chapter, being in business today is a complicated matter. Today's businessperson is faced with an overwhelming set of demands that often become more difficult as each year passes. To the individual who wants to open his own business and share in the American Dream, these demands can appear overwhelming and become a barrier, preventing him from taking the important steps to achieve success. But discouragement is an enemy, so you must soldier on.

I hope that as you read the story I am about to tell you that you will see that much of what I accomplished in my lifetime is still within the reach of the common man. Don't let the system fool you into thinking that it takes an MBA to be successful in business. I am proof that if you combine enough hard work, creativity, desire and ambition, and a few of my Smitty's Basics into your business practices, you, too, can be a success. Remember, we live in America, the greatest country on earth to be in business. When opportunity knocks, "open the door," rise to the occasion, and work your plan for success.

Worth Thinking About
Smitty's Secrets to Success

Dream, Envision, Conceptualize.
- What you do, and what you think, is everything.
- Always be positive.
- Think Success, not Failure!

Decide What Your Dreams and Goals Are.
- Write down your short-term and long-term goals.
- Develop a plan to reach them.

Take Action.
- Goals can be reached.
- Make decisions and then move on with your plan!

Continue to Learn All You Can.
- Read books, attend training sessions, and acquire new skills.

Be Persistent, and Work Hard.
- The harder you work, the luckier you become.
- Never give up!

Do Your Homework.
- Learn to analyze details.
- Get the facts, the input.
- Learn from your mistakes.

Stay Focused.
- Focus your time and money on each project.

Dare to Be Different.
- Be innovative; don't try to follow others.

Learn to Deal and Communicate with Others in an Effective Way.
- Getting work done through employees is the secret to success.

Be Honest and Dependable.
- Take responsibility.
- Learn the art of negotiation.
- Success comes in "cans," not "cannots."

Be Thrifty.
- Don't spend more than you make.
- Put your savings to work for you.

Be Committed and Determined.
- Have faith and trust in God.

2

Roots

"Each of us is the product of many influences."
—Mike Huckabee
from his book *Character Makes a Difference*

My Early Years

I was born January 12, 1919, in Numa, Iowa. The old-timers called Numa "lap land" because it is the point Missouri "laps" into Iowa. I was the third child born to Clyde and Ethel Smith. My dad worked in the coal mines around Numa. This was hard and dangerous work. It was also "winter" work, so dad had to find other jobs in the warmer months. Rural life in Iowa was tough, but my mom and dad somehow provided for us.

When I was five years old, in 1924, Dad loaded our family into his Model T Ford and moved us and all of our possessions to Beebe, South Dakota, in search of a better life. Jobs in Numa had been hard to come by, and Dad hoped that the move would provide better opportunity. My mom's sister and her husband, Frank and Vade Crooks, lived in Beebe, and they offered us a place to live until we could get on our feet.

When we arrived, it was in the fall, and the wheat harvest was going on. Dad got a job with a threshing crew and worked until the harvest was over, which was about thirty days. Later

Dad operated a small creamery where he would buy milk from the local farmers to separate and made cream and buttermilk for sale. Dad never made much money during the time we were in Beebe, but our family managed to get by.

Encounter!

My first experience with the evangelical church was in Beebe when I was six years old. A little friend and I asked our parents if we could go to see a "Holy Roller" preacher who was preaching in a big tent in town. After receiving their permission, we got to the tent and found a good seat in the middle of the aisle near the front.

When the preacher started preaching his message on "hell and brimstone," his yelling and enthusiasm stirred up the crowd. An elderly woman sitting behind us let out a big groan and started waving her arms and carrying on. This strange behavior from an adult somehow tickled us boys, and we started to giggle. At first, we kept our laughter under control, and the audience settled back down to hear the message. Just when things got quiet, the preacher turned up the volume and got the crowd going again. Unfortunately, the more he stirred things up, the more the woman behind us would wave her hands and the louder she would groan.

By this time, we were laughing uncontrollably, making quite a spectacle of ourselves. At this point, a man came to our seats and asked us to leave. As we were in the center of the aisle, the entire congregation watched as we were marched out of the tent. This was the first time I was ever kicked out of a church, and I hope it will be my last. But as I was to learn later in my life, God never gave up on me in spite of my juvenile laughter. In time, I also came to understand that this kind of behavior is not typical in most churches, and, thankfully, I didn't give up on God and the Church.

Early Formation of the Work Ethic

After nearly three years in South Dakota, my dad loaded us back up in the same old Model T Ford and we set out for Ames, Iowa. This is about the time America's Great Depression began to take hold of the country, and times were getting harder and harder. My dad's parents lived in Ames along with several other relatives. After we got there, Dad got a job as a street cleaner and later as a policeman. He quit the police department after a short time because the job required him to work at night.

When we arrived in Ames, I was supposed to be in the third grade, but they held me back because I was behind. Because we moved about every six months, my schooling was often interrupted. I was okay with this, but it probably contributed to my decision to drop out of high school in my sophomore year. I was to get my "real" education in the workplace, but I didn't comprehend this until later in life.

After my dad quit the police department, he got a job from a farmer shucking corn near Ames. On the weekends, I would go with him and help. I was eleven years old, and I can remember trying to keep up with him, as he could pick two rows of corn to my one. This experience of working with my dad started early in my life and would become a great influence later on in my life.

My dad was an extremely hard worker, and whatever he did, he did to the best of his ability. Whether it was working in the coal mine, picking corn, or cooking for a bridge-building crew, my dad worked harder and gave more of himself than any other person doing the same job. Later, when he and I worked in the coal mine together, he challenged me to "produce more." Something in me always wanted to "keep up" and win, no matter what the task. I guess I wanted to make my dad proud, so this forged a fierce determination in me at a young age.

Working in a coal mine as a teenager was a really tough job. If being pushed hard by my Dad wasn't bad enough, the coal mine was a dark and scary place. In those days, mine safety was not what it is today, and accidents always loomed just around the next corner. It is hard to imagine a young teenager today doing such a dangerous job, but the Great Depression forced lots of folks to do jobs and other things they would never do in normal times just to feed their families.

Looking back, I realize how blessed I was that my dad took such an interest in me. My older brother, Bill, who was the firstborn, and my dad were always at odds. Bill had a mind of his own, and nobody was going to tell him what to do. Children can acquire character traits of their parents, good or bad. Dad was also like Bill, so it was pretty much like adding gasoline to a fire. When I demonstrated an eagerness to work hard at an early age, Dad wanted to take me with him whether it was to work, hunt, or fish. It is amazing how much I learned from this simple, hardworking man.

Parents do influence their children, and my relationship with my dad is proof. As a youngster, I watched my dad work hard and demonstrate the values that I would later incorporate in my life. Unlike my brother Bill, I was willing to let Dad show me how to work. This sparked a fire in me always to do the best job possible. My dad showed me that you have to give of yourself in the workplace to be truly successful. He was always willing to put his muscle into every job to prove that point.

The example of learning from my dad also demonstrates that children should be willing to listen to their parents and keep an open mind when parents try to give them a push in the right direction. This thinking may be unfashionable in today's "doing it your own way" environment, but it is a critical part of growing up and the bonds we form as a family. Most parents try to give their kids the benefit of their life experiences, but kids have to be willing to listen, learn, and get involved.

Later in life, after coming into an understanding of biblical principals, I learned that parents are to train their children in the way they should go, and the promise is that when they are older, they will not depart from it (see Proverbs 22:6). I'm not sure my parents knew this, but perhaps instinctively they might have. At any rate, I did listen and learn, and it made a deep impression on me and helped to shape my work ethic.

The Start of "My Busy Season"

During my corn-picking years, our family moved near the small community of Fansler, Iowa. Fansler consisted of a community store with gas pumps and a dance hall that doubled as a skating rink. The entire population of Fansler was about a dozen persons. Our family increased the area population by eight as the Smith family now consisted of six kids: my older brother, Bill; older sister, Wilma; me; younger brother, Ervin (nicknamed "Swede"); younger sister, Mildred; and my brother, Doug, who was the baby.

In the fall of 1930, the economic depression that was smothering our country was at its worst. The house we moved into was a small three-bedroom home situated up against a hill. After settling in, the neighbor next door gave us boys a young billy goat to care for as a pet. As kids will do, we began teasing and spoiling him.

The billy soon learned that he could get on the roof from the hill behind our house where he would wait for us kids to get home. He would then jump off the roof in an attempt to ambush us. He would land stiff-legged on the ground, bounce around a bit, and then rear up on his two back legs with head lowered and try to butt us in the backside. We kids thought that this was great fun, but soon learned never to stoop over, as our rear ends made an appealing target to our young pet. This was all great fun until the billy began to get bigger and stronger and more capable of doing some real damage. Dad finally put a stop to this game, telling us that it was time for the goat to go. So, sell him we did.

In 1931, Dad moved the family about a mile down the road to a small and unwanted farm. For us, the farm was 120 acres of promise and lots of hard work. The farm had a small two-story home with two bedrooms upstairs for us kids and one bedroom downstairs for Mom and Dad. The kitchen had a wood-burning stove for preparing meals and doubled as a heater in the winter. The other source of heat in our little farm house was a coal-burning stove located in the living room. During the winter, we got to know our family really well, because the area around the coal-burning stove was the warmest place in the house. Coal-oil lamps provided light for reading and such the year 'round.

Our farm came with several old outbuildings that included a large barn for horses and cows and a place for hay storage. There was a building for chickens, a pigpen and shelter, and, the most important outbuilding, a two-hole outhouse for going to the bathroom. Drinking water was pumped by a windmill, and we got soft wash water from a cistern. The farm also had a large, fenced-in area where Mom planted her garden. There was a cave that maintained a cool temperature for storing the many fruits and vegetables our mother canned. The balance of the farm was devoted to raising crops for feeding animals and selling when the market and harvest permitted.

Farm life consisted of lots of chores, and our duty was to share in these. We would get up early and feed the animals, an assortment of hogs, horses, cows, and chickens; finish our chores by milking the cows; and then walk two miles to a country school. Bill, Wilma, Swede, and I attended the Victory #2 Country School down the road from our farm. The school was a two-room schoolhouse where grade levels one through four were grouped together in one room, and grades five through eight in the other.

When school was out, we would walk the two miles back home to our evening chores, which also included tending the fields and garden. While we managed to be kids now and then, our life was mostly centered on surviving and working to make the most out of what little we had.

One of the most bittersweet memories of my days at Victory #2 Country School was in the eighth grade. Our teacher was a young, male college graduate named Marvin Nolte, who was sort of rough and tough on us guys at times. This always posed a challenge to our budding manhood, so one day four or five of us eighth graders decided to bushwhack him on his way back from the outside john. The snow was really deep. I volunteered to tackle him, and the rest of the guys would help me wash his face in the snow. As he approached, I did my job, but my friends left me cold and ran back inside the school. I was no match for Mr. Nolte, and he roughed me up pretty good. I got a face full of snow and no help from my friends, who had let me down. At least it took my mind off the Depression for a few bruising moments.

I hope that no future generations have to experience the hopelessness and desperation that engulfed America during the Great Depression. During the depression years of the late 1920s and the 1930s, unemployment in America was at 30 percent and wages for existing jobs were sometimes as little as $1 per day for an eight-hour day. Things we take for granted today, like food and shelter, were always hanging in the balance.

For our family, we learned to make do in every way and to be conservative with everything. We learned to be creative and take nothing for granted. We also learned that being optimistic and living morally could sustain us through tough times. These were lessons and memories I carried with me all through my life, and I hate waste even to this day. Trust me when I say that even in times of plenty, being conservative with your money and spending habits, working hard, and living a moral and Christ-centered life, will always serve you well. Never spend more than you earn.

Swede and I

Ever since we were kids, my younger brother Swede and I were always really close. On the farm, we would do chores together and fish in the river for catfish to feed our family. Many times we would take the extra catch to town and sell them to help out at home with the little money we would get.

Swede and I lived a rugged, outdoor existence much of the time. There were lots of chores, and we grew up pretty fast. I remember during the spring thaw when the river water was high, we thought nothing of jumping on a sheet of ice that would be floating down the river and "surf" it downstream. Neither one of us thought of suffering hypothermia in the ice-cold river. We were tough boys; not even a freezing river could intimidate us.

Looking back, I realized that experiences like surfing down a freezing river, trying to out-pick my dad in the cornfield, and working as a teenage coal miner formed my personality and inner fiber. These experiences gave me the self-assurance that I could survive anything the world threw at me. They built an inner confidence that gave me the guts to take life head-on. At an early age, I knew that with hard work, dedication, desire, and a willingness to learn, I could accomplish just about anything I set my mind to. I am grateful that my mom and dad gave me so many chances to learn these principals at an early age, and that I lived in a wonderful country like America. This is a country that offers opportunity to those who choose to excel, no matter what the task at hand requires.

Swede and I would later share a great deal of our lives together. From our time on the farm, and through our many moves as a family, he and I shared so much. As kids, we learned the meaning of hard work, a theme that would echo throughout our lives. We later experienced the business world together, working side by side in the grocery business for years.

Due to my competitive nature, I tried just about anything that I saw done by someone else and would try to do it better. This sometimes worked out and sometimes it did not.

I am reminded of the time when I hitchhiked into Guthrie Center to see the circus. Like every red-blooded, Depression-era kid, I snuck in under the fence because I did not have the money for admission. I watched in wonder as a male circus performer put on a show riding horses bareback. With the horses tied closely together and running at a very fast pace, the rider would stand up on one horse then shift his weight by putting his other foot on the other horse, eventually riding both horses while standing straight up. I really thought this was cool, so when I got home, I decided to try the stunt using our old farm workhorses as substitutes for the highly trained circus ponies. Full of myself, I took our old nags down the road a couple of blocks, then urged them into a dead run. As I got close to our house, I stood up on one horse and shifted my weight, allowing me to place my other foot over on the second horse. Soon I was standing erect. By some miracle, both horses stayed together, despite being at a dead run. As I passed the house, I jumped back over to the first horse and began to thank God for keeping the horses together and allowing my goofy stunt to turn out okay. I also thanked Him for not allowing my mom to see my act of stupidity, as there is no telling what she would have done.

My Mom

It would be hard to go any further without mentioning my mom. Mom was what you would call a "homebody." Her life revolved around taking care of her children and my dad. She was the glue that kept our family bound tightly together.

Mom's life was made up of an endless list of chores, which included tending her garden, raising chickens, washing clothes on a washboard, and feeding a hungry pack of kids. Mom canned an endless stream of fruits, vegetables, and meats in the spring and summer months. This provided food for our family in the winter months, when life was more extreme and food was harder to come by. When Dad was gone, she was the disciplinarian. She used to switch our bare legs with a flexible willow branch when things got out of control. This got my attention no matter how tough I thought I was.

Life on the Fansler farm must have been hard on our mom, yet I never heard her complain. Given the severity of the times, she kept her focus on keeping our bellies full and being a good wife to my dad. She was an excellent cook and did miracles with so little. Every once in a while, she and Dad would go square dancing, and for just a few hours, the rigors of her farm life and rough existence would be blotted out.

Mom kept her whole net worth, a few simple coins, knotted up in a white handkerchief. I suppose this was her security blanket, and it took an act of Congress to pry those coins from their knotted nest. To this day, I have never seen anyone else with such a unique little ritual.

Mom always claimed that she was a "shirttail" relative of the oilman John D. Rockefeller. Once in a while she would drag out a bunch of old papers and show us her distant tie to one of America's great fortunes. This always fascinated us. We had no reason to doubt our rock-solid mom. As she would retell the story, I am sure that each of us quietly hoped that one day a letter might appear in our mailbox, dramatically changing our circumstances. Looking back, I can see how perhaps this gave a little comfort to a good woman with a fifth-grade education who stood so solidly behind her family.

Life on the Farm

While the Fansler farm gave our family a home, it was tough going most of the time. The land was of a very poor quality and hilly in many places. Our primary crop was corn, which was planted, tended, and then picked in the fall, the way early American farmers had done with muscle and grit for over a hundred years. When we cleaned the barn, we used the waste from our horses and cows for fertilizer to spread on our fields and improve the soil. I would later learn that the modern farms of today might get as much as 200 bushels of corn per acre, while the Fansler farm struggled to produce 25–30 bushels per acre.

Our scrappy little farm ended up with an assortment of milk cows, chickens, hogs, and a few horses. Our responsibility was to milk the cows twice a day, feed the chickens and hogs, and work in the fields when necessary. We never escaped from those chores. We sold any of our commodities when the opportunity presented itself, including taking our hogs to market.

In 1934, I signed up to go to high school for my freshman year in Panora, Iowa, which was about twenty miles away from the Fansler farm. This was quite an experience for me as I had to ride a rattletrap old school bus for the twenty-mile trip. The bus was unreliable and often caused problems coming and going. I got ten cents for lunch each day, which would buy a feast consisting of a half-pint of milk and a doughnut. To this day, I am still hooked on doughnuts.

If there is any regret I had about my high school years, it is that I never got to participate in sports. Because of problems with the bus, and my morning and evening chores, I couldn't devote the time to any after-school programs. I've often thought that because I was an outdoors kid, I was in tiptop shape and a pretty fast runner; I would have made a good football or basketball player. But times being what they were, helping out on the farm and being a good hand to Dad were my real priorities. Still, I've wondered what it would have been like if I had had the luxury of a few extra hours after school.

I was never a good student; C-'s and D's were my comfort zone. Once in a while I would get a B, but this was rare. I didn't take much work home. I knew there was always wood to be cut for the kitchen and living room stoves during the cold winters, plus repairing everything on the place. In 1934, the farm didn't have electricity. When I did study, it was by the light of a kerosene lamp, and that made poor light for studying.

During the fall of 1935, I somehow knew I was not going to make it through my sophomore year, much less graduate from high school. The Depression was getting worse, and the bus was still unreliable. Dad was about to start his winter's work in the coal mine, and I felt a keen sense of obligation to help him. Duty to my family seemed much more important than attending school. I was an able-bodied young man and capable of doing a good day's work for wages to help our family. Getting an education was important, but so was standing up to a worsening economy and the wolf that always seemed to be camped just outside our door.

The Last Move

In 1936, Dad decided to give up on the Fansler farm and moved our family to Guthrie Center, Iowa. Since we were accustomed to moving a lot, it was no big deal for us kids. Dad sold off what livestock we had and used the money to rent a house in Guthrie Center, which was a big improvement to the farm house in Fansler. Guthrie Center was a town of about three thousand people, so for us it was a big city. I did not know it at the time, but Guthrie Center would be my last move with the family I loved and with whom I had shared so much.

The winter of 1936 was one of the coldest ever recorded in Iowa. During an especially bitter, six-week stretch, the temperature never got above 20 degrees below 0. I was Dad's partner in the mine and now was committed to the working conditions and expectations of an adult. I was seventeen years old and a full-time coal miner in the wintertime, with a total of two years of coal mining experience.

Life as a Coal Mine Worker

When you go to work in a coal mine, you quickly learn the rules of the road. You learn to watch for dangerous gases called "damps" that could poison your lungs. When your pit lamp went out, you knew these gases were present and you needed to backtrack to the shaft. A coal mine is pitch black, and it's easy to become disoriented without your light, so you would have to run your hand along the iron rails that the coal cars came out on in order to get out and back to the shaft to fresh air as soon as possible.

When you are mining for coal, it is critical that you brace the roof before you start to extract the vein of coal so that the roof doesn't collapse. Dad taught me this and how to tell by using the end of my pick to test the roof. If it sounded hollow, it needed to be propped up. This, plus the dangerous gasses, was always on my mind when I was 400 feet below ground.

Dad and I made an average of $45 per week for working a forty-hour work week in the mine. This was more than the company-employed men made. Our pay was based on the amount of coal we produced, and it seemed like a good amount to us. Once in a great while, Dad would give me a few dollars from our check and allow me to spend the money as I saw fit. This was often spent on roller skating, a hamburger, and other such Depression luxuries.

On a spring day in 1936, and with the mine closing down for the summer, I emerged from the darkness of that Iowa coal mine into the sunlight after a hard day's work, wiped my brow, and muttered to myself, "There must be a better way to make a living. I've had enough!" Maybe it was the bitterly cold winter, the danger and dark oppression of the mine, or simply that I was tired of the struggles of a threadbare farm existence, but something in me said that a change was needed. I was determined that I wasn't going into that black hole anymore. I talked this over with my folks, and with their approval and five dollars in my pocket, l left Guthrie Center by hitchhiking nearly a hundred miles to Ames, Iowa. I wanted to strike out on my own and find a new life for myself. This was the springboard to the better way of life for which I longed. My Aunt and Uncle McKenna offered me a place to live in their home. The charge of five dollars a week would include room, board, and laundry.

A Message for You

I have probably spent too much time telling about my youth, but I wanted to give you some understanding of where I came from and the events that helped shape my character. I also wanted to share my experience about the Great Depression, which was an event that impacted most American families in some way or another. The Depression was a very difficult time for America, and it tested the principals and foundation of this great country. For our family, every Depression-era day was filled with keeping a roof over our heads, putting food on the table, and coming up with enough money to survive. Like other Americans, my family and I survived this time of hardship, emerging stronger, wiser, unified, and more disciplined from the experience.

What I want everyone to know is that early on I began to make choices for my life that set me on a course reaching for success and self-fulfillment. Granted, the Depression might have given me a push in the right direction, but I just knew the way to a better life was through developing ambition and a strong desire to succeed. What job I was doing did not matter. Whatever it was, I wanted to do my best. I wanted to mine more coal, till more land, and pick more corn than the next guy. I was always willing to give of myself just knowing that there would be a reward some day. Ambition and desire are the real ingredients to distinguishing yourself from the next person. When you combine this with the ethics of being a good dependable person and a good American, it will serve you well.

Your generation may never see the heartbreak of a national tragedy such as the Great Depression, but you may be tested in ways that are just as difficult. The culture of today provides much temptation and all manner of sin. People don't like to talk about "sin," or even use the word, but that's what it is when you succumb to desires that will take you off course. These can sidetrack ambition and lead you astray, leaving you struggling and as empty as we were during those hard Depression years. You need to be vigilant and say no to the things that can stifle your ambition and rob you of opportunities for future success. Indulging in the use of drugs and alcohol, and not keeping close relationships with your family, are poor choices to make. They will bring you only the heartache of self-defeat and move you further away from achieving goals and alienation from God and your loved ones. This brings us to the subject of choices and the next chapter of my life.

Worth Thinking About

- Don't succumb to desires that will take you off course.

- Be vigilant and say no to those things that can stifle your ambition and rob you of opportunities for future success.

- Ambition and desire are the real ingredients that will distinguish you from the next person.

3

Choices

"Success does not come by accident;
successful people make choices early that keep
them moving in the right direction."

—Clyde B. Smith

One of the blessings of my ninety-plus years is that I have been able to observe many successful people from all walks of life. While individuals reach success in their own ways, they usually share in the common traits of hard work, honesty, and a desire to be the best they can be. Success does not come by accident; successful people make choices early that keep them moving in the right direction. The thing I want you to know is that this is America, and you are free to make the right choices each day—no matter the choices you made yesterday. Wrong choices yesterday, or further back in your past, do not have to mean that you are stuck in that rut for life. You can move on, and you can extricate yourself from the things that have hindered you and caused you to stumble, fall, or experience failure. However, making better choices from here on is up to you. No one can make them for you. Hopefully, some of the things I have learned about making good and right choices will help you.

I'd like for you to know that I came to see that success is really not measured in material wealth. Yes, it's nice to have money and the things it buys, but the truth is, real success is getting up each morning and living up to your full potential. When you do that, the rewards will follow. It may not happen immediately, but it will happen. The rewards are not the same for everybody; much depends on how you define rewards. There are plenty of successful people I know who will never own a jet airplane, have a big bank account, or live in the biggest house on the block. Their reward and true wealth is in their satisfaction that they are living a moral and Christ-centered life, doing the best job they can, providing for and loving their families, and standing on their own two feet, not depending on government handouts. These are the true measures of success in a man or a woman. I hope that these things will be a part of your life and you will know the satisfaction that they bring.

By now, you know that I focus on working hard and striving to be the best I can be. To you this may sound like old-fashioned thinking, but trust me when I say that these principals are important, no matter what decade of life you may now be in. The sooner you learn this, the better your life will be.

Children, for instance, should be given the responsibility of chores around the house at an early age to help and encourage them to form good habits and develop a healthy foundation. Children should not resent their parents but recognize that this is preparation for learning how to take care of themselves in the real world. Sadly, the America of today is filled with people who have never learned to take responsibility for themselves. They are truly missing out on the American dream and the many opportunities this country has to offer.

One of the great things I learned in the Depression was how important family is in our lives. By our circumstances, we were bound tightly together in our need to survive. Today's family may not face the same set of circumstances, but being close is still vitally important. Always take time for each other and never forget to communicate. With today's working parents, busy schedules, cell phones, fast food, and the Internet, getting lost in our own little worlds and losing touch with each other can be too easy.

I suggest that you take the time as often as possible to turn off the TV, sit down together as a family at the dinner table, eat, and simply talk with each other. Enjoy eating together and being a part of each other's lives. Take time to share what is going on in your life and draw support from each other, never judging the other person. This is a ritual that is timeless and will strengthen both you and your family. Remember, Jesus set this example for us during the Last Supper as He ate dinner with the disciples, whom He loved as his family. Make room in the busyness of your lives for each other, taking time to do as Jesus did. Your life and that of your family will be richer for doing so.

Worth Thinking About

"The Victor"

If you think you are beaten, you are.
If you think you dare not, you don't.
If you'd like to win but think you can't,
It's almost a cinch you won't.
If you think you'll lose, you're lost,
For out in the world we find
Success begins with a fellow's will.
It is all in the state of mind.
If you think you're outclassed, you are.
You've got to think high to rise.
You've got to be sure of yourself before
You can ever win a prize.
Life's battles don't always go
To the stronger or faster man.
But sooner or later, the man who wins
Is the man who thinks he can.

C. W. Longenecker

4

Finding My Mentor

"As you go through life, watch and look for those
special people who are willing to share their knowledge and
skills with you. My mentor changed my life forever. "

—Clyde B. Smith

By the time I ended up at Keith Rushing's grocery store in Ames, Iowa, I had worked with threshing crews in the threshing season and been a corn picker, well digger, farmhand, painter, coal miner, garbage man, and a number two cook in a diner. My life experiences consisted of lots of hard work and growing up at an early age. When I met Keith Rushing, I was an eighteen-year-old kid who had a wheelbarrow full of ambition and a yearning for a better life. I also desperately needed a job.

The first time I met Keith Rushing, he was candling eggs in his grocery store. He bought eggs from the local farmers as part of the services he offered. I struck up a conversation with him, trying to get him interested in hiring me as he sorted the good eggs from the bad. I didn't get very far the first day as I recall, so I went back to see him the following day. Desperate for a job, I went out on a limb and told Mr. Rushing that if he would just give me a job, I would work for a week, and if at the end of that week, he wasn't satisfied with my work, he didn't have to pay me. Rushing thought that my proposal sounded like a "good deal," so he hired me on the spot.

Keith Rushing operated one of the best grocery stores in Ames, Iowa. It was located on Main Street, and he was known as a really good operator. He was married and had two daughters. Mr. Rushing was a slightly built man who had a reputation as a hard worker with a solid business reputation. He was a friendly individual, but he ran a tight ship. Besides being a good grocer, he learned how to buy and sell truckloads of produce, potatoes, watermelons, cantaloupes, and other produce from the truckers hauling for the growers out of the valley of South Texas. He would keep what he needed for his store, then sell the excess of the load to other grocers, making a few extra bucks for his wholesale efforts.

Mr. Rushing had a fellow named Clarence Iden who functioned as his store manager. When he hired me, Rushing told Mr. Iden to give me an opportunity to work and get experience in each of the departments in the store. For some reason, Mr. Rushing practically adopted me. When he saw that I was a very hard worker, he began to share his knowledge of the grocery business with me. Over time, I stocked shelves; took phone orders; and learned how to be a fast and accurate checker, package bulk foods, and merchandise the produce area. Mr. Rushing even apprenticed me to the meat department, where I learned a trade that would eventually help me start my first store.

At Rushing's grocery store, I was making eight dollars a week, working extremely long hours, and loving every minute I was at work. At some point, the grocery store quit being just a job and became my passion. Thanks to the interest Mr. Rushing showed in me, I found a business that I still love to this day. Mr. Keith Rushing changed my life forever.

Neither one of us knew it at the time, but Keith Rushing became my mentor and dear friend at a crucial time in my life. While I had made choices at an early age to be a hard worker and always to do my best, Mr. Rushing took these raw talents and helped me mold them into a meaningful life. Perhaps Mr. Rushing saw a reflection of himself in me, which made him so willing to share freely the principals of being a good grocer. Perhaps, Keith Rushing wanted to pass on his own legacy in the business through a poor farm kid who was taking on the world by himself. Whatever the reason, Mr. Rushing's legacy lives on in me to this day. It also lives on in the thousands of people I have employed and helped train in the oh-so-many years since Keith and I parted company.

Finding Your Mentor

As you can see by my story, a mentor such as Keith Rushing can be a positive influence in a person's life. Without Mr. Rushing there is no telling where I would have ended up. As my mentor, Mr. Rushing took the time to explain so much to me and share the business knowledge he had accumulated over the years. On my part, I was willing to listen and look for opportunity in every chance he gave me. I was also willing to give 110 percent of myself in every work day with just the promise of a small paycheck. I knew that doing so would eventually pay greater dividends as my life unfolded.

As you go through life, watch and look for those special people like Mr. Rushing who are willing to share their knowledge and skills with you. Seek out hardworking, successful, and moral individuals to observe and get to know as you go through life. If you are sincere about being the best you can be, these individuals are usually willing to give a hardworking person the benefit of their experience. Likewise, if you are at a point of success in your life, share your time and expertise with someone who will pass on your legacy to another generation of Americans.

Roller-skating to the Altar

Up until this point in my life, Ames, Iowa, had been good to me. I was working my tail off at Mr. Rushing's grocery store, and I was learning more about the retail business each day. When I wasn't at the store, I was batching with my brother Swede, who had moved into my small living quarters with me. Swede and I did our own cooking, washing, and ironing while keeping our little place clean and orderly. Swede was attending high school and working part time at Rushing's store. We both shared the responsibilities and chores of keeping our apartment in good shape.

Occasionally, I would be invited on a Saturday night to eat a steak dinner with Mr. Rushing, which was a special treat. My life mostly revolved around work and taking care of myself. For entertainment, I went roller-skating when time permitted. Roller-skating was a sport I had fallen in love with when we lived on the Fansler farm. Fansler had an old roller rink where we used to rent clip-on skates, where I learned to skate rather well.

The Ames roller rink was much more advanced than the Fansler one, complete with real shoe skates and a Hammond organ out in the middle of the rink floor. One evening when the organ played a song where I needed a skate partner, I chose a sixteen-year-old girl named Helen Daley. She was a good skater, and I admired her ability. Little did I know that when I chose her as a skating partner, I was also choosing her to be my partner in marriage. This would come about two years later.

Once I was dating Helen, my life became even busier. Most days and evenings I worked at the store. After closing up, I would go to the ice cream parlor where Helen worked. Helen would serve me my favorite flavor of ice cream while she cleaned and helped close up the parlor. Then we would go skating and, on occasion, to a dance.

As we dated, I realized Helen was a good match for me. We both were athletic and shared the same value system. Neither of us smoked or drank, and we were both kind of health nuts. After about a year and a half of dating, I proposed and she accepted. We were married in Ames, Iowa, November 24, 1940, where we started our life together as a couple.

Now that I was a married man, Mr. Rushing gave me a raise of two dollars a week. Helen and I were a married couple and living on a whopping eighteen dollars per week. It is hard to believe that Helen did not work and we were able to scrape by on such a small sum of money. Although we were content, I began to keep my eye on the job market to see if I could increase my take-home pay and improve our lot in life.

America and I Go to War

I had always been very happy with my association with Mr. Rushing and had never really thought about leaving the store, but an ad appeared in the Ames paper that I couldn't get out of my mind. A munitions plant in Ankeny, Iowa, had been advertising for a metallurgist at a starting salary of forty dollars a week. This was twice what I was making at the grocery store, and it was for a really good cause. America had entered the war in Europe, and the men fighting that war needed ammunition.

In my typical risk–taking, dare-to-be-different style, I decided to apply for the job at the munitions plant. I paid no attention to the section of the newspaper ad that said I needed a degree in chemistry to apply. Using every bit of my self-confidence and influence, I "white lied" my way through the interview, saying I had the required degree from Iowa State College. I was hired immediately as they were desperate for workers.

Once I was on the job, I took all of the unfamiliar chemistry words related to metallurgy home with me and looked them up in the dictionary. I tried to memorize each one to be able to have some idea of what was going on around me. Later, I became friends with an older chemist, who showed me the ropes and helped me write up any papers I had to submit. Like Mr. Rushing, he saw the sincerity in my efforts and helped me where he could.

Not long after I was employed at the plant, we began having trouble with the ammunition that was being manufactured. Somewhere in the process something was going wrong, and the shell casings were showing signs of possible cracks. It was our job to find out the manufacturing defect when God gave me the answer to our problem. It must have been God because I was not a chemist.

Soon after I found the problems and shared my findings with the boss, I was given a nice raise and promoted to being the assistant to the head chemist of the entire plant. He was an aloof kind of guy who thought he was above the rules. He would invite me to go to town with him for three-hour lunches and other such nonsense. This ate at me as I felt I was not actually earning my pay. It was like "backing up to the pay window," which went against everything I stood for. When I could take it no longer, I resigned my cushy job and enlisted in the military in the fall of 1942. If I could not help make the munitions for the country I loved, I was willing to fight for it instead. I loved my country and wanted to do whatever I could to protect the liberty that we had learned to enjoy and appreciate.

Worth Thinking About

"And so, my fellow Americans: ask not what your country can do for you—ask what you can do for your country."

—President John F. Kennedy (1917-1963)

5

On the Wartime Frontline

"My platoon buddies and I thanked God for many things.
By God's grace, most of us survived. Mountain by mountain,
town by town, one step at a time, the brave fighting men of the
10th Mountain Division certainly helped to liberate the people of
Italy by defeating the Germans and returning their
country to them."

—Clyde B. Smith

After several weeks of intense basic training at Camp Roberts, California, I found my way into the famed 10th Mountain Division of the Army in a roundabout way. When I first enlisted, I joined the Army Air Corps with the hopes of being a pilot. Learning that I was color-blind and unable to be a pilot, I chose the next best thing, which was to be a paratrooper. I served with the 82nd Airborne Division. This did not last long, as I got ulcers on my eyeball. These were caused by the California desert sun and sand where I had taken my basic training. With most of my other body parts intact, I joined up with the ski-troops of the 10th Mountain Division. We were shipped overseas to Italy and like the rest of my Army buddies, we were told to help rid the enemy from the country.

Most of the fighting we did was in the Italian mountains in winter conditions. A great deal of the time we were cold, wet, tired, and hungry. Fighting in the mountains is tedious as you chase the enemy from one mountaintop to another. There is always danger lurking behind each tree or draw. Every day my platoon buddies and I thanked God for many things. Mostly we thanked Him for our lives and asked Him to give us victory with honor. I also thanked Him for my favorite food rations, cans of beans and wieners, as they were the only rations I could keep down. Most of the rations we got on the front lines were cold and frozen. This unheated food gave me horrible indigestion, which amplified being tired, cold, and miserable.

One of the few comical moments during my fighting in the Italian mountains happened at the time when I was promoted. At this time, I was a squad leader and just a lowly private first class. However, as a squad leader I was very aggressive and had given the troops lots of calisthenics and conditioning. Evidently, the captain in charge was made aware of my work with the troops.

I was up on the frontlines when the captain called me to the rear echelon, saying he needed to meet with me right away. So, I double-timed it back to the rear where he was and we sat down to talk. He said, "Can I ask you a direct question? Can you whip everybody in your whole platoon?"

The question took me by surprise and I fumbled for the right reply. "Gosh, I don't know."

The captain snapped back, "Well, can you or can't you?"

I gave this last question a quick second thought and responded, "I might if I had to."

"Well, that's good enough for me," the captain declared. He told me I was now in charge, and he moved me up to the rank of staff sergeant. While there was not much ceremony to my promotion, it was a moment in my life that I will never forget due to the unique question I was asked and the promotion that came with it—staff sergeant. I was a platoon leader who was now responsible for forty-four tough fighting men who were dedicated and ready to serve Company C 2nd Platoon, 85th Regiment.

After the basic training at Camp Roberts, California, and other camps in America, I thought I was ready and willing to do what I could for our country, but further experiences were to test that resolve. One of these occurred on a mountaintop in Italy. The winter air in the Italian mountains was bitterly cold that predawn morning before we were to attack. At the time, I was the squad leader and my assistant was a really tough kid from New York who was a prize fighter in civilian life. Our objective was to sneak up to the top of the mountain before us and eliminate a machine-gun nest, allowing the rest of our troops to advance. When we were about thirty feet from the enemy, they heard us coming. The next thing I knew, I heard a grenade land close to me and knew this was probably the last sound I was to hear while I was on Earth. Quickly, I tossed my four grenades into the machine gun nest as the grenade behind me went off. The next thing I knew, I felt the sting of shrapnel in the back of my leg. Somehow, I was still alive.

After I realized I was not dead, I moved over to my assistant to see how he fared. There, in the cold morning air, the tough kid from the streets of New York seemed to be paralyzed with fear from the grenade that the Germans had thrown at us. I quickly grabbed his arm and yelled, "Are you okay?" Shaken, his answer was, "Yes, I'm okay."

Through the grace of God, on that early morning in the cold Italian mountains, the grenade the Germans had thrown and landed beside us was a concussion-type grenade, not a fragmentation grenade like I had thrown at them. Had we been in a foxhole, we both would have been dead from the pressure that a concussion grenade inflicts. Because God was watching over us, all I received was a piece of shrapnel in the back of my leg, and my fearful partner was left unscathed. However, the Germans were killed from the grenades, paving the way for our troops to take the mountain and continue with our plan to advance. There were many other conflicts, hard-fought battles, and injuries, but by God's grace, most of us survived.

Each day, our 10th Mountain Division continued to move toward our objective of defeating the Germans in Italy. Mountain by mountain, town by town, one step at a time, I am proud to say that the brave fighting men of the 10th Mountain Division certainly helped to liberate the people of Italy by defeating the Germans and returning their country to them.

As the war ended in Europe, I found myself on a ship called the Marine Fox, bound for the United States. Our unit was being sent back early to go to the Pacific theater to continue the fight with the Japanese. While at sea, the Japanese surrendered and the ship now became my ticket home. Never mind that our ship hit one of the worst storms of the season and was being tossed like a toy. The men of the 10th Mountain Division were coming home, and we all had just received our pay in cash, ten dollar bills to be exact.

Up to now, I have spent a great deal of time telling you truthfully about myself. By now, you know that I did not drink or smoke and that I was a health nut. You also know that I tried to live a moral life. What I have not told you is that I had a little off-colored habit called gambling when the opportunity presented itself. While I was not a dingy backroom card shark, I did enjoy a game of poker now and then. This was a habit I developed early while living on the Fansler Farm. During the cold winters, we kids would gather around the potbellied stove and play poker for matches. I became a pretty good card player during my younger years and refined this as I got older.

By the time I was on that boat bound for home, I was in the prime of my card-playing years. With nothing else to do, I joined every poker game on the ship that I could. By the time we got halfway home, I had won so much money that I had to stuff it into my pillowcase at night for safety. This, combined with all the pay I had sent home while in the Army, was to be my seed money for a new start in life. And in this new life, I wanted to get into business for myself. It was my long-term goal and dream that I would someday own and operate my own grocery store.

Why I Will Always Love America and Hope You Do Too

America means a great deal to me. I have always loved our country and been prepared to do whatever I can to help it. That is the reason at a young age and even with a family, my wife, Helen, and our new one-year-old daughter, Sandra, I enlisted in the military to fight and defend our country. I felt that America was the greatest country on Earth, and I wanted to do whatever I could to protect her and the noble principals on which she was founded. I strongly believe that having God as a part of America is the noblest of these founding principles.

Now, you may never be asked to lay down your life for America as I was, but I pray that you find ways to show your love of this country as I did. Embracing family values, being a responsible parent or child, and always striving to do your best will go a long way to strengthen this great nation. America is a land of wonderful opportunity for those who have desire and ambition. Making these fundamentals a part of your life will not only make you a productive citizen but will also continue to move this country forward.

Preserving the family unit is a way you can strengthen America. Taking time for family, taking care of each other, and growing closer is vital to the American way of life. When you have a personal crisis, look to each other and not the government to solve your problems. While America will always care for its citizens, make welfare a last resort to remedy your problems. Remember, if you are able-bodied, America is still the land of opportunity if you have the desire and ambition to make something of yourself. This was true when I was a poor kid trying to get ahead in life, and I hope it will continue to be true for many years to come. America will be what present and future generations choose to make of her. It's good to be reminded that each of us can do our best to preserve the integrity of this land at all times. One of my friends, Dr. Gary Frazier, points out in his book *America at the Tipping Point*, "Unjust laws are being written, political cowardice and greed mortgages our progenitor's futures, spending is out of control, and we cannot ignore immediate concerns like these." We would do well to ask, "Is it too late? What can be done to take back our country?"

We can take back our country; we can be a public voice for the eternal truths of God.

Worth Thinking About

President Abraham Lincoln, in speaking to a minister of the Christian Commission, an organization that ministered to the soldiers during the Civil War, said, "If it were not for my firm belief in an everlasting Providence, it would be difficult for me, in the midst of such complications of affairs, to keep my reason on its seat. But I am confident that the Almighty has His plans and will work them out; and, whether we see it or not, they will be the best for us."

President George Washington, in his 1789 Inaugural Address, said, "The propitious smiles of Heaven can never be expected on a nation that disregards the eternal rules of order and right which Heaven itself has ordained."

6

Coming Home

"The secret of joy in work is contained
in one word—excellence. To know how to
do something well is to enjoy it."

—Pearl S. Buck

The war was over; it was time for my wartime buddies and me to come home. Oh, how welcome that was! After the boat docked, they shipped us to Colorado, where we were discharged from the Army. Not wanting to spend a dime of my seed money, I stuck my thumb out and began to hitchhike home. I was soon picked up by a truck driver heading to Omaha, Nebraska. This guy was a real character and entertained me the whole way. When we arrived in Omaha, the truck driver was not going to let a rock-hard, battle-honed young buck just walk away after a free ride. He insisted that I help him unload his truck, which was packed full of canned goods. Once this was done, we parted company and I was on the last leg of my long journey home to Ames, Iowa.

When I finally arrived back home, all I wanted to do was see my family, my wonderful wife and two beautiful daughters. My youngest daughter, Linda, whom I had never seen, was now two years old and had been born while I was serving in Italy. I was thrilled with such a loving family. After getting somewhat acclimated, I decided to take a nice, long, hot bath. It's kind of funny what you think about when you are freezing cold and hungry on the battlefield. I couldn't wait to get into the tub and wash all the misery of the war from my pores. I was ready to make a clean start and that tub was the first step. After a long-looked-for soaking, my next desire was to find a good restaurant and order the biggest and best steak they had! Wow, what a treat that would be!

As I soaked in the tub enjoying every drop of warm water, I noticed that my young, four-year-old daughter, Sandra, had quietly slipped in the room and was watching me intently. Our bathroom was quite large and gave her ample room to observe this strange man. Uncomfortable, I asked her to leave, but she just stared at me without moving. Quite a smart little thing, she intentionally stayed out of my reach and ignored my pleas for her to leave. Finally, yelling for my wife, Helen, to rescue me, I noticed the bewilderment on her little face that seemed to be silently protesting, "Who is this strange man in our tub?" It then dawned on me that she didn't realize that I was her daddy.

After getting some much needed rest and good home cooking, I went to work helping Helen's dad, Ray Daley. He was a carpenter and contractor around Ames who built and remodeled houses. Soon afterwards, I purchased a home for Helen and me to live in, and Ray helped me convert the home into a duplex. Later, I would sell this house for a nice profit that would help supplement my objective to buy a store.

At some point, after returning to Ames, I went to see Keith Rushing, and he offered me my old job back, but I had made up my mind that I wanted my own store. I politely turned down his offer. Mr. Rushing then offered me a deal that seemed genuine and heartfelt. "Smitty," he said "come back to work for me, and I'll help you find your own store." A man of his word, he did just that.

My First Store

After working about four months at Rushing's store, Keith located a small butcher shop in Roland, Iowa, that was for sale. Roland was a small town located about fifteen miles north of Ames and had a population of about 900 people, many of whom were of Norwegian descent. The building was owned by Mr. Josendahl and was used only as a meat market, but it was rather large and had a full basement. The shop itself was located in the front part of the building. Mr. Josendahl, Keith and I came to an agreement concerning the lease, the fixtures, and the inventory involved. The meat market was profitable at the time, but the owner, Mr. Josendahl, was old and tired of the business responsibilities.

The purchase price for the business that included all furniture, fixtures, inventory, and goodwill was $65,000. This was a steep price for an army veteran even with the $15,000 I had managed to save. I thought that it would be a deal breaker, but Keith Rushing did something that changed my life forever. He offered to take me to the bank in Roland and personally guarantee a loan for the balance of the money I needed to purchase the store. He went on the hook for $50,000, which was a great deal of money back in 1946.

Like so many adventures in my youth, I asked my brother Swede to be my partner in the new store. Swede had saved $2,000 that supplemented our down payment and gave us operating money. After some training, Swede became an apprentice meat cutter, with the butcher, Amos Quam, teaching him the basics about breaking beef down and the necessary merchandising of it for the most effective sales.

One of the strong points of the butcher shop was that it came with a slaughter permit that allowed us to kill and butcher two cows per month. As meat was still rationed during this period after the war, it gave us the advantage of having hard-to-get items for our customers, which helped create a built-in cash flow.

The building was rather large, but within ninety days of purchasing the butcher shop, Swede, the staff, and I had completely remodeled the store building, the shelving, and the display tables. I wanted to make the butcher shop into a complete grocery store, so we pushed the meat counters and the meat cooler to the back of the building. This then gave us the room we needed to add fixtures for groceries and a nice produce department.

Remodeling that first butcher shop was probably the real start of my career as a grocer. For the first time, I was able to design, build, and merchandise the layout of a store. While this challenged my level of previous experience, there is no better way to learn a job than rolling up your sleeves and getting it done on the frontline. As a result, I developed a passion for store design and merchandising that was to stick with me for the rest of my career.

In the period after World War II, being an army veteran was a revered position. I was proud that the public at large showed respect and consideration to veterans whenever it could. Patriotism in America was at its peak, and being a veteran opened a lot of doors.

Being a newly discharged fighting man of the famed 10th Mountain Division, I used my veteran status whenever I could as I prepared for the grand opening of my new store. Multiple times I used this advantage on suppliers to get hard-to-come-by items that were still rationed. With each success, I squirreled away these treasures in the basement of the store in anticipation of the grand opening I was planning.

As the day of the grand opening of the store drew near, I was thankful to have my brother Doug come and join our operation. Doug came to Roland to work in our produce department. He was sixteen years old and an ambitious guy. After high school and college, fate tossed Doug and me together for the next thirty-some years. This is a business and personal relationship I have always been proud of. Doug has always meant so much to me. He is a first-class guy and a really hard worker; he learned the supermarket business in depth and became one of our key executives later as our company grew and expanded into a multistore operation.

With the store ready for the grand opening, I put a full-page ad in the Ames, Iowa, newspaper announcing the big event and a list of the hard-to-get items. I knew this would get a reaction, but didn't expect the crowd of people who had lined up for a block when Swede and I got to work at seven that morning. As I opened the door, I saw total chaos. People were scooping up these rationed items that I had run around the state collecting! I just could not believe what I was seeing.

Now you have to remember that I was a twenty-eight-year-old who had put his heart and soul into merchandising this store. To see the chaos unfolding was so much more than I'd expected. It was definitely not how I had envisioned things going for our grand opening. This was not going to work out well at all!

Being aggressive and determined to do whatever was necessary at this point, something just snapped in me and I jumped up on the front checkout counter and began to address the mob of frantic shoppers. "Well, I know most of you folks and you are from Ames, and a lot of you are my relatives and friends. What I want you to do is go back and get a shopping cart and shop like you would at any other market. If you do that, then you are entitled to these hard-to-find items, but otherwise, we don't have enough for our own locality. We have plenty of meat, produce, and other grocery items. That's the way it is going to work best for all of us. I would appreciate your cooperation as I do value your patronage."

This was a gutsy move, but it brought the crowd under control. They did as I told them to do, and we had a record day and weekend. I had driven the wheels off of my pickup truck gathering the items for our grand opening, and I was not going to sell them in a rummage sale atmosphere.

From the grand opening on, our weekly volume began to grow. At first, we turned our inventory once every two to three weeks, which was good, but not great. There was another little grocery store in Roland, and we encountered some resistance in shopping with us because these owners were locals and we were not. It took some time to overcome this prejudice, but we managed to do so with better customer service, a variety of good meat, and a better inventory mix. Soon, we were turning our inventory about once a week and business was getting stronger each month.

I did not know at the time, but I probably owe a great deal to our Norwegian competition in Roland. When we first en-count-ered the resistance, I began to focus on the customer; this was the start of a lifelong passion for putting the needs and wants of the customer above all else. We began to win the market share with a superior level of customer service and a well-trained staff. Throughout my years in business, I have become a fanatic about this. You have to invest in people if you are going to compete effectively in the market place. Whether it is a national chain, or a small independent compet-itor, focusing on the customer with the best variety and latest merchandise and training staff is the way for an organization to grow and prosper.

For the next year and a half, I settled into a routine of working six days a week. Monday through Thursday, I worked from 7 am to 6 pm, and on Friday and Saturday I often worked until midnight. This was a seventy to eighty hour work week, but fortunately the store was closed on Sunday. On Sunday, Helen and I would take our girls to the local church, and then out to a good lunch. After lunch, I would go back to the store for the afternoon and complete the book work of the past week. This would allow me to be on the sales floor on Monday morning, filling the shelves with the necessary product.

Not long after the grand opening, Swede decided that he wanted to go to northern Iowa and open a tavern. I offered to buy him out at a fair price and he accepted. While I would miss him, our parting was amicable and good for both of us. We would later rejoin forces.

Life Tosses Me a Curve

It was a cold winter night in January with the temperature expected to get twenty degrees below zero. I stopped to check my antifreeze at the local gas station, which was a couple of blocks from the store. The last thing I needed was a broken radiator from the bitter cold. As I was checking my antifreeze, I heard the local fire siren go off that indicated that there was a fire in town. The fella that owned the gas station ran out and said, "Smitty, you stay here and take care of my customers. I'm a volunteer and need to go and help put out the fire." Agreeing to do so, I waited for his return.

In about ten minutes, the gas station owner raced back to the station and yelled to me, "Smitty, it's your store that's on fire!" Now my heart was racing as I hustled back to the store. Sure enough, it was my store and there was water everywhere from the efforts of the firefighters. There was about a foot of water in the store and it was freezing cold. I ran into the building several times to do what I could to salvage as much as possible. Most of the merchandise that was not soaked had some smoke damage. The store had an apartment upstairs, and those poor people were smoked out.

It turned out that the fire was due to an electrical short. After the fire, Mr. Josendahl told me he would not rebuild the store, effectively canceling my lease. He had a grandson who worked in a grocery store in another town, and he wanted to put him into business. I guess he figured we had done such a good job of building the business that his grandson could take advantage of our misfortune.

I made a deal with Josendahl to sell him the fixtures that were left and made plans for a huge liquidation sale. I really marked down prices, and we did well. With this money, the money from Josendahl, and what we had saved, I started to look for another store. I soon found one in Jefferson, Iowa, and made the deal to rent the building in the early part of 1948. The store was called the Friendly Food Store.

Store Number Two in Iowa

Jefferson, Iowa, had a population about three times the size of Roland. The new store had a better location than my first one and ended up doing more volume in spite of being smaller. I moved my family to Jefferson, purchased a home, and threw everything I had into the new venture.

In just under two years, the store was doing great volume, but the size of the store had limitations. I had a lady who worked for me whose brother was the president of a small bank near Jefferson, Iowa. One day I suggested to her that her brother should buy my store, as I knew he was always looking for a business opportunity. When the banker came to see me, I made him a proposition that was similar to the one that I made with Keith Rushing many years before. I told the banker that if he was not satisfied with the store and its earnings after six months, I would buy it back at exactly what he had paid; he bought it immediately. When I returned in six months to see if he wanted to execute my guarantee, he was making so much money he just smiled at my offer. He was as happy as a lark.

Besides the many things I had learned in my first two stores, I realized I wanted a bigger store as the next step in my grocery career. By this point, I was beginning to get a sense of how I wanted to merchandise, train my staff, and give better service to the customer. I also had many promotional ideas that I wanted to try, but the small stores limited my abilities. I was now ready to take my small organization to the next level and to bigger and better stores — stores for the foreseeable future.

Worth Thinking About

"Always do right. This will gratify some and astonish the rest."

—Mark Twain

"Success is for those energetic enough to work for it, hopeful enough to look for it, patient enough to wait for it, brave enough to seize it, and strong enough to hold it."

—Garry Kinder

"There's lots of opportunity for youth in this country, but you must reach for it; No one hands it to you."

—Clyde B. Smith

7

On the Retail Frontline

"One of the keys in retailing is to take a product
and create a visual picture for the customer in a manner
that makes them want to trade with you and purchase that
item—this is called merchandising."

—Clyde B. Smith

My Biggest Store Yet

After selling my Jefferson store to the small town banker, I located another store in the fall of 1949 in Marshalltown, Iowa. The previous owner had gone out of business, and the store was available for lease. The store was 3,200 square feet (40 ft x 80 ft) and had a great location. Unlike my previous two stores, the Marshalltown store didn't have a full basement for storing stock and preparing merchandise. The back room of this store was only ten feet wide, which would challenge us to be somewhat frugal and to be extremely careful when ordering our store merchandise.

The flipside to having a small back room was that the Marshalltown store would have the largest merchandisable floor space I had ever worked with on my own. I sensed that this increased space could pay huge dividends in growing our volume. Since going into business for myself, I had seen our weekly sales volume grow from a peak of $3,000 per week in Roland to over $4,000 per week in Jefferson. I had a good feeling about this new store in spite of the previous owner's run of bad luck.

I quickly made a deal on the Marshalltown store and leased the building for five years at five hundred dollars per month. One of the first things I did was to hire Max Strain, an old friend with lots of experience, from Ames. He was to be my first employee and manager of our meat department. Within sixty days, Max and I had remodeled the interior of the store with fixtures we built ourselves, a complete paint job, new checkout stands, and signage. I called the new store "Smitty's Super Valu Market."

One of the first business relationships I had as a grocer was with a company called Winston and Newell located in Des Moines, Iowa. This fine company had been my grocery supplier since day one in Roland and we had a good relationship. Besides supplying groceries, they also did some of my bookwork and prepared reports such as my financial profit and loss statement. Winston and Newell would sometimes act in an advisory capacity as they reviewed my sales reports. This was valuable to a young merchant who was learning the business daily on the retail frontline.

Prior to leasing the Marshalltown store, Winston and Newell changed their name to Super Valu. Because of our longstanding business relationship, I christened the Marshalltown store with Super Valu also in the name. This was a good move as it tied me closer to my supplier as well as making a statement about the value of their services.

With the store now finished, Max and I were preparing for the grand opening when we developed an electrical short at the front checkout stand. We found out that we could not use both cash registers at the same time without blowing fuses. Max and I had done the electrical work in spite of neither one of us being an electrician. That's how retail was done in those days with the owner and managers wearing a variety of hats to save time and money. I guess that our electrician's hat was on kind of crooked when we wired the checkout stands.

Max and I worked all night before the grand opening using a jackhammer to tear up the concrete around the cash registers to get at our electrical short. Once this was done, I had a real electrician repair our problem so that it was done properly. We then poured a new layer of fresh concrete over our dug trenches to patch the slab. Fortunately, we had access to some good plywood to place over the new concrete. This kept the shoes of our grand opening shoppers clean as they visited our store for the first time to check out this new merchant in town. While this was a "just in time" job, it was indicative of the commitment a small businessman must have to do whatever it takes to get the job done or, in this case, get the store open as scheduled and honor our ad specials.

The Start of Promoting Big

With a successful grand opening behind us, I knew after a few months in business we had to do something new to attract more customers to the store and increase our volume. I decided that we should start buying eggs from the local farmers; I figured this could possibly increase store traffic. I had seen Keith Rushing do this when I worked for him in Ames, and as it turned out, it worked for us as well.

When the farmers started bringing in their eggs, it struck me one fall day that what I needed to do again to increase our volume was to challenge any farmer in the area to a corn shucking contest as a promotional stunt. This challenge was bound to get lots of attention as most every farmer worth his salt at the time thought a lot of his corn shucking skills. As I had done my share of corn picking/shucking in my day, and I was in tip-top physical shape, this sort of challenge appealed to my competitive nature. This was just the bait for the hook that I had been looking for.

Shortly thereafter, I put a full-page ad in the local paper challenging any and all area farmers to a corn shucking contest. The format for the contest would be that we would shuck corn for four hours. At the end of the allotted time, whoever shucked the most corn would be the winner, with the loser having to buy the shucked corn from the winner at market value. The proceeds from the sale would be donated to the Girl Scouts and Boy Scouts for their troop activities.

While I never had even one farmer challenge me, the promotion really shook up the town and put Smitty's Super Valu Market on the map. Farmers from all over the countryside would come into the store, size me up and wonder, "Can I take him?" Finally, they would browse around the store, discover what great merchandise we had, and sample our superior customer service. I really do regret that no farmer took me up on my challenge, but our steadily increasing volume of sales more than made up for any regrets I had.

Now that I had a larger store, I was free to think more creatively than ever before. One of the keys in retailing is to take a product and create a visual picture for the customer in a manner that makes them want to purchase that item — this is called merchandising. In a small store, it is hard to create this atmosphere as inventory is often packed into the space to meet a broad variety of needs. A larger store allows you to devote more floor space to merchandising for the customer's imagination and needs, ultimately selling more of a specific product.

Shortly after we were in the Marshalltown store, I went to Minneapolis to the Super Valu headquarters to check out a line of private label coffee. When I say private label, I am referring to a manufacturer who will take a product, made to your specifications, and then put your name and logo on it. After tasting several of their coffees, I settled on a distinct coffee blend that impressed me, and I named it "Smitty's Red Rooster Coffee." I gave it the tagline "Something to Crow About," which I used in our advertising.

When I received the first shipment of coffee, I built a large display to draw attention to our new product. I asked a friend who worked at the local radio station, a real funny little guy,

Jerry, to make a red rooster costume that he could wear to run up and down the aisles of the store to help promote the coffee. He was also the radio announcer who presided over the new Smitty's Super Valu Radio program that aired every morning from 7:45 to 8:00.

I decided that a great way to promote our new coffee was to have a contest that aired during our radio show. I came up with the idea that when my friend, the announcer of the show, called local residents, if they answered their telephones, "Smitty's Red Rooster Coffee—Something to Crow About" instead of "hello," they would win a cash prize. If nobody answered with the required response, the jackpot of cash would continue to grow until someone answered correctly.

This turned out to be a very successful promotion and was the start of my never-ending quest to develop ways to distinguish my store from the competition. It showed me how tying the right merchandise to a promotion could not only increase store volume but also awareness of our store in a given community. Most small town grocers in those days did things very traditionally to promote their store, if they promoted at all. I was never content to be "ordinary" or "traditional" and was constantly looking for ways to be different and daring, with fresh ideas to increase sales.

I knew we had hit pay dirt with the coffee promotion when word started to spread around town that our competitor, Mr. Clifton, of Clifton's Supermarket, was not too happy with his attorney. It seems that Mr. Clifton called his attorney during our morning radio show and the attorney answered the phone— you guessed it—"Smitty's Red Rooster Coffee—Something to Crow About." Mr. Clifton was none too pleased with his attorney for his obvious support of his direct competitor and his unprofessional greeting on the office phone. In the poor attorney's defense, the jackpot was almost a hundred dollars and in those days, that was really something to crow about!

During the formative period while we were building the volume of the Marshalltown store, I came up with another promotion that got a lot of attention. It was during the flying saucer days when there was a national fascination with spacemen and their aircraft.

I decided to buy a large quantity of white paper plates that resembled "flying saucers." The staff and I wrote on each plate a message entitling whoever found the plate to a free gift item at our store. This might be a box of Jell-O, a pound of ground beef, or some other consumer staple. We used multiple items that had strong consumer appeal so that the customer would make sure to redeem the plate as soon as possible.

Once we had written on all the plates, I went up in a small two-seater Piper Cub airplane and tossed the plates out over every farm and small town in our county. I asked the pilot to fly really low, especially when we saw people, and I would open the door and lean way out of the plane and toss the plates. It was incredible to see the reaction of the people on the ground when they saw the plates coming down at them. It was even better when they realized that they were entitled to a free item at the Smitty's store!

I am sure that a promotion of this type was a first for any retailer at that time in Iowa. I can't tell you how many plates we redeemed and how successful this promotion was. Like the corn shucking contest, the coffee promotion, and our unique approach of buying eggs from area farmers, the "flying saucer" promotion distinguished us from the competition and moved us towards a healthy sales volume of $7,000–$8,000 per week.

Marshalltown was truly a turning point in my career as a retailer. The space I leased turned out to be a real winner when combined with creative promotions, excellent staff, and superior merchandising. We had been well received by the community and our sales volume was strong. I was never one to stand still for long, so in our fourth year of business, I began to develop my boldest retail plan yet. This unfolded almost five years to the day after we leased our Marshalltown store.

Worth Thinking About

"A man is a lion in his own cause."

—Scottish Proverb

"Every man must carry his own sack to the mill."

—Danish Proverb

"Look well into thyself; there is a source of strength which will always spring up if thou wilt always look there."

—Marcus Aurelius Antoninus

"Let him that would move the world, first move himself."

—Socrates

"Your word is a lamp unto my feet. And a light unto my path."

—the Bible, Psalm 119:05

8

An Adventure in Shopping

"I was convinced that shopping in our
store should be an adventure for our customers."
—Clyde B. Smith

In the fall of 1954, we opened a brand-new Smitty's Super
Valu store in Marshalltown. It was a monster at 15,000 square
feet! The store was our first custom-built market, and it replaced
the original 3,200-square-foot store we had leased five years prior.
The new store boasted a full "scratch" bakery and coffee shop,
departments that were unheard of in a grocery store at the time.
We were probably the first grocery store in Iowa to put in a real
scratch bakery and a coffee shop. Both were well received by the
public. The store was over four times the size of our original store
in Marshalltown, complete with expanded meat, grocery, and
produce departments. The new store offered the kind of space
where I could do things in an expanded way. The size allowed us
to have a bigger diversity of products to entice the customer each
time they shopped the store. It also gave us space for a one-of-a-
kind promotion that would build on our reputation of "daring to
be different." By now, I was fully convinced that shopping in our
store should be an adventure for our customers, not just the same
old grocery store design and layout.

One of my favorite promotions in our new expanded store was our first truckload sale of fresh fish. In the winter of 1955, with temperatures in Iowa at ten degrees below zero, we brought in fresh fish from all over the world and treated the community of Marshalltown with a promotion beyond their wildest dreams. To tantalize them, we hung a huge flounder outside the store that created a strong visual effect. We even brought in a big, live sea turtle to further draw attention and to get people talking. Then to top things off, we treated them to a shipment of live lobsters from Maine.

Customers in our part of Iowa had never seen anything like this before. It amazed me that people would run into the store and scoop up armloads of fresh frozen pike and other fish, oblivious of the smell that they got on their clothes, all because it offered a variety not usually found in the normal supermarket! As a merchant, I was gratified to see such an acceptance of our promotions and our registers ringing nonstop. Soon, our expanded market was hitting a volume of over $35,000 per week and our team of dedicated, trained staff was just as happy as I was. Personally, this energized me to try harder and to accomplish more! It was very gratifying.

The Supermarket Institute

My dear friend and mentor Keith Rushing was an active member of the Supermarket Institute. He would often take me to their conventions to help further my education as a retail grocer. The Supermarket Institute was a worldwide organization, which attracted hundreds of thousands of people. They were the lead trade group in our industry and offered a wealth of educational and networking experiences. We would go to the meetings and be exposed to all the new products, fixtures, and other merchandise developed for the supermarket business, as well as products to make stores more complete, efficient, and competitive. Whatever your needs as a grocer, the Supermarket Institute was a clearinghouse of ideas, products, innovation, and education for the retail grocer. I was always grateful to be invited to these trade shows as they helped me to better understand the magnitude of what a modern, up-to-date supermarket could be.

It was during my time in Marshalltown that I became very active in the Supermarket Institute organizations — eventually being invited to sit on their board of directors. This is a relationship that I would cherish for the next several years. Being a member of their board of directors offered me a window into the supermarket world that stimulated me as a retailer. As a board member, I got to experience firsthand the new concepts as they happened — many of these I would incorporate into an existing or a new future store design that I was planning to build.

As a retailer, I wanted to be the first or the most progressive operator in my market when it came to new ideas and concepts. I was zealous about exceeding the customer's expectations and wanted to excite them at every turn in our store. It was not uncommon for me to put several of our managers in a car and drive all night to a new store opening if I heard through my contacts at the Supermarket Institute that a new and innovative concept was to be revealed. I was not too proud to admit that other retailers had great ideas or a new merchandising concept. In fact, if I really liked it, I would stock the idea away in my memory and try to replicate it back into one of our stores. Of course, I would try to improve on the concept if at all possible.

Building a First-Class Team

Since my first store in Roland, Iowa, I knew that if I was going to be successful as a retailer, I would have to build a first-class team. I believed that you are only as good as your people, no matter how talented you are. I embraced this concept and devoted much of my energies as a businessman in hiring, training, and investing in the right type of people who could help me build the business so as to try to be number one in the industry.

Early I learned the importance of delegating authority, giving the right people a job and then letting them do it. I always knew what was going on, however, and kept a tight rein. Developing personnel has always been a part of my work.

I also was adamant about sharing the wealth with our managers as a reward and incentive for exceeding their job expectations. By the time we built the new Marshalltown store, I had developed a business plan that allowed our department managers to share in the profits from each department and the store as a whole. This was in direct contrast to most small town grocers who were content to keep the profits themselves. My objective in doing this was to get them excited and thinking about "our" store instead of just "my" store. Once I helped them achieve this mode of thinking, I could then concentrate on moving the business forward, and the staff would take care of our store and its many needs.

The strategies I used to forge a first-class team in those early days are almost comical. It makes me smile and laugh when I recall things like getting the staff together on a Saturday night after a long day of hard work to see who could do the most push-ups or arm wrestle. This was an odd way to end our work week, but it was a great team-building exercise. Instead of buying a case of beer and lounging around at informal meetings, we would do calisthenics or dance on one leg like a Russian Cossack. We had a game where two people would grab the same broomstick with both hands and hold it out from their chests. They would then try to pull the stick down until the opponent's hands broke their grip on the broomstick. This was a real test of strength and got lots of catcalls from the group. While these games might seem odd in the context of today's work force, in the 1950s world, they brought us closer together as a team.

In the three markets I had competed in up to this point, I knew one of our biggest assets was our people. I became a stickler about training and kept this at the forefront of our business plan for all my years as a retailer. I learned a good lesson from that Norwegian competitor in Roland when the Norwegians in town resisted shopping with us. I just trained my team harder and better, ultimately winning them over with a level of superior customer service.

One of the training traditions I started in Marshalltown was to send everyone in our organization that was destined to advance through our ranks to the Dale Carnegie Course. This self-improvement course taught these individuals how to be leaders and more productive team members, and improved their customer service skills. The course taught them to be passionate about their job and their team. The overall objective was for them to learn to think and talk on their feet. It developed their personalities.

While my first objective in sending these individuals to Dale Carnegie was to make our organization better, I also hoped that this training would add value to their personal lives. I knew that an employee who was happy and fulfilled from within would be better and more productive at both work and home. Later, I would add the Toastmasters program to this training ritual.

What I Had Learned So Far

By the time we got into the new 15,000-square-foot Marshalltown store, I was beginning to develop more fully my business principals and core values. I started with the philosophy of "dare to be different" and incorporated this principle into everything we did as a company. I was passionate about this and tran-slated it into our crazy, one-of-a-kind promotions and our store mass-merchandising. I wanted to be first with the latest merchandising ideas and scoop our competitors whenever possible. I purposely built enduring relationships with our suppliers so that they would always keep our business at the forefront of their distribution chain.

This passion to be different also built a passion in me to be the best. In order to do this, I had to be willing to work hard and motivate those around me to do the same. I had to learn to trust my staff and let them do their job. I also knew that to do their job effectively they had to have training, more training, and training on top of that.

I had also learned that I should share the wealth with those key staff members who really made their departments grow. If they were willing to work long hours, spend extended time away from their families, and really dedicate themselves to being the best, they were entitled to share in the financial rewards that were created. If they were to enrich my life, I needed to enrich theirs. I felt this was good business and the honorable thing to do.

I learned that if we were going to be the best, I could never take my eyes off the needs of the customer. Once those crazy promotions got them into the store, we had to take the customer on a shopping experience that made them feel good about shopping at Smitty's. My goal was that when customers went home and unpacked their purchases, they still felt good about where they had shopped and what they had bought. I knew if I accomplished this, it would help establish a solid foundation, and then the shoppers would tell their friends and neighbors, which would ultimately grow the business.

By the time we got into that big store in Marshalltown, I realized how grateful I was that as a small boy, teenager, and young man, I had learned the principals of hard work, integrity, the value of a handshake, and being the best that I could be at all times. I was fortunate that my father took an interest in teaching me the value of hard work, pushing me beyond those limits I set for myself. My dad and mom helped develop in me a competitive nature that fueled a truckload of desire and ambition. These became my foundation as a retailer and ultimately the guiding principles of the company I founded. I had learned a lot about retailing and serving the public.

Worth Thinking About

"If you want to become the greatest in your field, no matter what it may be, equip yourself to render greater service than anyone else."

—Clinton Davidson

"Nothing can bring such peace but the triumph of principles."

—Ralph Waldo Emerson

"To be able to look back upon one's past with satisfaction is to live twice."

"I had to be willing to work hard and motivate those around me to do the same. I had to learn to trust my staff and let them do their job."

"I should share the wealth with those key staff members who really made their departments grow. If they were to enrich my life, I needed to enrich theirs."

"I must never take my eyes off the needs of the customer."

—Clyde B. Smith

9

Growth Opportunities

"Tomorrow's growth depends on the use
we make of today's materials and experiences."

—Clyde B. Smith

Things Really Start to Roll

In 1956, Keith Rushing took me to a grocery store he owned in Monticello, Iowa, for a look around. After we looked the store over, he asked me if I would consider buying it from him. As I had been looking for another growth opportunity, the purchase sounded interesting. Unfortunately for Mr. Rushing, the store had never been in the black no matter how hard he tried. Of course, this type of challenge suited me just fine, especially after reviewing the sales, the gross profits, and the opportunity I felt it offered. Mr. Rushing and I made a deal.

I transferred Carroll Vaughn from our Marshalltown store to Monticello to be the manager of the new store. I also took a few other store persons with me to help Carroll get things in order. The team and I merchandised the entire store according to guidelines we had developed in the Marshalltown store, along with a general "spruce up" and overhaul to attract customers to come look and shop.

As we were going about the conversion, I discovered that the only real problem with Rushing's operation was that it had been merchandised poorly. Keith had a lady manager who put too many "loss leader" items at the end of each aisle. These made it too easy for the customers to cherry-pick the store and miss the items with a better markup. As we merchandised the store, I kept this in mind and did not repeat the mistake of the previous owner. I immediately got acquainted with the suppliers and negotiated special deals to better merchandise and offer better products and prices to our customers.

I was pleased that when we took an inventory three months later, the Monticello store was in the black. Carroll and his team had worked extremely hard, and being profitable was their reward. I believed that each store must pull its own weight to make a contribution to the company's overall efforts, and that if it did not, not much had been accomplished except to dilute the profits from the other stores. With the Monticello store being in the black in just three months, I was very happy with the results.

Other Growth Opportunities

With the two stores now showing a good profit, I decided to build a 20,000-square-foot store in Waterloo, Iowa, in 1957. Waterloo was a big town and would challenge my retailing abilities. While building the new store, I made a deal to buy two additional stores in Waterloo, which created a synergy and allowed me to spread the cost of overhead line items such as advertising, distribution, supervision, and training over a larger retail base.

I hired a manager from Waterloo named Gil Hoeg. He had many years of experience and a wonderful personality; he fit well into our operation. Gil knew the market and helped us hit the ground running. This was important because Waterloo had the largest population base of any market we had competed in so far. It also had the most competition.

Later in 1957, we opened another new store in Mount Vernon, Iowa. The store was 12,000 square feet, much smaller than the prior two stores we had built, but it was tailored for the size of the market. Mount Vernon was a nice little store complete with all the basic departments. While it was smaller in size, it had the Smitty's feel and was merchandised as well as any of our other stores.

By the end of 1957, about a two-and-a-half-year span, we had gone from the one store in Marshalltown to six Smitty's Super Valu Markets spread over four different towns. They pushed our team into the big leagues with its own set of challenges. I was grateful that we had developed an organizational structure and the policies and procedures to support it. But given my competitive nature, I was soon looking around the corner for the next challenge to test my skills and those of my topflight staff.

In the fall of 1958, we had opened a beautiful new 25,00-square-foot store with bakery and restaurant, in Iowa City, Iowa, and it took off like a rocket. The store was managed by Everett Larson, who was assisted by my brother Doug. Because of the store's success, and lots of Everett's and Doug's hard work, I was able to sell this store in 1960 to a supermarket friend, Doc Randal, who had a chain of food stores out of Mitchell, South Dakota. This sale turned out to be very good for us, and it provided the seed money we needed to begin the move to Phoenix and to get started with our first store there.

Worth Thinking About

"There is nothing as laborious as not to labor. Blessed is he who devotes his life to great and noble ends, and who forms his well-considered plans with deliberate wisdom."

—St. Augustine

"This is the only chance you will ever have on this earth with this exciting adventure called life. So why not plan it, and try to live it as richly, as happily as possible?"

—Dale Carnegie

"Happiness does not consist in getting something; it consists in becoming something."

"One's eyes are placed in front because it is important to look ahead. Cultivate foresight."

"Self-confidence is a first requisite of great undertakings."

"What the future has in store for you depends in large measure on what you place in store for the future."

"Remember that what you possess in the world will be found at the day of your death to belong to someone else; but what you are will be yours forever."

—Clyde B. Smith

10

The Smitty Stores Go "James Bond"

"Nobody was thinking about the customer. . . . I decided to do some 'retail espionage.' The undercover work of my grocers enabled us to take the Phoenix market by storm."

—Clyde B. Smith

Vacation in Phoenix

In 1959, Helen and I took a one-week vacation in Phoenix, Arizona. After about 48 hours, I was starting to get restless. I decided to do some retail discovery work by checking out the supermarkets in the Phoenix area, the Valley of the Sun. This was a delightful habit that I had developed over the years; I was always curious about other retailers. Wherever I traveled, I ritually tried to visit a sampling of the supermarkets in the immediate area to get a sense of what was going on from a retailer's perspective. Always on the lookout for a unique idea or a clever merchandising technique, checking out grocery stores in different markets was very stimulating to me. As you may have surmised by now, I had an insatiable appetite for finding the "next cutting-edge retailing idea" that I could take back and incorporate into my stores. I wanted shoppers in our area to be the first to experience any new and different marketing ideas available.

In 1959, Phoenix had a population base of about four hundred thousand people. This was a huge market compared to the size of the Iowa markets in which we competed. At the time, Phoenix was home to many of the major grocery retailers, including Safeway, Bashas', Bayless, Food City, and a host of other independent operators.

To my surprise, after I took a hard look at the grocery stores in the Phoenix market, I discovered that most of these stores were really "Plain Jane." Many were not as well merchandised as our stores in Iowa, and none had the amenities such as a scratch bakery and coffee shop. These lackluster square boxes seemed less intimidating as I took a closer look. Maybe they were not as bulletproof as they originally appeared to be.

One of the first mistakes I noticed that the grocery stores in Phoenix were making was their building locations in the shopping centers that they occupied. Most of these grocery stores were located in the middle of the shopping centers, and, in my opinion, were as poorly located as you could get. Most of these centers were built in an L shape, putting the grocery store in the corner of the L. This made it more difficult for their customers to park close to the entrance, ultimately creating parking frustrations.

A supermarket is very important to the future success of a shopping center. As the primary anchor tenant in most strip centers, the supermarket should be on the end to facilitate ease of access for their customers. Laying out a functional parking lot is critical. Doing so allows customers to park closer to the entrance, making the unloading of groceries easier after shopping. While this might seem trivial to other retailers, it showed me that nobody was thinking about the customer as these stores were planned. If such an important item was being overlooked, I figured that there must be more weaknesses in the Phoenix competition.

Our week's vacation in Phoenix came to an end; by the time we were ready to leave for home in Iowa, I had made up my mind that we were going to move our company and open up some supermarkets in Phoenix. After my retail search and discovery, I just knew we could compete. Unlike the corporate bureaucracy of today, there was no detailed business plan or strategic planning session, just me making a decision that felt really good. Once my mind was made up, it was full steam ahead — no looking back!

I once had a small town banker call me a "plunger." He thought that I charged off in the dark without doing my homework and thinking about the consequences. Truthfully, I'm the type of person who likes to see the light at the other end of the tunnel before I go in, but I am also the type of person who is not afraid of going in the tunnel. While moving into the Phoenix market may have seemed like "plunging," my competitive nature told me that we had the new business designs and concept, plus the resources to compete effectively. If there was one thing I knew, it was the grocery business — I didn't need a team of Harvard graduates to tell me whether I was doing the right thing or not. If this was considered "plunging," then that's the way it was going to be.

Going "James Bond"

With Everett and Doug out of the Iowa City store, I hatched a novel plan to do some retail espionage. Realizing that I needed good firsthand information in the Phoenix market and needed to learn the buying habits of the residents, I decided to take Everett, Doug, and four additional key people to Phoenix while I was building the first store. Instead of helping me, I told each of them to get a job at one of the better chain or independent grocery stores in town. Their mission was to gather as much firsthand information about the local grocery business as they could. I knew there was no better way to understand the Phoenix consumer and his shopping habits than to be on the frontlines where the action was. Wanting to be fair to my undercover grocers, I told them that our company would subsidize any difference in their pay if necessary.

Within days, every one of these Smitty's employees was working for one of our soon-to-be competitors. These were first-class grocers, and they started to move up the ladder right away. As time permitted, we would secretly meet, and they would debrief me on what they were experiencing and all the good things they were learning about the Phoenix market.

I cannot tell you how much I owe these individuals. The information they were able to gather was invaluable as I began to plan the merchandising of our first store. I soon learned the many commodity differences that there were between Phoenix and Iowa. I learned that the climate played a big role in what products we should buy and in what depth. For instance, in a warm weather store, you cut way back on your candy department. People buy more candy in a cold climate than in a hot. There were so many differences in the two regions that the undercover work of my "James Bond" grocers saved us thousands of dollars on possible mistakes. Through their work and team dedication, we were able to take the Phoenix market by storm with the right merchandising plan!

I acknowledge these great friends for their valuable contribution in helping us get it right at the outset in the original Phoenix Store:

Everett Larson — Store Manager
Doug Smith — Assistant Store Manager
Arnold Eggers — Bakery Manager
Tony Witte — Produce Manager
Al Larson — Receiving Manager
Dick Greenley — Accountant
Carl Mattox — Restaurant Manager

Taking the Competition Head On

While our team was garnering valuable information about the Phoenix grocery market, I was busy designing and preparing a floor plan that I felt would be a big attraction for the twenty-six-acre location I had chosen at 16th Street and Buckeye. The location appealed to me because I wanted to be close to the Food City store and the huge volume of business they were enjoying. I wanted to share and enjoy part of the high volume sales in this area of the Phoenix market.

In my typical risk-taking style, I decided to take a fifty-year lease on the twenty-six acres. I figured by doing so, I was making a long-term commitment to the Phoenix market. Once I struck the deal, I personally wrote up the agreement, which drove my attorney, Arley Wilson, of Marshalltown, Iowa, crazy. "Smitty," he used to say, "I will stay out of the grocery business if you stay out of the attorney business!" Of course, he thought I was goofy for wanting to sign a fifty-year lease.

After I nailed downed the location, the next thing I did was get with a fixture and store design company in Phoenix called Parmenter. I teamed up with their key design man, Burton Barr. He and I then spent hours at the drawing board drawing and redrawing that first store. I knew if we were going to take on Food City and the Phoenix market, we had to have the right store design and merchandising concept.

I finally settled on a store design that ended up at 56,000 square feet. This would be the largest grocery store in Phoenix and all of Arizona. Burton Barr and I laid the store out with a unique floor plan that was designed to take the customer on a really enjoyable shopping experience. We even incorporated aisles that were so big and wide that you could drive a car between them. This concept was highly unusual at that time as most grocery stores tried to pack as much as they could into what floor space they had.

I was glad I had chosen Parmenter to be my store design company as I really enjoyed working with Burton Barr. He was a great guy, and we were destined to spend a lot of time together in the coming years. He did have one habit that irritated me at times. Just as we would be about finished with a working drawing, he would come up with some new idea and begin to scribble on the nearly finished plan. "Hey," I told him, "if you want to show me something, do it on a piece of scratch paper!"

In the end, the store design I signed off on was huge compared to the other stores we had built! Newspapers were to call the store a "Goliath" in the food market industry. The actual floor plan was almost twice the size of our immediate competitor, Food City. As we finalized the store plan, we felt confident that our concept and management team were ready to show Arizona a new, modern approach to supermarket retailing.

As the new store was being built, I began to line up our suppliers. Since I now had been in the business some fourteen years, I had already dealt with many of the suppliers through our Iowa stores. Most suppliers were happy with our plan to bring a new supermarket concept to Phoenix. They looked forward to the increased sales their company would enjoy. In turn, they offered us exceptional deals to take on their products.

I did have one situation that still puzzles me to this day. For some reason, the ice cream suppliers in the Phoenix area wanted to charge me almost double the price that I was paying per gallon in Iowa. I surmised that these guys were talking with each other because none of them would back off the price. The harder I tried to break this pact the worse the situation got.

I have to admit that at first I was stumped on what to do with what seemed to me like "price fixing." I knew that ice cream was a huge seller in a warm climate such as Phoenix, and it was vital that our store be competitive. I was about to run out of ideas when I remembered a manufacturer in Cedar Rapids, Iowa, the Cherry Burrell Company, who manufactured ice cream-making equipment. I went back to Iowa and set up a meeting with the manufacturer. We decided that what we needed to do was purchase the equipment and install a complete ice cream manufacturing plant right in our new store!

Burton Barr and I identified an area up over the meat department that would be perfect for the ice cream plant. I envisioned putting a glass wall around this section so that the customers could watch their ice cream being made as they shopped. I would then have demonstrators passing out samples. I knew that if I could just get the shoppers to taste the quality and flavor being made, we would sell a ton of ice cream. While this idea would require some additional expense and experience, I thought it really fit well into my philosophy of "daring to be different." I was just about to sign the equipment order when I thought perhaps I would give the Phoenix supplier one more chance to break the price they were asking.

I had done quite a bit of business in Iowa, so a national manufacturing company and I used our new plan to appeal to them one last time. When the regional manager came to the conclusion that I was serious, their company finally agreed that they could not charge me such a large difference for the same product in the two different markets. They knew my reputation and figured that I was really going to move forward with the in-store plant. Just in the nick of time, they sent out one of their "big shots" with a proposal that they would sell ice cream to me at the price I was paying in Iowa.

Naturally, I was not very trusting when he made their proposal because of what I had been through. I then looked the guy in the eye about the offer and asked the question he did not want to hear, "How long are you going to honor this price?" The shocked ice cream salesman stammered, and then he said, "Five years." I was elated with the outcome of this situation because I had locked into a favorable pricing structure on a key product for the next five years. I learned early in my business career that it usually pays to be a good negotiator. In this case, it really paid off!

Worth Thinking About

- Little bantams are great at crowing.

- Never cackle till your egg is laid.

- Never forget a customer; never let a customer forget you.

- Customers don't need us; we need them. Customers are not interruptions of our work; they are the purpose of it. Customers are people who bring us their wants. Our job is to handle them profitably for the customers and us. Customers are not outsiders to our business; they are a vital part of it.

- He who prevails most, dares. Fortune favors the daring. No one reaches a high position without daring.

11

Translating Your Vision of Merchandising into Reality for Your Customers

"Sweat + Effort = Success"

—Clyde B. Smith

Our First Store in Phoenix

About four weeks before our first store in Phoenix was to open, I called my "undercover" grocers back to resume their respective positions with the company. Since we were in the critical last stages of the opening process, I needed my best staff to stock the entire store, train the new employees, and translate our "Smitty's Vision" of merchandising into a reality for our potential customers. Largely thanks to their reconnaissance, I was confident that we had the right insight and merchandise mix for the market. I felt sure that we could wow the Phoenix consumer with our physical facility, plus our well-trained, friendly employees and the superior product offering. Again, I owe thanks to my undercover team.

We were determined that Smitty's Big Town Market was not just going to be a place to buy groceries, but a unique and exciting shopping experience for the customer. This store was to bring together all those innovative ideas we had refined in our Iowa stores, along with some new ideas I felt would work well with our expanded store size.

Our new store included a large, complete scratch bakery, and a first-class butcher at the meat department, which included a well-merchandised, self-service meat section. It also included a deli, a 120-seat restaurant, and what was soon to be one of the best merchandised produce departments in the entire Phoenix area. Tony Witte was a first-class produce man and knew how to appeal to the customer through product mix and quality presentation. He also had a talent for buying the right merchandise direct from the local farmers, and at the right price!

Back in the late 1950s and early 1960s, having specialty departments like a scratch bakery and a full-service restaurant inside a supermarket was not common. These were the departments we had pioneered in our Iowa stores, and I wanted to introduce them to the Phoenix consumer. I believe that you have to "scoop" your competition if possible and be first at whatever you do in business. This was a passion I had developed early as a retailer. With our first store in Phoenix, I was willing to take on the increased expense of departments like these to put some distance between us and our competitors.

As the final few days before our opening unfolded, I felt very sure about what we had accomplished. Not only was the store big and beautiful, but I thought the merchandise flow was really going to be first class. Burton Barr and I had agreed that, by making the shopping aisles wider at seven feet, the customer would enjoy the extra room while shopping. Furthermore, the wide aisles gave the store a very open and inviting feel. Our departments were outstanding with our department heads working their magic at every turn. Our store managers, Doug Smith and Everett Larson, did a great job of coordinating the flurry of activities that inevitably happen just before an opening. I also knew I could count on our baker, Arnold Eggers, really to put on a show with the first "in-store scratch bakery" in town.

As an ex-butcher, I was also very proud of the meat market. We specialized in custom cuts of prime meat at very attractive prices. Also, rather than tossing a bunch of pre-sliced meat in a case like most grocers did at the time, we had a self-service side of the meat market that had a boutique feel. Surveying the store shortly before the opening, I knew our management team and our well-trained staff were ready to meet the competition head-on.

Looking back, I realize that we must have been in the crosshairs of every supermarket operator in Arizona before we opened that first store. Those grocers who hired our people had now figured out our motives and would be gunning for us with the hopes of a speedy failure. Was there anything illegal or wrong in doing this? No, or I certainly wouldn't have done it. Here was this guy from Iowa who had competed in small markets and now had the nerve to try to compete in one of the largest retail markets in Arizona. Our competitors must have looked at the size of our store and the associated overhead, and thought that we were crazy to take on such a huge obligation. Little did they know that I had spent the last fourteen years building a business model that I felt sure could compete in any market in the country. As we put the finishing touches on our first store in Phoenix, I was ready and willing to find out.

Just a Peek

As we prepared for the grand opening of our first Phoenix store, I decided that we should have a "sneak peek" the evening before. We had utilized this method multiple times in prior store openings in Iowa with great success. In a sneak peek preview, you whet the appetite of potential consumers by inviting the who's who of the area where you are opening, in this case, some of the citizens of Phoenix and Arizona, into the store and giving them a peek at the new facility before the general public was invited in. Traditionally, the groups who are invited to the sneak peek are dignitaries, politicians, the media, and others of influence who can mold consumer opinion for weeks to come after the store is opened.

Once in the store, these dignitaries are tempted with a wide variety of quality foods to sample and enjoy as they are toured through the store by management and staff. We worked with our key vendors to provide their products as samples for the many visitors in hopes of growing both our business and that of the vendor. During the sneak peek, nothing is sold, which further builds excitement for the grand opening the following day.

I am happy to say that our sneak preview, held in February of 1961, at Smitty's Big Town Market was highly successful. Hundreds of dignitaries came from all over the Phoenix area to check out the new competitor in town. Since we needed their tongues to wag for some time after the sneak preview, our people and vendors pulled out all the stops for this blue chip group. We could tell that everyone really enjoyed themselves as they toured the largest supermarket to date in Arizona history. Things could not have gone better, and I was happy and thankful about the entire event.

"Merchandise by the Acre"

Phoenix newspapers headlined their take on the store with "Merchandise by the Acre," explaining that the concept was so new that the merchandising industry hadn't gotten a name for it yet, although it was being dubbed variously as a "super supermarket" and as a "combination store" or "a combo complex." Mainly the store was a grocery supermarket along with some new departments not usually found in a super-market, such as a scratch bakery and restaurant, that expanded into a wide range of nonfood products.

More than a Grand Opening

The day of our grand opening, people came from all over the Phoenix area to see the new store. The volume of people and the merchandise they bought was staggering. I was glad that we had trained our staff well; they executed their duties as close to perfect as you can get. It was one of those amazing days where everything about the store, our customers, the merchandise, and our staff seemed to work. I can't remember the exact promotions and special ads we ran, but whatever we did worked. Most every shopping cart was full as our new customers shopped the exciting, well-merchandised departments of the store.

After we opened the store on the first day of the grand opening, I was walking around, greeting the shoppers, making sure that everything was in place and everybody was working according to plan. I looked out the store front and saw a group of guys trying to steal a car. I quickly ran out of the store and confronted the would-be car thieves. I didn't carry a gun in those days, but I guess I was so aggressive that I scared the tar out of them, and they quickly abandoned their objective and took off before I had a chance to get the police involved.

There were five more attempted car thefts that day, which was unbelievable to me. While our promotional activities had brought out the shoppers, they also brought out a group of bad guys who were determined to take advantage of us and the chaos of our first day. This was something none of us had experienced or planned for, and it took us totally by surprise. While I had faced many challenges as an Iowan retailer, I had never been confronted with such brazen individuals! In Iowa, we would occasionally have a petty shoplifter, but that was about the extent of it.

I had chosen the location of our first store to be near the Food City store because it was one of the highest volume supermarkets in Arizona. Unfortunately, this location was in a very tough part of south Phoenix, which presented us with a whole new set of problems. Phoenix at the time had a population of approximately 400,000 people with its share of an unsavory element. We soon learned that a great many of these individuals lived in our trade area. This was a whole new wrinkle for a group of Iowa farm-boy-type retailers who were used to competing in towns with less than 50,000 in population.

In short order, our team learned the questionable habits of the neighborhood and devised ways to deal with them. We soon had standard operating procedures to deal with shoplifters, car thieves, and purse snatchers. We learned the unique responses of the different ethnic groups as they were confronted with an alleged crime. Some would pull a gun or start swinging the moment they were confronted. Others would be more passive until they knew what you were going to do. If they did not like what they were sensing from you, out would come the knife, and the fight was on.

I found out that our first store would consistently supply us with more than our share of adrenalin. In our first year, we saw more guns, knives, and swinging fists than we had in our entire time in Iowa. At one point, my brother Doug was shot; at a later date, my good friend Clim Gonzales was shot in the shoulder. Both of them turned out okay, and I thanked God for watching over them. We had come to Phoenix to be retailers, but this was something we hadn't envisioned. After fifteen years in business, I knew retailing was tough, but this took tough to a whole new level.

From the day of our grand opening, we were elated with the volume the new store was doing. It appeared that our attention to the merchandise mix, promotions, and our customer service was really paying dividends. I knew this was true when, at the end of the second mont we took an inventory and I was pleased with the results — the store was making a profit.

It is almost unheard of to get such a large store profitable as quickly as we did. Normally, it takes several months to absorb all the training that is necessary, plus paying for front-end costs and other overhead associated with putting together a new store. Because we were turning our inventory so fast, we shortened the path to getting the market into being profitable. These accelerated inventory turns also helped us build up our cash reserve due to the lag time in paying for purchases. This looked good to me as I contemplated future expansion into the Phoenix arena.

Could what we did be replicated by someone else wanting to start, grow, and expand a business such as this? The answer is yes.

Worth Thinking About

"Be grateful for each new day. A new day that you have never lived before. Twenty-four new, fresh, unexplored hours to use usefully and profitably. We can squander, neglect, or use it. Life will be richer or poorer by the way we use today."

—Ralph Waldo Emerson

"Success is reached by being active, awake, ahead of the crowd, by aiming high, pushing ahead, honestly, diligently, patiently; by climbing, digging, saving, by forgetting the past, using the present, trusting in the future; by honoring God—having a purpose, fainting not, determining to win, and striving to the end."

—Russell Conwell

"Determine that the thing can and shall be done, and then we shall find the way."

—Abraham Lincoln

12

Promotions, Profitability, and Good Business Practices

"With numerous promotional activities, we put a lot of distance between us and our competition."

—Clyde B. Smith

Promoting That First Year

In Iowa, I experimented with numerous promotional activities to grow our business and had become pretty good at them. In fact, we put a lot of distance between us and our competition that way. I wanted to be first with an idea, or new concept, in reaching the customer. We had become known for our semitruckload sales, mass merchandising, and quirky promotions. These promotions had worked; I wanted to continue to build on these successes in our new Phoenix market.

After putting some thought into what would be one of the most unusual promotions that would draw attention to the store, I decided that we should introduce our full-service restaurant as the "featured lead" in our advertisement. In those days, it was highly unusual for a supermarket to have a full-service restaurant, and I knew that this would be a promotion that our competitors could not duplicate.

I decided that we would promote a complete chicken dinner in the restaurant for only 29 cents! This would include two pieces of chicken, mashed potatoes, gravy, green beans, and a drink of your choice. Back in those days, a typical dinner like this would have been around $1.29, so this was a real bargain. I knew that this promotion would garner attention but was not prepared for the crowd of people who lined up and out the door into our parking lot when the promotion broke.

Inside the restaurant, the scene was chaotic. Every table was full, and the kitchen was operating at full speed. The staff was moving as fast as they could, while the people in line eyed the chicken dinners being served to the lucky patrons who were sitting and enjoying the great quality meal.

When you do a promotion such as this, you must be careful that it doesn't backfire. I was confident in our staff's performance but was concerned that the people in line would get tired of waiting and leave. This would be counterproductive to the intent of the promotion, so I turned my attention to solving the wait problem.

Moving through the restaurant, I gathered all my "brass" and started to target those tables with patrons who had finished their dinner. I would introduce myself and ask, "Did you enjoy your dinner?" Everyone was pleased and complimented me on the meal and said they were just enjoying sitting and having another drink and such. At this point, I gestured to the line of hungry patrons needing to get seated and politely suggested they might want to consider those who were waiting.

I must have had a smooth delivery as most of the patrons hurried to conclusion and vacated their table with a smile, making room for the next group. This was a relief as I was walking a fine line between making the diners angry for hurrying them up, while those in line might also get upset for not being seated fast enough. These are the kind of risks that are involved with daring to be different. Fortunately, by the time I got to Phoenix, I was getting more or less used to doing this.

We were very pleased with our chicken dinner promotion. We had taken one of our unique strengths and utilized it to draw attention to our entire store. Many, if not most, of the people shopped after their meal, but the real intention was to expose our organization to shoppers all over Phoenix who could become patrons. I knew that with our big, new store, our well-trained staff, superior merchandising, and good pricing, we could convert them into becoming regular Smitty's customers. And I was willing to risk selling a chicken dinner for 29 cents to do so!

I must have been hung up on the figure of "29 cents" at that time in my retail career because some time later, I decided to run a special featuring a gallon of milk for only 29 cents. This was to be one of our most successful promotions, but it brought us an unintended consequence that I did not anticipate.

To get things in motion for our milk promotion, I called a new supplier friend of mine named Dave Vandervoort who owned and operated an independent dairy, called the Sweet Milk Company, in the Phoenix area. I asked Dave if he could supply me with lots and lots of milk. I explained to Dave that I wanted to sell a gallon of milk for 29 cents during a big promotion I was planning. This was a crazy loss price leader even in those days so I wanted to make sure that I could get enough milk to supply our customers during the promotion. If there was one thing I hated, it was going into a store for a promotional ad item and they had "just run out." To me, this was unacceptable. My theory is, if you are going to do it, do it well and be prepared!

Dave assured me of a steady supply of milk during the pro-motion, and I pulled the trigger on the event. When the ad broke in the paper, people came from all over Phoenix. It was a stampede of buyers, just as I had hoped for. Every cart that checked out had milk in it, and every buyer had a big smile from the savings on the basic commodity. I was happy at providing such a bargain for our customers and grateful that almost every shopping cart had a good variety of other retail items in their carts, which helped to offset the money we were losing on the milk.

I was feeling really good about the promotion when I no-ticed that the labor union had set up a trailer out in our parking lot. They had put word out to their membership about our promotion and were offering a dollar to each union member to go into the store and buy three gallons of milk. The union knew I was losing money on the milk, and I guess they wanted to make it more painful by adding to my losses. What this had to do with "worker's rights" baffled me. The union was just being spiteful because our people up to this point did not need them and were doing well on their own. So far, we had resisted their overtures to organize, which I am sure infuriated them.

At first, I was madder than a hornet when I found out what the union was up to. My first instinct was to ask them to leave our property, but with all the customers coming and going, I decided the last thing I needed was a confrontation with the union in my parking lot. So, I decided to take a different approach.

I walked out to the union trailer and really turned on the personality. I said, "I want to thank you guys for kicking in a buck a piece for all these shoppers." This was not the response that they expected, and it blew their mind. If the union was causing me any pain, those boys in the trailer certainly could not tell it on my face and by my warm reception.

What the union men did not think about was that even the union members shopped for more than just milk when they were in our store. Their promotion of my promotion simply added volume to our business and probably created some goodwill with union members as they told their friends about the good buy they got at Smitty's. The union men also did not know that I would continue to sell milk at a loss if necessary, if it meant keeping them out of our store and out of our business. The union would never care for our people as much as I did; that was plain and simple.

I would cross paths with the Labor Union a few years later, and their efforts would become more pronounced. They did not like the fact that our people were not organized and, more importantly, were not being represented by them. This was to become a battle of wills, and I was not going to bend easily. I had stared down the barrel of a German machine gun during my combat duty in Italy. The union in Phoenix did not scare me one bit.

Worth Thinking About

"Necessity makes even the timid brave."

—Sallust

"Necessity is the mother of invention."

—Latin Proverb

"It is no use saying, 'We are doing our best.' You have got to succeed in doing what is necessary."

— Winston Churchill

"Public opinion in this country is everything."

—Abraham Lincoln

"The secret of success in life is for a man to be ready for his opportunity when it comes."

—Benjamin Disraeli

"Your greatest pleasure is that which rebounds from hearts that you have made glad."

—H. W. Beecher

13

The Right Managers

"Taking risks is an essential part of business and must be embraced if you are going to move forward and stay ahead of your competition."

—Clyde B. Smith

Managerial Qualities:
Desire, Determination, and Dedication

Everett Larson and Doug Smith—what a great pair of store managers! I had chosen them to take on the leadership role in our first Arizona store because both had the desire and determination to do whatever it took to make the store work. This was no easy task, as they found themselves in charge of the largest supermarket in Arizona. As I have pointed out, this store had multiple departments and was far more complex than the average supermarket at the time. While they relied heavily on their department managers to use their expertise to bring in our projected bottom line number, both Everett and Doug had to have generalist expertise to keep all the parts of the store working together.

Everett and Doug had come out of our Iowa store operation and were the most experienced men we had. Everett was an outgoing fella who just loved the supermarket business. He would meet me early in the morning to open the store and, like me, would usually be the last one to go home. He was a great merchant and really understood the direction the company was planning to go. He was 100 percent dedicated to our success, and his special efforts showed me this.

My brother Doug had come to work in my first store in Iowa when he was sixteen years old. This was the butcher shop we converted into a complete grocery store in our first few months of business. Doug came to work in the produce department during his summer vacation from school. Later, when his schooling was completed, he decided to build a life and a career with us. I bet he never imagined that his summer job with the store in Roland, Iowa, would become a lifelong commitment in Arizona. Those are wonderful mysteries of life that unfold for us each day.

Doug was my younger brother, but he was always a true professional on the job. As the assistant store manager of our first store in Phoenix, he played an integral role in helping to make the store successful and profitable. Like Everett, Doug was good with people and set a positive tone at all times for the customer and staff. He had the desire and ambition that is found in all successful people. To this day, he is a happily retired, first-class guy.

Commitment

Doug and Everett represent what was the true success of that first store in Phoenix. In my later career, I was always asked by many what made this first store so successful. Without a doubt, it was our people. For some reason, we had the good fortune of attracting and keeping a staff that was totally committed to making that store and all the stores that followed work. Let me highlight the word "commitment."

In those days, our managers and key personnel worked between 50-70 hours a week. If there was a problem that needed to be solved, they would work tirelessly until there was resolution, even if it took more hours per week. They did this with enthusiasm, dedication, and a sense of pride that made us a team rather than a group of people who simply worked together. While I was the owner, they all demonstrated the same attitude toward success and building the business that I did. To them it was "our store—our future."

One of the Primary Fundamentals

One of the most important lessons I learned from our stores in Iowa was that if you are going to be truly successful, you have to spread the wealth around with your key employees. By the time I got to Phoenix, this had become one of the primary fundamentals in our corporate culture.

If you were a department manager for Smitty's, you were given the responsibility of growing your department as if it were your own business. I encouraged our department managers to take this ownership attitude to heart by giving them the ability to hire and train their own staff, buy for the department, and merchandise their purchases. I believed in sharing every bit of information I had about their department with them, which included their profit and loss statement. I learned by sharing information that it reinforced their ownership attitude while giving them the tools to run their department better.

Too many businessmen like to keep their employees in the dark about the fundamentals of their business. To them, keeping their employees out of the "numbers" leaves the owner in absolute control and the lord and master of the money chain. The owner then is free to manipulate whatever reality he wants the staff to believe.

Profit Sharing

As our stores in Iowa grew rapidly, I took the exact opposite approach with our staff. I wanted them to know as much about the business as I did. Unlike most small-town grocers in Iowa, I wanted them to share in the information chain and in the profits of their departments. I learned early that personally, I could only accomplish so much. If I was to really grow my business, I would have to be willing to share the profits with those individuals who helped make the company grow and prosper.

By the time we opened that first store in Marshalltown, Iowa, I had developed a formula that paid our department managers 10 percent of the net profit of their department. This, combined with a decent living wage, was my way of motivating and rewarding them for the long hours and unwavering commitment they made to be a Smitty's manager. As we grew, I would later make company stock available to them at 10 percent above book value per share as an additional incentive. In the event they left our company, we would pay them 10 percent over our current book value. Our turnover was rare, as 99 percent of them believed in our company and its future and wanted to stay and be a part of the wonderful success we were experiencing.

A few weeks after we opened our first store in Phoenix, we were doing around $250,000 per week in sales. To put this into perspective, this would be like doing more than a million dollars a week in today's dollars. Not long after, our store would level off at approximately $400,000 per week, which was a tremendous amount of business for a supermarket in the early '60s.

Creating and Merchandising a Department

One of the ways we achieved this type of volume was our belief in how you create and merchandise a department within a supermarket. It is my belief that if you create a department, you cannot abbreviate the department and achieve success. To be successful, a department must have three important components: (1) a critical mass and diversity of inventory, (2) an adequate amount of square footage, and (3) a manager who is totally dedicated and responsible for the development and success of that department. If any of these ingredients is missing, you cannot pique the interest of the customer, and you are not adding extra volume to the shopping experience.

Within these departments, you must merchandise "like kind related" items to make the shopping selection easier for the consumer. This also increases volume as the customer will purchase more if they can see the items together and how they complement one another. To this day, it gets on my nerves to go into a store and have to hunt for items that should be merchandised in close proximity. I still believe in developing a happy "shopping experience" for the consumer, and this should not include a scavenger hunt for items on a shopping list.

By devoting adequate square footage to a department within our store, we were better able to concentrate on the success of that department, rather than dabbling in a few items and then expecting the consumer to respond. It also gave us the ability to pay a topflight department manager to take an ownership position and develop a merchandising plan that works. This gave us a lead person who could train the staff of that department to be totally familiar with the demands and intricacies of what it takes to make that department successful.

It also gave me a manager who was willing to take risks, an essential part of business that must be embraced if you are going to move forward and stay ahead of your competition. Department managers were encouraged to take on calculated risks, knowing that there was a sufficient reward. In business, you have to dare to be different, and there is no better place to accomplish this in a supermarket than at the department level. Whether it is a special product buy, truckload sale, or being the first in town with a new product, our department managers were great at taking risks and reaping huge rewards. Because they had some skin in the game with the profit-sharing plan, I was always confident in their assessment and the degree of risk they took. Not all of their plans worked out, but the velocity of our merchandise turns told me that most of the risks they took were right.

Worth Thinking About

"Behold the turtle; he makes progress only by sticking his neck out."

—James Conant

"No great honor ever comes to the man who has not ventured something."

—Roy L. Smith

"Why not go out on a limb? Isn't that where the fruit is?"

—Frank Scully

"The people I want to hear about are the people who take risks."

—Robert Frost

"It's a good rule never to send a mouse to catch a skunk or a polliwog to tackle a whale."

—Abraham Lincoln

"We have committed the Golden Rule to memory; let us now commit it to life."

—Edwin Markham

"Salesmanship consists of transferring a conviction by a seller to a buyer."

—Paul G. Hoffman

"Management is the art of getting things done through people."

—Lawrence Appley

"Management is the marshalling of manpower, resources, and strategy in getting a job done."

—M.E. Dimock

"It is more important to choose well those who are to work with you, and under you; to put the square man in the square hole and the round man in the round hole."

—John Lubbock

"You can employ men and hire hands to work for you, but you must win their hearts to have them work with you."

—Riorio

"If you mean to profit, learn to please."

—Winston Churchill

"No one would ever have crossed the ocean if he could have gotten off the ship in the storm."

—Charles Kettering

The greater part of progress is the desire to progress.

—Seneca

14

Mass Merchandising

"The reason you mass merchandise is to create a special atmosphere that captures the attention of the shopper and achieves long-term market share, while saving the consumer money."

—Clyde B. Smith

In the early '60s, the nation was just beginning to embrace "mass merchandising." This was before the Walmart strategy was fully developed by Sam Walton, which dealt with purchasing in volume and then selling to the consumer at a discount. We had already tried some mass merchandising in Iowa and had become pretty good at it. We had experimented with truckload buying volume and special merchandising within our stores, but none of our Iowa stores presented us the opportunity to mass merchandise like the square footage of our Phoenix store. The name of the game is capturing additional volume by understanding the customer's needs.

I believed that the reason you mass merchandise is to create a special atmosphere to capture the attention of the shopper and to achieve long-term market share, while saving the consumer money. When you mass merchandise an item or a series of items, you buy in volume at a reduced price from the manufacturer and then pass the savings on to the customer. This builds loyalty and a belief in the customer so that they will continue to shop with you in confidence for the items they need, while also saving money.

Due to the large size of our first Phoenix store, we were able to take the mass merchandising concept and really put it into action. We removed a row of our center gondolas, which gave us plenty of room to draw attention to our special items. Our department managers would then buy truckloads of popular products such as chips, canned goods, paper products, or beverages and display them in mass in special center areas we had provided. This would create a wonderful savings for the customer and allow us to scoop our competition because we were buying in truckload lots.

For most grocery stores at the time, mass merchandising was very difficult, if not impossible, because the average store was about half the size of our South 16th Street store. This did not allow those merchants the luxury of devoting a large amount of space to merchandising products in mass. Most of the merchants put a few items on the end of a gondola and that was it. This, in my opinion, wasn't the best way to accomplish the volume you needed to buy and sell in truckload lots.

I had learned about square-foot limitations firsthand as I started my career in a store that was only about 2,200 square feet. As our stores in Iowa became larger, we were able to begin to understand the concept of better mass merchandising but were not able to utilize it fully until we were in our larger, new Marshalltown store. Mass merchandising then was a concept that we would continue to learn and refine all through our years in Arizona. In 1962, I could see it was the future of retailing, and it soon would be one of the most effective ways of creating value for the consumer and loyalty for our stores.

You cannot talk about mass merchandising without talking about how it affects the bottom line profit. In those days, the average supermarket was throwing net profit to the bottom line of about 1 percent per year. In our South 16th Street store, we were consistently able to beat this number with our net profit ranging from 2 percent to 4 percent. We were able to do this with the help of effective mass merchandising and our specialty departments, plus many other factors that contributed to this healthy bottom line.

Mass merchandising is like a double-edged sword. You can substantially increase your volume and net profit if both the buy and the sell go well. If either does not, you can be left with a whole bunch of merchandise that is slow to sell and a pile of your cash tied up in it. Only through extensive experience can you get your arms around this process and minimize the associated risks.

Our general managers and department managers knew how to buy, merchandise, price, and sell whatever merchandise that passed through the store. They were in their respective jobs from sunup to sundown and developed valuable expertise in knowing their customers and what items they would purchase. They built long-lasting relationships with our suppliers, who in turn gave us the edge on first best buying and pricing of the new product offerings. I tried to be first in the market to introduce a new product, and if we could sell it below the competition, it was a homerun. Our managers and their supplier relationships helped us to maintain an edge.

Our managers also knew when to mark down an item and get it off the shelf as soon as possible. I have always maintained that your first markdown is usually the best; therefore, it should be rather deep to get the attention of the shopper. It is better to get some of your cash back and reinvest it quickly than to stick with an item hoping that things turn around.

Potential eroding of the bottom line is the reason we had to develop an expertise in mass merchandising quickly in that South 16th Street store. I was pleased that our dedicated team of managers in short order accomplished this and that we had many more winners than losers. I was always watchful and grateful for our accomplishments and our first-rate team.

Worth Thinking About

"Determine that the thing can and shall be done, and then we shall find the way."

—Abraham Lincoln

"Watch your thinking; your thoughts become actions. Watch your actions; an action soon becomes a habit. Be careful of your habits; your habits form your character. Watch your character; for character turns into destiny."

—Author Unknown

"Set yourself earnestly to use what you were made to do, and then set yourself diligently to do it; and the loftier your purpose is, the more sure you will be to make the world richer with every enrichment of yourself."

—Phillips Brooks

15

Paying Attention to Details

"**Nordstrom Rules No. 1:** Use your good judgment in all situations. There will be no additional rules."

—Clyde B. Smith

Early in my grocery career I learned from Keith Rushing that you had to pay attention to detail if you were going to create a healthy bottom line. With the national average of only 1 percent net profit as the industry standard, there is very little room for waste. Losses from theft, squandering supplies, or a payroll that is out of whack are all things that can eat away your net profit. Only through careful attention to detail can you control these overhead expenses.

I had developed an unusual habit of working a profit and loss statement backward, a system called a weekly recap of sales and projected grosses. I would anticipate and project what the possible volume would be from each department and then apply their average overhead to project what our gross margin should be. This would allow me to work the figures backwards as I plugged in our associated costs such as labor and markdowns. I could then project a possible bottom line to give our team some numbers to shoot for. As sales unfolded, we would carefully monitor our actual results compared to projections. This attention to detail helped us to react quickly if there was a problem that was beating up our projected bottom line.

Nowhere was the attention to detail more obvious than in our staff meetings and training sessions. Since my time in Iowa, I had become a fanatic about training our people. I believed that investing in people was as critical as any investment we could make. As I have said, we had our managers go through the Dale Carnegie course and, later, the Toastmasters program. I felt programs such as these built confidence and professionalism in our managers that not only helped our stores but also helped them develop as individuals.

Training your staff is as critical as making the right merchandise purchase. This became even more important to us when we opened the first store in Phoenix. With the size and depth of that store, the overhead could have devastated us if we got it wrong. A poorly trained staff would have been like an anchor around our neck if they failed to live up to our standards of workmanship, cost control, and efficiency.

I believed in allowing our managers and department heads to choose and train their own staff. There is nothing like learning the business from someone who is on the frontlines. Typically, the new hires would shadow someone in the group for a period of time until they were capable of functioning on their own. Our managers would teach them our policies and procedures and help them understand our corporate culture. To assist them, we developed a comprehensive employee manual, which covered everything from dress code to defining the benefits. Since pleasing the customer was of all importance to our success, the managers were careful to hire for appearance, attitude, and personality.

Let me give you a few examples of how a properly trained staff can make a difference in a supermarket environment and how it relates to the bottom line.

Most people look at the "sackers" as one of the low men on the totem pole. Why would you care about training them?

Just teach them to toss the items in a bag and you are done. In most supermarkets, the sacker is often the last person with whom the customer comes in contact. That sacker can make a huge impression on that customer at the store and when the customer arrives home. We recognized this.

At the store, the sacker must work efficiently to package the customer's purchases while being cordial and courteous. He or she must package the merchandise properly, using just the right number of sacks for the merchandise bought. Put too little merchandise in each sack, and you waste money on supplies; too much in each sack, and you run the risk of damaging the purchases. When the customer gets home, a properly packaged purchase will leave a lasting impression, good or bad, on the customer. I might have been a great guy and loved that customer dearly, but the last person to leave an impression was our sacker, and many times, that was the impression customers remembered.

When you analyze this scenario in the context of thousands of customers, you can see how vital well-trained sackers are to an organization. If they are wasteful or careless in their packaging, both the store and the customer suffer. If they do not smile while loading the groceries or handing them to the customer, the customer thinks we do not value their business at Smitty's. This is the reason we were relentless in our training drills that would time our sackers for their speed, while grading them on their correct use of proper packing techniques. We would also evaluate them on their demeanor with the customer as they performed these critical functions.

Cashiers, or "checkers," as we called them, were trained with the same attention to detail. To be a good checker, a person had to have a good personality and be accurate. They also had to be fast! The job required using both the left and right parts of the brain, similar to a bank teller.

We would train our new checkers early in the morning before the store opened or late in the evening after the store closed. Like most new hires, they would shadow an experienced checker before we would let them go on the line.

A poorly trained checker can really affect your bottom line. At the time of our 16th Street store, there were no scanners or fancy electronic cash registers. Cash registers were manual, requiring that the checker input each price for an item by hand. This required a great deal of concentration and dexterity. If a wrong price was input, the store ran the risk of losing money, or worse, making the customer mad for overcharging. If the checker missed too many items or undercharged, it could dilute the bottom line quickly. This could mean real trouble when you are working with such tight margins.

Like all frontline employees, checkers helped set the tone with our customers. While they were required to be accurate, we also required them to be friendly and outgoing. This would mean making a bit of small talk while they were ringing up their purchases. A good checker knew how to balance conversation, while getting the items rung up and moved to the bagging area. This was a delicate balance if we were busy and there were other shoppers in line.

Just like our sackers, the checker always left a lasting impression on the customer. For that brief moment, they controlled the relationship with the customer and were the most visible face of our company. If they were properly trained, the customer would hand over their hard-earned money and feel good about their purchases.

One of the unsung heroes in a supermarket is the guy who works in the back room and is responsible for the back door. This person controls the flow of inventory in and out of the store. While you don't have to have a lot of personality, you have to be extremely accurate and faithfully honest. A checker might cost you a few dollars missing an item; a back room manager could cost you serious money if a case of product goes out the back door.

We brought Al Larson, Everett's brother, with us from Iowa to be our back room manager. Al was a back room manager in Iowa, and he was a good one. Like his brother, he performed a valuable service to the company, only in a less public venue.

Al had been trained in our Iowa stores and knew the critical role he played. Without his unwavering control of our back room in that huge store, we could have lost plenty of inventory or been shorted by unscrupulous vendors. If your back room manager is not doing the job, talk about punching a hole in your bottom line! It is like driving a tank through your profit and loss statement. Al Larson may not have been the most visible manager in our company to the customers, but he played an important role in keeping our prices in line and our shelves brimming over with product. He also took on the huge task of price stamping each item before stocking. This was done by hand in those days and had to be accurate. Our night crew of stockers was responsible for all items being correctly priced and displayed. This also fell under Al's area of responsibility.

From my examples, I hope you can see what an emphasis we placed on training and how each job description in our supermarket contributed to a healthy bottom line. Our managers and department heads were the most obvious, but we considered all jobs within the store critical, because like Keith Rushing showed me so many years prior, no detail or job was unimportant when it came to building a healthy client base and a healthy bottom line.

Worth Thinking About

"Honor lies in honest toil."

—Grover Cleveland

"We placed an emphasis on training and how each job description in our supermarket contributed to a healthy bottom line."

"Pay attention to detail if you are going to create a healthy bottom line."

—Clyde B. Smith

16

The Private Label Business

"Seriously ponder over and thoroughly examine
any project to which you intend to give your attention."
—Baron Rothschild

Private Label Merchandise: What It Is

For years grocers have been using the concept of selling "private label" merchandise to augment their bottom line. Private label merchandise is merchandise produced for a grocer by a manufacturer to a certain specification under a brand name that the grocer develops. Usually the manufacturer has reduced the cost of the product due to the absence of national marketing costs, sales, and development expense. The manufacturer then passes these savings on to the grocer, who in turn passes the cost savings on to the customer. In addition, the customer learns to associate your private label with your supermarket.

It is customary for private label merchandise to be somewhat more profitable to the grocer due to the decreased costs from the manufacturer. Supermarket operators like this concept and often devote volumes of shelf space to private label products. The good news is that this often saves the customer money, but the bad news is that some of the time the product produced is of poor quality. Like mass merchandising, the private label sword can cut both ways and cause the loss of customers and money if one is not careful.

We had been in the new store about six months before we decided to bring in a private label line on certain items. We were experiencing great success with our national brands but knew that a private label line would add something different for our customers. It also just might help the bottom line.

Unlike many of my peers, I was always a stickler with private label merchandise. My goal was to have a product that was every bit as good as or better than the national brand but at retail price that was 10 percent or more below the national price.

To achieve this standard, we would invite numerous manufacturers into our store office for a cutting test of these products. Manufacturers like Del Monte, Green Giant, Libby's, and others would be asked to bring in their product and compete for our private label business. During our cutting test, we would take like kind items and compare them for taste and quality. Not satisfied with ending it there, we then would put the items in unmarked containers and invite others into the office to sample the product and then ask their opinion. Based on both of these methods, we would then make a decision on who would get our business for a particular item.

I was passionate about quality, and getting into the private label business was no exception. At Smitty's, we set a high bar for our private label partners to get over, and we moved it higher from time to time. If we were going to devote shelf space to a private label product, this meant that some other brand got left out. I could not risk disappointing our customers if our private label brand did not measure up. In chapter 7, I related the story of our private label for "Smitty's Red Rooster Coffee — Something to Crow About." We had a lot of fun promoting this, and it earned satisfied customers for us.

Worth Thinking About

"It is best not to swap horses while crossing the river."

—Abraham Lincoln

"God save us from hotheads who would lead us foolishly, and from cold feet that would keep us from adventuring at all."

—Peter Marshall

"The prodigal son's father did not say to him, 'You stay in the pigpen—we're going to make it a better pigpen.'"

"Have you ever thought that in every action of grace in your heart you have the omnipotence of God engaged to bless you?"

—Andrew Murray

17

The Customer Was King at Smitty's

"As corny as this may sound, we asked our (store) team to treat the customer as they would want to be treated. There was no exception to this rule."

—Clyde B. Smith

In the past thirty years, there have been thousands of books and articles written on achieving great customer service. These have grown an army of consultants and practitioners who have made lots of money teaching businesses of all sizes the basic concept of treating the customer right. There are few businesses today that do not mention the importance of customer service in their mission statement or core values.

In reality, delivering great customer service has almost become a cliché in today's business environment. The term "great customer service" has become so overused that it has lost some of its impact and intent. Most businesses today go through the motions but rarely deliver what I consider exceptional customer service. Nothing evidences this more than how 99.9 percent of today's transactions are ended with the checker telling the consumer—you guessed it—"Have a nice day."

We were fortunate that we learned our customer service skills in the small towns of Iowa. There is nothing like doing business in a small town to sharpen your customer service skills and keep you on your toes. The reality of being a small town merchant is that you see your customer not only in your store, but all over town. This teaches you to build a relationship with the customer that is genuine and more heartfelt than simply telling them to "have a nice day" as you hand them their receipt.

We learned that delivering exceptional customer service is vital to becoming a successful small town merchant. There was always the pressure of hoping our staff was delivering the type of service expected and not making the wrong person angry, because in a small town, ill will can spread at lightning speed. Likewise, if you go beyond what is expected by the customer, chances are they will influence the thinking of their friends and neighbors. You might remember the resistance we encountered at our original store in Roland, Iowa, by mostly the Norwegian population. It took building an exceptional team with superior customer service skills to warm their hearts and get them shopping with us. I might not have written this book if the opposite had happened.

Delivering on Great Customer Service

Because of our small town training, our team knew what great customer service truly felt like when we opened our first store in Phoenix. Our challenge was to translate this feeling into our daily interactions with the customer. We knew we would have to work extra hard to make our new home as customer-centric as our much smaller stores in Iowa. Our staff was up to this challenge.

To build a foundation of great customer service in that huge store, we asked that all frontline personnel speak to or acknowledge each customer as they shopped. We asked our team to smile at all times as they went about their daily routine and to look for situations where they could go out of the way to "wow" the customer. We also empowered many of our staff with the ability to resolve customer questions or problems right on the sales floor. Most importantly, we asked our team to treat the customer as they would want to be treated. There was no exception to this rule.

Our Employee Handbook

We laid the groundwork for our customer service ethic in the first few pages of our employee handbook. The handbook was prefaced by the following letter:

To All New Associates:

Welcome to our business family at Smitty's Big Town!

We are glad you have joined our organization. We want you to become a part of our team. Our major objective is to serve our customers promptly and courteously with all their needs.

We are proud of our stores and the part they play in serving their respective communities.

We know our business grows as each one in our organization grows in his or her job. It is our sincere desire to help you improve your skill and gain the useful experience which will help you to grow mentally, morally, financially, and physically more important to your company and your community in the years ahead.

With your help, we will move forward together.

Thank You,
Clyde B. Smith
President

We further reinforced our commitment to the customer after my cover letter with the first five principles in our employee handbook. I feel that they are worth mentioning because this demonstrated where our thinking was in the 1960s.

1. **Our Customer is the Reason We Have Jobs** — We are happy to have customers in our store. Our friendly, courteous service will bring more customers to our store than any type of advertising. Satisfied customers tell their friends, and will bring more customers to our door.

2. **Greeting** — Nothing we do is as important as serving our customers, so let's stop whatever we are doing to welcome them with a smile and a greeting. We know our customers will like what they see—so when they say, "Just looking," say, "Thank you, but if we can be of further service, please let us know." Make them feel welcome.

3. **Returns** — If a customer has occasion to return merchandise—for exchange, credit, or refund—remember that they believe their reason for the return is a valid one. We are for the customer, so we greet our customer pleasantly and we take care of their return as graciously as when we made the original sale. There Is No Exception To This Rule!

4. **Our Guarantee** — If a customer has a complaint about merchandise purchased at Smitty's Big Town in any department or area, regardless of the reason for complaint, we take the position that the customer is always right. We never argue or contradict the customer. Merchandise will be replaced, or a refund or credit given in a cheerful, pleasant manner. Department managers or the store manager will authorize this type of transaction. Remember, our fellow employees are customers, too! The same basic policy of courteous service and fair adjustment applies to all Smitty's Big Town employees as well.

5. **Phone Manners** — We smile when we answer the phone. In a phone conversation our voice is all our customers know about us. A voice that smiles says, "We are glad you called." The friends we make by phone today may be our best customers in person tomorrow.

By now, I am sure that the consultants I referred to earlier have a more comprehensive and fancier way of saying what we did in those first five principals of our employee handbook. In those days, these five simple principals written in plain English spelled out our total commitment to the customer and acknowledged their importance to our success. They were what our managers, our staff, and I worked tirelessly to live up to each day. We had been privileged to learn our customer service skills in small town America, and I knew that if we were going to be truly successful in this much larger market, the Smitty's stores must translate this feeling to our big city customers.

I maintain that a happy customer is a good one. To me, you start this process with building your customer service skills and then support these skills with policies and procedures that put the customer first. These should then be practiced over and over again until they become part of your corporate culture.

One of the interesting things I have learned in my retail career is that delivering great customer service involves both verbal and non-verbal communication. A staff member who is not dressed appropriately, has poor grooming, or arrives late for work may send a mixed message to the customer on a nonverbal level. This can conflict with the store's objective of superior customer service. To achieve truly great customer service, I discovered that our staff could not lose focus on the customer in all we said, did, and how we created customer perception. It was a total commitment we had to make on a daily basis.

The Shopping Experience

My experience was that we should offer our customers an interesting tour of our store. That is the reason Burton Barr and I spent so many hours on the drawing board coming up with a cutting-edge design for our first store in Phoenix. We agonized over the placement of each department and how the trip unfolded for the customer. I was convinced that there was a natural order to the flow of the departments, and I wanted to tap into this to make our store not just a place to buy groceries, but a unique shopping experience for the consumer. When they came to Smitty's Big Town, we wanted to immerse their senses in a collage of sight, sound, and smell.

With such a large footprint, our first store in Phoenix allowed us to experiment with a variety of concepts that a smaller store would be limited in. We were able to merchandise departments as larger cohesive units and in much greater depth. The larger space allowed us to bring related items together to tempt the consumer by playing to their imagination. If they were going to buy the pasta, I wanted to sell them everything else they needed to make and serve the meal, but sometimes the customer needs a little help when visualizing the end result. We gave them a nudge by putting all the pieces close by so they could see the end result more clearly.

A good merchant understands this and learns to place merchandising displays and product racks strategically in such a manner that they guide the customer thoughtfully through the store. This allows the shopping experience to unfold in a methodical manner and helps the customer experience things that otherwise might be overlooked. At Smitty's, we felt that when a customer entered the front door, we had to lead them on a shopping tour that created a positive experience. If we did this properly, it was stimulating for the customer and increased our sales per square foot.

Appealing to the Customer's Senses

I have mentioned merchandising numerous times. I don't want this to sound repetitious, but I want to make sure you understand what I am referring to. Merchandising is taking a product, or a group of products, and displaying them in an alluring manner that makes the customer want to purchase that item or items. Good merchandising creates an image in the mind of customers where they can see themselves associated with the product by fulfilling a conscious or subconscious need. It creates a bond between the consumer and the product by appealing to their sense of sight, sound, and smell.

In a supermarket, we primarily used strong visual appeal, but merchandising can also be a pleasing aroma or a pleasant sound. We took great care in how we displayed a featured product and what signage we used. Often we would add props to complete an image in the mind of the consumer. To me, this was like painting a picture for the customer by allowing them to see the product in the proper context. We would also price units in multiples, such as 3 items for $1, to motivate and add a value proposition to the merchandised display. This has the added advantage of helping to increase sales.

We were very fortunate to have first rate department managers who took our merchandising concepts and translated them daily into a wonderful reality for the consumer. On any given day, you could walk into one of our stores and get excited by the sights and sounds that surrounded you. Everywhere you looked, there were larger than life displays of everyday items that were creatively merchandised to facilitate an excitement in the consumer, and hopefully a purchase for us. Our managers took great care with their end displays, product placement, inventory levels, and signage. They were adamant that the shopping experience for the customer must be uncomplicated and inviting. At Smitty's, we took the approach that shopping with us should be pleasing from the time you entered the store until you unpacked your purchases at home. If we fulfilled this objective, we did our job.

There is a lot of work that goes into creating a unique shopping experience for the customer. It is a job that starts long before the store opens and continues well after closing. I believed that every shopper deserved to be greeted with the same quality of merchandising, no matter what time of day that you shopped in our store. This put a tremendous amount of pressure on the perishable department managers and their team to keep the store looking fresh, fully stocked, and inviting at all times. It was a high standard to meet each day, but my team never let me down.

One of the most powerful elements of the shopping experience is our sense of smell. We learned to use this effectively in our first big store in Marshalltown, Iowa, by piping the wonderful aromas generated by our scratch bakery through the ceiling and into the various departments. These aromas teased our shoppers with nurturing smells, appealing to their sense of well-being and empty stomachs. There is nothing like the smell of warm bread to get a shopper in the mood to shop or to plan a home-cooked meal.

A Consistent Emphasis on Attention to Small Details

Our management team became totally committed to the shopping experience and how this affected the customer. This required us to pay very close attention to even the smallest details. We did little things like layering our steaks and chops in the meat cases with butcher paper so that when the top row of meats sold, the paper would come off and the next row of meats would just "bloom." This ritual said "freshness" to the customer no matter the time of day.

Each day, retail merchants have a choice of how they will be received by their customers. I believe that this is directly tied to the experience that shoppers have when they are in their store. If the store is interesting, clean, uncluttered, and well-merchandised, chances are that the shopper will think favorably of the merchant. If you combine these "must haves" with a customer and a focused staff, a merchant has a good chance of being rewarded with their continued business. If the store does not live up to these basic standards, the merchant is deliberately sabotaging his own success.

Simulating the Shopper's Experience

To get a feel for how the customers perceived our store, I would grab a shopping cart and go through the store just as our customers did. This must have panicked the staff a little, but it was the only way for me to simulate the experience our shoppers were having. On these little tours, I would pay close attention to how the shopping cart navigated the store, the impact of our displays, and if items were properly grouped together or orphaned and hard to find. We were fanatics about cleanliness, so this was always at the top of my list.

I would also take a hard look at our departments that had to be perceived as "really fresh" by the customer. Our bakery, meat market department, and produce areas were always a challenge due to the perishable nature of the goods and the inventory turns, so I would give them an especially close look in my role as a shopper. These departments were critical to the shopping experience, and they sent volumes of information to the consumer about our philosophy on quality and freshness. Although we might be a supermarket, I always wanted the customer to feel that we were as close in the supply chain as you could be to the source, be it the farm or the oven.

I would really get into the role of the customer by pretending that I had a lot of things to buy for a large family. I needed to be thrifty but I wanted to bring them a real quality product, plus the quantity needed. Was I able to meet the criteria at Smitty's? Were the items easy to find? Was the store inviting? How did we measure up? If I was not satisfied with my answers, we would work until we got it right.

In reality, our department managers were shopping on an ongoing basis each day. They usually did not need me to point out their deficiencies, but once in a while, I would make a suggestion for the better. We were blessed that we had highly competent managers that had the unique ability of seeing their department through the eyes of the consumer and making changes when necessary. Like me, they were fully committed to making each shopping trip for the consumer a unique and exciting experience.

Seeing the Big Picture through the Eyes of the Customer

While our department managers were responsible for their area of expertise, the merchandising "buck" stopped with our store managers. Both Everett Larson and Doug Smith, whom I have mentioned before, were key staff members I looked to for creating consistency and excellence in the shopping experience. Both of these individuals spent a great deal of their time walking the store to ensure that our message and image was properly conveyed. Their job was to see the "big picture" through the eyes of the customer.

Worth Thinking About

"Our managers were not content to sit behind a desk and pontificate what the shopping experience for our customer should be. These strong and highly competent managers believed in being on the frontlines—orchestrating the shopping experience daily. I cannot tell you how valuable their contribution was and how I admired the big job they did. One cannot fully understand a large operation such as Smitty's from behind a desk in a remote office. A successful manager has to be side by side with the troops. Again, it's getting work done through people."

—Clyde B. Smith

18

When Things Get Out of Hand

"If you let the bad guys get the best of you,
they can destroy the success of your future business."

—Clyde B. Smith

After several months, we were finally settling into the supermarket life in Phoenix. Our store had made a major impression on the consumer, and we were steadily gaining market share. Our sales were increasing weekly, and we had moved into the "black" at a breakneck speed. The entire staff was working long hours, but we all loved every minute of it. Phoenix was turning out to be our kind of town.

As I have said before, the one thing that caught us off guard when we opened our store was the amount of crime that we would encounter on a daily basis. The neighborhood around that first store was as tough as it gets. It was filled with rough individuals who were fearless when it came to the law and us. We soon recognized that if we let the bad guys get the best of us, they could destroy the success of our future business. We weren't about to let that happen.

As small town merchants, we were shocked at the outright disrespect for the law that we saw at our grand opening. You might recall that we had six attempted auto thefts that day. We also encountered numerous shoplifters who were testing us to see how much they could get away with.

This was to be a recurring theme at our store for quite some time. In that first year, we had numerous encounters with bad guys that often ended in a rush of adrenalin and swinging fists. It was not unusual to see one of our people give chase into the parking lot in pursuit of one or more shoplifters. During one of these pursuits, a big, tough shoplifter ran behind a shed and then bushwhacked one of our sackers with a two by four. When my brother Doug caught up with him, the fight was on. He was later turned over to the police department, probably a little sore and ego-bruised from his brush with Doug.

We might have been small town merchants, but most of our Iowa team was worldlier than they looked. I had been through the war and was in tip-top shape, and so was the rest of our team. If we were intimidated by these bad guys at first, this dissipated quickly as defending our store became a matter of principle. By the time the first six months had passed, we had seen most everything the neighborhood could dish out—that is, until the day things almost got out of hand.

In this first store, our offices were located above the restaurant, which was accessed by a staircase on the outside of the building. The offices surrounded a central foyer.

We had been in business about eight months when I heard my brother Doug confronting a couple of shoplifters in the foyer. From what I could hear, Doug had caught them shoplifting and was interrogating them about the theft. When the couple would not cooperate, Doug reached for the telephone to call the police.

As Doug picked up the phone, the male suspect—who was a really big guy—grabbed the phone out of Doug's hands and then ripped the phone out of the wall. Sensing a deteriorating situation, Doug jumped on the big guy and wrestled him to the floor.

As they hit the floor, from my office I heard a loud "crack" like a gun going off, so I ran out into the foyer. I saw Doug on top of the guy and blood was all over the suspect. I ran up and grabbed Doug, yelling for him to ease up on the guy, thinking it was the shopper's blood and that Doug was doing some serious damage.

Doug then rose up and put his hand to the side of his head. It was then I realized that the blood spewing everywhere was Doug's and that he had been shot. I could clearly see a hole in the side of his head where the bullet had gone in at an angle and ricocheted out.

The woman who had evidently fired the shot and was almost as big as the man ran out of the foyer and started down the steps. I was in hot pursuit, about twenty feet behind. When she hit the bottom of the stairs, she ran straight to a waiting car with three black men inside. Throwing open the door, she tossed her purse on the backseat and slammed the door shut. She then turned around and headed back up the stairs.

At this point, I was not going to let her get away with anything, and more importantly, I wanted to see what was in her purse. I flung open the door and jumped into the back seat, paying no attention to the car's occupants. I grabbed the purse and turned around to pursue her as she headed up the stairs to help her husband.

As she nearly got to the top of the stairs, the excitement level really turned on as I was going up the stairs and Doug was chasing them down the stairs with a blood-soaked towel wrapped around his head. Then all of a sudden the woman's wig came off. I thought to myself, "That's a man!" The lady was bald as a cue ball with huge muscles and manlike features. As I closed in on the pair, I did not care if it was a male or female. I was determined that the person I was chasing was going to pay for shooting my brother!

Fortunately, our staff in the office had called the police when things started to turn ugly. As we closed in on the couple, two police cars roared up to our building. The officers jumped out and met this big gal as she was coming down the last steps and arrested her. The officers slapped on the handcuffs and put her in the backseat of their patrol car. When they turned to do something with her husband, she kicked out the back window of the police car! I thought to myself, "This is one mean, tough woman!" Later, when the police emptied the purse I had chased so hard to get, they found a small Derringer handgun that she had used to shoot Doug at close range.

With the police fully in control, I rushed Doug to the nearest emergency room where they looked after his wound. In no time, they patched him up and sent him home to rest. But like a true professional, the next day Doug was at work with a patch on his head and a story to tell that few people could ever match. It was amazing that he lived to tell the story.

Doug had been shot point-blank in the head by that bald-headed, man-like woman. After the emotion died down, it sunk in how tragic the incident could have been. To this day, I thank God that the bullet had not gone straight in. If it had, my friend and wonderful brother, with whom I had spent so much of my life, would have been dead. This story still haunts me to this day.

Worth Thinking About

"One of the great discoveries man makes, one of his great surprises, is to find he can do what he was afraid he couldn't do. Most of the bars we beat against are in ourselves—we put them there, and we can take them down."

—Henry Ford

"I believe that crisis really tends to help develop the character of an organization."

—John Sculley

19

In the Forefront: The Emerging Discount Superstore Concept

"Combining a supermarket with a department store
made perfect sense to me. Smitty's would become a one-stop-shop
store for the consumer, saving them valuable time and money.
We were on our own in building the merchandise model."

—Clyde B. Smith

I had been involved with the Supermarket Institute as a board member for many years. When we opened our Phoenix operation, I stepped up my participation in an effort to understand better the direction of the industry. It was my desire always to keep our stores at the forefront of store design, merchandising, and product trends. I knew if we did so, we would offer a better shopping experience for the consumer, which had now become our passion.

Each month, I would devour industry publications in search of a new or unusual concept that we could incorporate into our stores. If some other operator had opened a new supermarket with unusual features and a new concept that appealed to me, I would get a group of our managers and travel to wherever the new concept was. We learned never to be shy or to let our egos get in the way. When someone showed us a better mousetrap, it was our job and intention to serve our customers and give them the best the industry had to offer.

Through my involvement with the industry and the Supermarket Institute, I became infatuated with the emerging discount store movement. This was 1963, just as Walmart and the discount store concept was still evolving. In those days, I really liked how the discount store operators packed their stores to the rafters, using a "big box" type building to house a diversity of merchandise. In fact, the progressive discount merchants had taken the same mass-merchandising approach we had used in our first store in Phoenix. Perhaps this was the root of my attraction.

At Smitty's, we understood mass merchandising from our volume buys and the discount positions we took on many of our grocery items, but we had no experience in the hard and soft goods that the discount retailers sold. Theirs was a world of ready-to-wear clothing, electronics, jewelry, hardware, sporting goods, and a variety of sundry departments. These were retail items that came with a larger profit margin but were unfamiliar to us when it came to market fundamentals such as how the supply chain worked and the diversity of market trends.

A Foundation upon Which to Build

I cannot remember if it was a sudden decision or if it evolved over a period of time, but somehow I decided that combining a supermarket with a department store operation was going to be our next move. This made perfect sense to me because it was consistent with our philosophy of serving the customer and improving the shopping experience. Smitty's would become a "one-stop-shop" store for consumers, saving them valuable time and money. Our team had become very good merchants in the supermarket business, and I knew that this expertise would give us a foundation from which to build a department store platform. After all, it was still just retail to me!

My experience in the supermarket business had taught me that most consumers shop for groceries one big day a week.

They would then drop in as many as two times per week for items they either forgot or suddenly needed. This provides a supermarket with a frequency of visits per customer that is way above the statistical average of a typical department store. Industry standards at the time showed that most department stores received only one to two visits per customer per month.

I believed that, based on the frequency of visits to our supermarkets, we could increase the sales in a department, store-type operation if it was housed under the same roof. It seemed perfectly logical to me that while consumers shopped for meat, bread, and milk, they could shop at the same time for jewelry, shoes, and a car battery. This unique merchandising format would offer a wide range of products to the consumer, with groceries and other goods feeding business to each other.

One of the appeals to a department store operation is the much higher markup and gross profit potential of the individual merchandise. This is in contrast to a typical supermarket where your standard markup on a can of peas for example might be only a few cents. In a department store, items like ready-to-wear clothing and jewelry are typically marked up to double or more of what the merchant pays for them. In the department store world, if you buy it for a dollar, you sell it for two. These items might not sell as fast as a can of peas, but the much larger profit margin potential makes the slower merchandise turns acceptable.

It Made Perfect Sense to Me

At Smitty's, with our high volume sales we turned our entire grocery inventory about once every week. The typical department store at the time turned their inventory about once every quarter — if that often. I believed that if I could take our frequency of store visits per customer and direct them at department store merchandise in the same store, we might increase the velocity of these turns. This would not only push profitability in these items but also just might garner us some additional sales volume from merchandise that our customers were buying elsewhere. In 1963, combining a supermarket with a department store made perfect sense to me.

What made perfect sense to me was like running into a dark cave as far as the industry was concerned. There was not much of a road map pointing the way, with few other retailers having been down this road. This was years before retailers like Kmart, Target, and Walmart joined their hard and soft goods departments with groceries. I had heard of a miscellaneous operator or two that was experimenting with the concept, but we were mostly on our own when building the merchandising model.

Our Number Two Store in Phoenix

Once I made the decision to combine our next supermarket with a department store format, I felt that it was important to run the idea by our store managers. I knew that both Everett Larson and Doug Smith would be good sounding boards, based on their years of retail experience. I valued their opinions and felt that their acceptance of the concept was crucial. They would also keep our conversation confidential, which is vital in a highly competitive business. Until we had it thought out, I wanted our new concept store to stay under wraps.

I called Everett and Doug to my office and informed them of my decision. Neither seemed that surprised. Both had been around me for years and knew my ambition to serve the customer. I explained my rationale about using our strong supermarket volume to feed traffic to the proposed department store operation. They seemed to understand this logic, as I never sensed any hesitation in their demeanor. Later, I would broaden our inner circle on the expansion to include our department managers and other key personnel. Everyone agreed that it would be a positive move for the company and would keep us at the forefront of expanding the customer experience.

Prior to my meeting with Doug and Everett, I knew it was critical that I get their support and that of our management staff. One of the most valuable lessons I had learned in business over the years was that I was only as good as our people. To undertake such an ambitious project, our staff must be 100 percent behind this next move. My experience had taught me that even in a perfect scenario we would need all of our staff to excel at their jobs.

By 1963, we had built a corporate culture at Smitty's that focused on two things: our people and our customers. For our people, we devised monetary incentives, personal improvement initiatives such as Toastmasters and our Dale Carnegie program, and a relentless training regimen that added value to their jobs skills and personal development. Many years ago, when we began to operate two stores simultaneously back in Iowa, it became apparent to me that I could not grow our company without the daily commitment of a dedicated staff. There was only so much I could accomplish on my own. It also became apparent that Smitty's had to enrich the lives of its people in multiple ways if they were going to give their best performance on the job.

One of the Key Ingredients to Any Business Success

Getting work done through people is one of the key ingredients to any business success. Many businesses struggle with this fundamental. We were fortunate that at Smitty's we were able to cultivate a culture that celebrated hard work and developed family-like ties. As I said before, if we had a problem, our entire team would work as many hours necessary to find a solution. To me, this is the hallmark of a winning team.

In our corporate culture, I saw my role as the team member that set the pace, rather than the boss. I was fortunate that God blessed me with a tremendous capacity of extra energy to do the job. I am sure that this goes back to the times I worked side by side with my dad. Through my experiences working with him, I always wanted to be the first person on the job and the last person to leave. There was no job beneath me, and it was important that the staff knew this. How could I ask more of them than I would of myself? It was up to me to demonstrate the hard work that was required to grow the business, especially the type of growth that would be required with our number two store.

Many business people never fully grasp the concept of hard work and the relentless commitment it takes to succeed in business. Often being the boss is seen as an excuse to go home early or skip the drudgery of the menial tasks that make a business successful. Running a business requires sacrifice, which I learned every day. I spent countless hours away from my wife and beautiful daughters in my pursuit of serving the customer. I regretted this sacrifice many times over the years, but I had countless employees, suppliers, and the public depending on my commitment to the business.

When an owner is not willing to make a 110-percent commitment to the business at all times, you send the wrong message to your staff. There is no greater motivation for them than to work in the trenches side by side with the boss. If you do not lead by example, how can you ask them to follow?

Every Staff Member on Board

Once our staff was fully on board with the "hybrid" store concept, I decided to go back to Parmenter's for our store design and fixture needs. I had really enjoyed my relationship with them and their lead person, Burton Barr, when we had worked on our first store in Phoenix. Burton suggested that we bring his coworker Ted Frohs into the planning process for added dimension. Together, the three of us became the design team of the Smitty's store number two.

I was confident in our capacity to design a wonderful supermarket but was much less confident about adding the department store concept to the layout. I had done lots of reconnaissance on discount and department stores, but there was very little to draw from when combining the two concepts.

I spent hours on the drawing board in my office refining the new store's layout. I also kept a drawing board at home. It was not unusual for me to get up from a dead sleep and rework an area of the store with a new idea. I spent countless hours with Burton and Ted, brainstorming department layouts and putting them on paper. The three of us were plowing new ground, and we would occasionally hit a pile of rocks. When we did, both of my drawing boards saw lots of action.

In the end, our design team came up with a store layout that was a massive 135,000 square feet! The store would dedicate approximately 45,000 square feet to the supermarket operation, with the balance devoted to the department store: ladies' and men's ready-to-wear, shoe department, jewelry department, hardware, sporting goods, domestics, a sundry department, and a pharmacy. The store would have a central concourse when you entered, with the grocery store on the right and the department store on the left. In the central concourse, there was a snack bar that handled candy and other items that would pump out the hunger-provoking smells of hot, fresh caramel corn and popcorn to tempt the shoppers. Along with these various departments, we would also operate a barber and beauty shop.

I made the decision early that Everett Larson and Doug Smith would take on the responsibility of the supermarket portion of our new store. I had ultimate faith in these seasoned veterans and knew that they would be up to such a challenge. I would also take other key personnel out of South 16th Street store, which meant that all of them would have to hire and train their replacements. Given our depth of staff, and our penchant for promoting from within, the new store would provide plenty of opportunity for our existing staff.

As I planned our second store, I became aware of a distinct department type store on the west side of Phoenix that catered only to government employees. I liked the store layout and how it was merchandised. Through my visits to the store, I became friendly with the store manager and struck up a relationship with him based on our mutual love of the retail business. While getting to know this manager, I learned that he was responsible for the entire store operation. He told me that he did the buying for the store as well as the merchandising, staffing, and pricing. As the manager, he was involved in most every area of the store and talked a good retail game.

I saw in this man the ambition and desire that I always looked for in a person and, more importantly, a prospective employee. With his apparent broad department store background, I began to see him taking a lead role in our number two store. After several discussions, I offered him the position of department store manager. He would be in charge of all phases of the department store operation, including buying, merchandising, and hiring the staff.

Location, Location, Location

With our store layout completed, and our management team in place, I concentrated my efforts on finding a location and getting the building built. I settled on a location in Scottsdale at 83rd Street and McDowell. The location was big enough for the large size of the store and our rigid parking requirements. We had developed a three-to-one minimum parking ratio plan that gave our customers ample parking. We had learned through our years of experience that customers will happily walk further to access the store if they can see the front door. Parking on the side of the store may be a shorter hike, but not seeing the front door is a psychological barrier. This was one of the little things we had learned that merchants often overlook.

When we opened our supermarket and department store hybrid in December of 1963, it was the talk of the town, if not the state. At the time, it was probably one of the largest stores of its kind in the country. Our store boasted a full-service, sit-down restaurant for 200 persons, a Smitty's supermarket, a complete bakery, and a department store operation. Under its 135,000-square-foot roof, our customers could now shop for all of their family needs. The store was to be the first of its kind in Arizona and was specifically designed to be a new one-stop shop for the Arizona shopper. We had developed the "superstore," but like the public, even we did not know it at the time.

Worth Thinking About

"This is the only chance you will ever have on Earth with this exciting adventure called life. So why not plan it, and try to live it as richly, as happily as possible?"

—Dale Carnegie

"Running a business requires sacrifice. When plowing new ground, you will occasionally hit a pile of rocks . . . . Keep on . . . it requires lots of action."

—Clyde B. Smith

"Put up with small annoyances to gain great results."

—American Proverb

"The reward of a thing well done is to have done it."

—Ralph Waldo Emerson

"It ain't braggin' if you can back it up."

—Dizzy Dean, St. Louis pitcher

20

Challenges: Confronting the Complex Problems

"There was no manual on running a 'superstore' concept; we were writing the manual each day."

—Clyde B. Smith

For every success we had with our first store in Phoenix, our second store was to challenge us twofold. From the beginning, the store began to bleed red ink, and the losses did not stop for the next eighteen months. It seemed that every time we turned around, a new set of problems would confront our team and we would be forced to make changes to our operating procedures or the store itself. Remember, this was 1963, and there was no manual on running a "superstore" concept; we were writing the manual each day.

It became immediately apparent that I had underestimated the scope of running a department store operation. I had been a bit simplistic in thinking that a department store with all its hundreds of items was "just retail." Over the years, we had built a great business model to be successful in the grocery portion of the store, but did not have the expertise in running a department store with such product diversity. I quickly learned that the department store business was cash intensive, which was a real problem if you had 90,000 square feet of department store merchandise that wasn't selling as well as we had projected.

Identifying the First Problem

One of the first problems that we encountered in our first few weeks of business was in the store layout itself. We had segregated the department store from the grocery store operation by using a central concourse. Each entity had its own set of cash registers facing the concourse for checking out their respective customers. This seemed logical to me when we designed it, but it proved nonfunctional. Each set of registers became a psychological barrier to our customers, keeping them from crossing over from one side to the other. If a customer did, it was hard for our staff to tell what merchandise the customer had really paid for if they brought sacks of merchandise from one side to another.

The central concourse concept effectively eliminated the reason we had combined a grocery store with a department store format in the first place. Our original premise was that the grocery store would funnel business to the department store because they were both under the same roof. With our central concourse, we soon found out that a customer who went through the check stand on the grocery store side usually was ready to leave once the shopping was done. Perhaps this was due to the perishable nature of our many products or the large variety of frozen foods we sold. Maybe it was just how the grocery store shopper was hard wired in the 1960s. Who hasn't said, "I would love to stop and talk, but I have groceries." At any rate, it was not working out as we had planned.

I could tell right away from the shopping patterns and the poor department store sales that we had to do something about the central concourse design—and fast! I pulled our team together and we concluded that the dual register system had to go. A single checkout platform would encourage the shoppers to spill over from one department to another using a seamless transition. It would also give our staff a better handle on inventory control by not bagging purchases until the customer had actually paid for their items and was exiting the store.

Right in the Thick of Things

Undoing that dual checkout system was one of the hardest and most complex problems we had ever been confronted with at Smitty's while a store was operating. It taxed our team both physically and mentally. In our number two store, there was a massive number of utilities and steel cable buried in the concrete floor. We would have to deal with these imbedded pieces of infrastructure by rerouting many of them within the slab while we were reconfiguring our checkout stands. Given my "hands on" style, I was going to be right in the thick of things as it all unfolded!

We began this process immediately after we closed the store one evening at nine. I assembled a team of about twenty people who would be responsible for the conversion. Each night for three consecutive nights, we would work until nearly dawn with jack hammers, concrete saws, sledge hammers, and lots and lots of muscle. This was tedious and dirty work, which had to be completed and cleaned up by the time we opened each morning. Like we did in Marshalltown, Iowa, when we had a similar register problem, we laid plywood over the holes in the slab to keep our customers shopping and safe from our mess.

As we worked night by long night, our team was functioning on adrenaline and virtually no sleep. I was proud that no one complained about the long hours, showing up each night 100 percent ready for the grueling job. Each and every one of us wanted to solve the problem, and we were committed not to let a bunch of concrete and steel stand in our way, no matter how tired and exhausted we were!

Critical Decisions Have to Be Made

Relocating the registers to a single location looked to be a huge task, but I was convinced it was absolutely necessary. As a businessman, I knew that each day we waited was costing us serious money. Little did I know that this was the first of several critical decisions I would have to make before our number two store was even eight months old!

Once the register project was complete, things began to get a little better regarding our volume. The supermarket side of the store was going gangbusters, as it was very well received by the consumer. Sales were comparable per square foot to our first store on 16th Street, with merchandise turns increasing weekly. But—and this was an expensive but—our department store area sales were still doing poorly.

We had been right in our assumptions regarding our checkout stands and how they were restricting the flow of customers to the various departments. Shortly after the project was finished, there was a distinct shift in the shopping patterns of our customers, with our department store area beginning to see more traffic. This had proved to be a good decision but had not solved our problem of slow sales in the department store area. Frankly, I was stymied; I knew we had a great selection of merchandise, and it was as good as any retailer in the trade area. If I knew one thing about retailing, it was merchandising, and our store looked first rate. Perhaps time would rectify our poor performance.

We waited a few more weeks for the floor plan change to work, but we were still bleeding red ink. The department store side of the business was losing more money than the supermarket side could make. In search of an answer, I started to walk the aisles, visiting with our regular customers regarding their impressions of our department store merchandise. I would say things like, "I see by your cart you shopped in our supermarket, but there are very few items from our department store." This would elicit a response from many of our customers that became a reoccurring theme. "I really like the quality and selection of your merchandise, but your department store prices are much too high."

I guess I had probably known this down deep, but hearing from our customers that we were overpriced caught me somewhat by surprise. Up to this point, I had felt reasonably good about the manager I hired and the team he had put together. He had merchandised the store beautifully, and it complimented our supermarket merchandising really well. But the losses incurred from very high labor and handling costs, plus the customers confirming that our pricing of product was extreme, told us that we must change things immediately. We had fixed the floor plan, but it was time to start looking elsewhere for a solution.

Discovering, Confronting, and Finding the Way Out of a Problem

As I was looking for a way out of our problem, a Kmart store opened down the street, and I decided to do a little price checking. My wife, Helen, had done most of the department store shopping for our family; I was unfamiliar with current department store prices. Going into Kmart that first time really opened my eyes to just how far off the pricing was at our number two store. No wonder there was a resistance from our customers!

When I confronted our department store manager, the real story began to unfold. While he had portrayed himself as having a well-rounded background in retail, the truth was that most of the things he said he had experience in—such as purchasing and dealing with the vendors—had really been done for him by his previous company.

The corporate headquarters of his prior company was located in San Diego, California, and they did most of the ordering and delivering for his store in Phoenix out of their warehouse. The warehouse stocked a broad assortment of inventory that was just a few hours away. He did order for his store, but it was done on a "just in time" basis from their ware-house operation. This allowed him to keep the right inventory, with the right quantities and without much effort on his part.

His job at Smitty's was way more complicated than the basic arrangement he had at his former employer's place of business. Ordering for a 95,000-square-foot department store with hundreds of items was far more involved. At Smitty's, our needs required longer lead times for product delivery, and the dollars at risk were far greater. With a department store operation, there are seasonal issues, style changes, and product-specific knowledge that is required to be successful. To be effective, you have to know which item to buy, when to buy it, and how to price it properly. You also need to know how to negotiate "mark-down" money and how to buy "off price" to be competitive.

I found out that our manager was actually buying most of our merchandise from wholesalers and jobbers who marked up the items as much as 10 to 25 percent before selling them to us. This conduit of suppliers was convenient for spot purchasing, but to really be price effective, he needed to be buying directly from the manufacturers. He also allowed his department managers to buy important items like ready-to-wear, which was above their abilities. Buying for a full-fledged department store required a whole skill set that our manager and his staff did not have.

As I dug deeper into the problem, I also learned that his payroll was way out of whack. He probably had three times more employees than he really needed. Most of these employees had fancy titles and came with large salaries and benefits. I was distressed when I found out that he was not only overpaying for product but was too inexperienced to know that he was overstaffed. To add insult to injury, his high-priced staff even had difficulty putting a proper bank deposit together!

When I confronted our manager with what I had found out, he was unhappy with the straight talk I gave him. At first, he threatened to make trouble for us if I let him go but soon realized that his shortcomings would be exposed if he did. He finally decided to go quietly, which was a big relief for both of us.

Now out of a manager for our department store, I went to see a guy I knew who was liquidating some equipment from his office and some miscellaneous department store fixtures. He had managed a discount store in Phoenix that had gone out of business. I was familiar with the store and had actually been at the location several times. I liked the way the store was merchandised, which I assumed was a reflection on him.

Somehow during our visit, we discussed the possibility of him coming to work for us and managing our department store operation. His plan was to go back to Chicago, where he was from, but he would consider staying in Phoenix to be part of our team. It appeared he had the experience we needed — in spite of the fact that the store he managed had gone out of business. At any rate, he presented himself well and knew much more than our first manager did when I quizzed him. We made a deal, and he agreed to join our staff.

Unfortunately, the guy turned out to be what I call a "schlock" operator. I soon learned that he was not what he had portrayed himself to be. He would arrive late to work and wanted to stay holed up in his office all day. He would summon his staff to his office and hold court, giving the staff mostly hot air for direction. I found out that the store he managed was really a collection of independent department vendors who banded together under one roof. His real role was more of a coordinator than a manager.

The guy had been with us about sixty days when he made some disparaging comments about my brother Swede. My brother had come back to work for us just before we opened our number two store. Seizing on the comment he made about Swede, I realized it was a good excuse to rid ourselves of another mistake. Of course, firing the guy was the kind thing to do. Had I told Swede about what he said, there is no telling what would have happened to him.

Costly Mistakes, Honest Reappraisal, Facing Adversity, Tough Decision-Making

By now we had lost nine months and several hundred thousand dollars on our department store operation. We were fortunate that our first store in Phoenix was still doing well and the grocery side of the number two store was beating projections. However, our losses were hurting our cash flow and I was becoming concerned that the department store might sink the whole Phoenix operation. The overhead for a 135,000-square-foot store is huge even in good times. It gets magnified immensely when sales are not up to projections and inventory turns are slow. The management team and I were very concerned about our future!

The good news was that we still had several stores in Iowa that were really doing well. While I had sold a couple of them, the other stores were providing a good, positive cash flow. The stores were in a separate corporation and maintained their own financial identity.

As our losses mounted, I began to consider different ways to prop up the Phoenix stores to keep our cash flow strong. It was very important that somehow — and very soon — we get profitable. We could not let our creditors see us in a weakened position because we could lose or have our trade credit reduced. Over the years, our ability to get credit and repay our creditors ahead of time had allowed us to grow new locations mostly on accounts payable.

I called my attorney and explored the idea of combining the Iowa Corporation that held our stores with the Phoenix Corporation that was losing money. He told me it would take some time to accomplish this union and we needed approval to merge the two companies. What he did not know was that we were running out of time and money and that I had to do something right away. When he hesitated, I told him that I was going to merge the two corporations immediately in spite of the obstacles.

I moved quickly to consolidate the two corporations to affect a positive cash flow. While my attorney might have been worried about the legal logistics, and the IRS complications, I knew what had to be done and proceeded to combine the two entities. I was fortunate that my wife and I owned the stock in both corporations, so there were no dissident shareholders to deal with.

This was just what needed to happen and our losses became positive thanks to the Iowa Corporation. Combining the two strengthened our balance sheet and cash flow. It was a tough decision to make, but we were facing dire times. We had faced months of adversity, and our entire staff was committed to making the "superstore" concept a success.

Looking back at those uncertain times, I was very fortunate that everything worked as planned. By combining the two corporations, I had placed a large bet that we could get our number two store in the black. Had this not happened, I risked losing both sets of stores as now there was no shield to protect the Iowa stores from the possible losses.

I was also very blessed to be surrounded with a management team and staff that wanted to prove our concept right. Those individuals gave so much of themselves to make that number two store successful. I thank God that I did not have to face all those problems by myself. God was truly looking after us. Only years later would I fully comprehend and come into an understanding of this.

Redefining the Shopping Experience without a Road Map

With the two corporations now merged, we had bought ourselves some time to get things right. We were all focusing our efforts towards getting the department store areas profitable when I got the opportunity to hire a seasoned department store manager and his wife. Jim and Muriel Palmer were from Chicago and were good, genuine retailers. They had a strong foundation in the department store business, with years of experience. Jim's responsibility was to manage the overall department store side of our operation, while Muriel's strength was on the sales floor. Both turned out to be wonderfully qualified people.

Jim was also a seasoned buyer and knew what was required to keep us competitive. He was an experienced manager who knew how to get the best out of the department heads. Muriel took over as manager of our Housewares Department and looked after some of the store merchandising. The Palmers brought credibility to our department store operation that had been lacking from the start. They also provided leadership to the department managers and became a valuable resource to them in most of the retail area.

It took another few months to get the department store operation turned around for the good of all concerned. The Palmers, along with our core staff of department managers, played a big role in getting this troublesome area into the black. Jim reengineered our purchasing procedures, and we finally became competitive in the department store merchandise, just as we had always been in our supermarkets. He also streamlined our staffing and brought our labor costs in line. Likewise, Muriel brought change to our sales floor that reflected better merchandising and product turns.

Both Palmers ended up staying with Smitty's for years and became our good personal friends. Had we hired them in the beginning, much of our retail grief could have been avoided.

Worth Thinking About

"The business world is always ready to test your abilities and teach even seasoned veterans a little humility—especially when you are redefining the shopping experience without a road map."

—Clyde B. Smith

"There were plenty of pitfalls and chug holes on the road that took Sam Moore from door-to-door salesman to CEO of a company listed on the New York Stock Exchange. And through it all, Sam relied on an inextinguishable faith, giving him the confident trust that his God would guide him."

—Max Lucado
in speaking of the remarkable story of Sam Moore,
President of Thomas Nelson Publishers, Nashville, Tennessee.
(Nelson is one of the world's largest Bible publisher.)

"Some of the best men I know have all had major setbacks. Those who know how to rebound and come back are the ones who succeed in life."

—Sam Moore
from the book *American by Choice*

"Life has no smooth road for any of us; and in the bracing atmosphere of a high aim, the very roughness only stimulates the climber to steadier and steadier steps."

—Bishop W. C. Doane

"In the crises of life . . . our words show where our souls have been feeding."

—H. E. Fosdick

21

Lessons Learned, Tuition High!

"When you are 'shaking up' conventional thinking, question everything that you know to be true down to the last detail."

—Clyde B. Smith

What I Learned from Our Number Two Store: "Supermarket 101"

People always talk about the tuition for a college education being expensive. Well, the tuition I paid to get my diploma on that number two store was significant. When we opened that superstore in 1963, I had been a successful retailer for almost sixteen years. I had seen lots of adversity in business and loads of hard work; however, I was not prepared for the challenges that we encountered building the model for that "superstore" concept. There were so many lessons I learned and the tuition was high!

One of the most important lessons I learned revolved around the mistake we made with the central concourse and the dual cash register systems. By combining a supermarket with a department store under one roof, we were redefining the retail paradigm as it was known in the early 1960s. We correctly gauged the emerging logic of the combination but fell short when we separated the two entities by a separate set of cash registers. Though they were both under one roof, which was innovative, they might as well have been two distinct stores that shared a common wall.

What we failed to do was question everything we knew to be true about retail at the time. We got it 90 percent right by combining the two retail entities but missed the other 10 percent with our segregation of the two areas. I learned that when one is "shaking up" conventional thinking, one should question everything that one knows to be true, down to the last detail. Getting it 90 percent right in many cases is good, but when you are blazing new ground as we were, the other 10 percent can impact you directly in the bottom line.

Another important thing I learned is that when you are working outside your area of expertise, don't assume that you can do things as you have done in the past. I had hired numerous managers over the years to work in our supermarkets but had never hired a department store manager. I probably thought that the two retail disciplines were the same and approached hiring a department store manager just as I would a supermarket manager.

I found out the hard way that I had needed either more expertise or expert guidance when I hired our department store manager. Due to my lack of specific knowledge regarding the department store business, we had to suffer for almost nine months with two poor performers. This cost us significantly and disrupted our focus. Perhaps if I had dug a little deeper, educated myself better, or engaged a "head hunter" in the search, I might have averted a great deal of the stress that engulfed our entire organization while we were trying to get that "superstore" concept right.

Perhaps the most valuable lesson I learned from our experience with that number two store was that hard work alone will not solve your problems. It certainly helps, but as a manager/owner, you have to be willing to make the hard decisions that your business requires. During that first year in business, I was confronted with firing decisions, floor plan decisions, and a decision to merge our two corporate entities. Had I waited to make these decisions or failed to look them squarely in the eye, I might have had a whole different outcome to my retail story.

One of the toughest jobs a business person has is to make the really critical decisions on a timely basis. Making a tough call often concerns matters that are unpleasant or will alter the course of a business from its familiar path. These decisions are gut-wrenching, but hiding from them can be disastrous. Will you make the right decision 100 percent of the time? No, but if you take no action, most problems will not fix themselves.

As I made those tough decisions regarding our business, I did not make them in a vacuum. I had a crack management team that I consulted with over and over. Their guidance was valued and important to me. I also spent hours upon hours examining the various consequences. These were decisions that were made with careful thought and deliberation from all the variables that I knew at the time. Most importantly, I did my best to gather all points of interest and input and then made a decision based on my interpretation of the facts.

What I did not do is let the various points of interest paralyze my decision-making capacity. When you are in charge of a business, at some point you have to take action in an attempt to solve the problems that are in front of you. If you do not, you run the risk of not only damaging your business but also depriving the people who depend upon your success of the leadership that they expect and deserve. Remember, when confronted with the tough decisions, get the facts, weigh them carefully, gather input from trusted resources, encourage open debate, and then take action!

Worth Thinking About
Smitty's Big Three

- When you are working outside your area of expertise, don't assume that you can do things as you have done in the past.

- Hard work alone will not solve your problems. It certainly helps, but as a manager/owner, you have to be willing to make the hard decisions that your business requires.

- One of the toughest jobs a business person has is to make the really critical decisions on a timely basis. These decisions are gut-wrenching, but hiding from them can be disastrous. When confronted with the tough decisions, get the facts, weigh them carefully, gather input from trusted resources, encourage open debate, and then take action!

22

Getting Back on the Path to Growth

"While I knew in my heart that the superstore
concept we had pioneered . . . was the future of retailing,
I was reluctant to put our group into another superstore until
I was sure we had gotten the concept right."

—Clyde B. Smith

It took almost three years for us to digest our number two store and resume our objective of growing the company. The problems we encountered with that superstore had really challenged us for a time, putting our plans to build additional stores on hold. Although it had not brought us to our knees, it had taught us many valuable lessons at a great expense of money and manpower. As I have said before about that store, the tuition to get my degree was very expensive.

I was delighted that my brother Swede had rejoined our company in 1963 as an assistant manager of our number two store. Swede played a valuable role in getting that store moving in the right direction. Likewise, my brother Doug took on more responsibilities in both our stores and continued to be a key player in our organization. Doug had a winning way with people. Doug's people skills really helped in building our growing organization into a first class team.

In 1965, we opened our third store in the Phoenix area. The store was only 45,000 square feet and was strictly a grocery store operation. We were still bruised from our superstore experience, and I felt we needed to go back to our roots. Our team knew the grocery store side of the business really well and had a formula for success that had been proven in both Phoenix and with our chain of stores in Iowa. It was a business model we had refined over the years, and it had been profitable for us time and time again. I was reluctant to put our group into another superstore until I was sure we had gotten the concept right. I knew in my heart that the superstore concept we had pioneered with our number two store was the future of retailing, but our organization needed a little breathing room. We also needed some strengthening of our balance sheet.

The bottom line was that our team needed more on-the-job training and a great deal more of "hands-on" learning experience in several of the departments. We needed to prepare our entire staff for the growth and profitability that would be needed for us to take on the competition that would surely come our way. If our future was to be in the superstores, I wanted to expand our operation in a professional and businesslike manner, with the entire organization fully prepared to go to the next level in retailing.

We would not open another superstore until we opened our sixth store in 1969. By this time, our stores were achieving huge volumes per square foot and were very profitable. During the years between our first and second superstore, we continued to learn the department store business and became quite good at retailing both the hard and soft good items that completed the superstore concept.

The three grocery stores between superstores were very successful and provided the type of cash flow and profitability that gave us the confidence to move forward in a positive manner. So in 1969, we built our second superstore. The superstore would be our format of choice until we built our thirteenth store in 1976. We put a few grocery-store-only formats in our mix; then it was superstores only until we built our twentieth store.

A banker friend of mine with some retail experience constantly asks me how we grew from one store in Phoenix in 1961 to twenty stores in 1980, doing over $750 million dollars per year in sales and employing over 6,000 people. He likes to remind me that in today's dollars, this would equal over $2 billion dollars in sales! Being a banker, he is always trying to get me to dissect our growth and give him some fancy business model or technique we used to achieve the level of success we experienced. He is always asking me about how we controlled our growth and kept our stores profitable. I guess in his line of work, he has seen more businesses fail from spectacular growth than actually make it.

The truth is, I never thought much about our growth as it was happening. I just knew that we wanted to grow by creating a unique shopping experience for the customer, while simultaneously creating opportunity for our staff. I also had the desire and ambition to be number one in the Phoenix market and to be at the forefront of supermarket retailing. I knew down deep that if we did these things really well, the growth of the business would take care of itself. For me, this translated into a business model that centered on four basic principles:

1. Always focusing on the customer,
2. Hiring, training, and involving the right people,
3. Striving to be number one through innovation, and
4. Ongoing personal leadership.

It Takes the Right People

There is no way a business can be truly successful unless it has the right people performing the right tasks. Smitty's achieved the level of success it did because of its people and their abilities. I learned early in my business career that if you were going to grow your business, the key was in "getting work done" through people. No matter where they landed on the pay scale, top wage earners or entry level, each member of your staff is vital to your success. At Smitty's, we never lost sight of this.

As I was building my career and stores in Iowa, I would often see single-store operators start to grow by adding additional stores. Unfortunately, many would soon be making half the money and saddled with twice the overhead. Worse, they often would begin to lose money in their main store, which was the primary source of their profits!

Many of these individuals were successful in their original store because they could control the operation from sunup to sundown. Having just one store and focus, they would mold that single store into the type of store and culture they wanted. The staff would take their cues from the owner and perform like he or she wanted them to because the boss was always there. Unfortunately, when the owner started to devote time to another store, store discipline would begin to fall apart. For some reason, many of these single-store owners failed to understand that a multistore operation calls for training, delegating, and preparing store personnel to be productive at whatever they do, even if the owner is not on site.

My mentor and dear friend Keith Rushing was no exception. Keith was a great operator, but he had a very difficult time making money in multiple stores. Keith fit the profile I just outlined. He had all the knowledge in the world and delivered a high quality of customer service but could not translate this into more than one location. Though he tried owning multiple stores more than once, Keith was most successful when he could see both the front and back door.

Watching Keith and others try and fail at multiple stores taught me that if we were going to grow as a company, I would need to hire and train the right people. Even though I was willing to work as many hours as it took and make countless sacrifices such as time away from my wife and young girls, to be really successful, I had to surround myself with the type of people who mirrored the same desires and ambitions that I had. I needed people who were willing to work the long hours and challenge themselves to produce more and beat the goals that they and the company set. Even as a little kid, I was fiercely independent, but when growing a company, I was fortunate to learn early that I could not do it alone.

I also learned that besides finding the right people, you had to train them really well. We were relentless with our training regimen in Iowa and brought this passion for training with us to Phoenix. One of the biggest problems that faced many of my contemporaries in Iowa as they grew into multiple locations was that many did not invest the time and energy it took properly to train and empower their staff. This often diluted the growth potential of the remote store because the manager and his team were cast more in the role of "caretaker" than "decision maker." As we began to add multiple stores, I was determined not to let this happen to us.

At Smitty's, we grew a passion for training our people and then encouraging them to take the position of ownership in their area of expertise. Without a doubt, this was one of the pivotal keys to our success. Whether they were a store manager, department manager, or carryout staff, I knew that if we invested in their success with a disciplined training regimen and honest communication, they would grow as individuals and help us grow as a company. Of course, we always hoped that this investment would foster a sense of "ownership" among our staff and they would look upon Smitty's as theirs. I always used to say that when "my store" becomes "our store," good things begin to happen for everyone concerned.

I am amazed to this day that many of the carryout staff we hired for our first few stores in Phoenix became managers for us in later years. I always liked to hire them when they were young and full of energy and hungry for an opportunity to show what they could do. For some reason, God gave me the insight to be able to see that spark in our young staff and to cultivate the ones that really wanted a career with us. My brother Doug was also good at this, as were many of our original managers. It was not uncommon for us to find young carryout persons with what it took, relentlessly train them as they were being rotated through our various departments, and then one day in the future be standing in front of one of our stores handing them the keys as manager. Nothing made me prouder.

Ongoing Leadership

I always believed that as the owner I must provide consistent and ongoing leadership for the team. I found that our business became even more effective and successful if I was willing to get in and set the pace. Whether it was on the sales floor, pitching in to unload an extra large shipment, or mopping up after a flood in a store's dairy department, I found that if I was willing to give 100 percent and get in the trenches with our staff, chances were that the staff would give 110 percent back. I learned early in my career that if I was willing to set the pace, the managers wanted to outwork me and their staff wanted to outwork them! This built the needed energy and discipline within our organization that fed off itself as we grew.

As our organization grew from that one store in Phoenix to twenty stores with over six thousand employees, I continued to block portions of my time to be visible in the stores. Nothing motivated me more than to be in one of our stores on a busy day and to pitch in and help our staff. By the time we got to twenty stores, I had done just about every job in the supermarket business and nothing was out of my comfort zone. I always felt that if I gave a hand, it showed the staff that I respected what they did.

I remember one time on a Sunday evening when one of our stores was hit by a twister during a rain storm. The twister took off portions of the roof, and the driving rain that followed flooded the store. When I got the call from the manager, Clim Gonzalez, I raced over to the store after I made multiple calls to contractor friends of mine for help. When I got there, I told Clim he would be back in business by the next morning. He just looked at me as if I were crazy.

To this day, Clim laughs when he remembers the sight of me in my "fancy, $100 leather shoes" as he called them, mopping up the water in the store. Sure, there were other people there to help, but I felt that if I was going to keep Clim and his staff most of the night, it was up to me to set the pace by giving them a hand. Although it would be impossible today to reopen due to health regulations, Clim and his team did open the store the next morning, and it was business as usual.

I am sure that in today's "work smarter, not harder" society, setting the pace for your staff seems a bit old fashioned. I still believe it is a great tool to build a framework of team spirit, while keeping in touch with the people who add so much value to your business. My years in business have taught me that the staff's dedication to your business will be a direct correlation to the dedication you demonstrate to them on a consistent basis. If you are willing to set the pace, the right people will see this and become caught up in the process. To grow a successful business, you need the right people, and they need your leadership to complete the circle.

Worth Thinking About
Some of Smitty's Key Management Thoughts

1. Provide strong, effective leadership and offer direction.

2. Show and tell—explain "why" as well as "how." Good training is a must.

3. Know how to delegate authority.

4. Four "Bes": Be objective; be enthusiastic; be strong and courageous; be creative.

5. Stimulate and motivate.

6. Use common sense.

7. Know and care about what you talk about. Put the mind in gear before you open your mouth.

8. Know your job—take ownership and pride in what you do.

9. Recognize that you don't buy respect, you earn it.

23

Being Number One

"How do you become number one?
To accomplish this, I knew we would have to be more
creative and innovative than the next guy; we would have to
differentiate ourselves from our competitors."

—Clyde B. Smith

As you have probably gathered by now, I am a very competitive guy. For as long as I can remember, I've challenged myself in most everything I've undertaken. When I worked in the coal mine with my dad, I wanted to mine more coal and work harder than the next guy. In the army, I was very intense in leadership and wanted to do more push-ups and calisthenics than anyone else in my platoon. Naturally, when I got into business, I brought this competitive nature to my supermarket career.

In both Iowa and Phoenix, I wanted our company to be number one in the marketplace. I knew how to accomplish this; we would have to be more creative and innovative than the next guy. In Iowa, I used "out of the box" marketing and promotions to make the small towns we operated in sit up and pay attention. We were the first to incorporate unique departments into our stores such as a scratch bakery and full-service restaurant. If there was a new product coming to the market, we wanted to be the first to bring it to the marketplace and have the best pricing. I always wanted us to be number one.

In Phoenix, we used these strategies along with our bigger stores to differentiate us from our competitors. Our stores were clean, well-merchandised, and staffed with the best trained and knowledgeable grocers we could hire and train. While we always kept a keen eye on our bottom line, we routinely tried to pass on any savings we could to the customer to keep them coming back. I was convinced that the shopping should not be a chore; it should be an experience. It was up to us to provide the excitement in this experience if we were going to get to the number one slot.

I was fortunate that I got to be involved as a director of the Supermarket Institute early in my supermarket career. I always thought that this helped our team stay at the forefront of the industry. As we grew, I would take several of our managers to the conventions and assign them responsibilities at the meeting. We all would scour the event for that "latest item or concept," which we could then take back and be the first to have in our market. While some other grocers might use the convention to party or vacation, our team saw it as a tool to becoming a leader in our respective markets.

So you don't get the wrong impression, I was not one of those guys who lay awake at night obsessing about being number one. For me, it was more about getting up in the morning and trying to do things a little bit better than I did yesterday. I truly loved the supermarket business, and I had the overwhelming belief that if we applied ourselves daily, we would one day achieve our goal of being number one. If we did, it would not only fulfill my long-term goal, but it would also enrich the lives of thousands of team members, while creating ongoing value for our many loyal customers.

By the time we had ten stores in the Phoenix area, we reached that number one slot. This said volumes about our team and how we ran our stores. The media portrayed us that way. This isn't just us patting ourselves on the back—news stories featured our unique complexes, calling attention to our displays with great photo coverage. Phoenix was a big city and was home to many of the large chain stores which still dominate the grocery business today. By the time we had twenty stores, we had over 35 percent of the entire market share and were besting the national profit margins for supermarkets by several percentage points. This meant that over one in three consumers shopped at a Smitty's store for their grocery and department store needs. Even by today's megastore standards, this is an overwhelming statistic when it comes to a major metropolitan market.

Focusing on the Customer

God truly smiled on me that day I was hanging around the back door of Keith Rushing's grocery store when Keith decided to give me a job. Working for him gave me the opportunity to learn the grocery business from the ground up. This learning curve continued on with my first store in Roland, Iowa, and spanned many more years to our stores in Phoenix. When I was in the prime of my career, there was not much about the grocery business that I had not been exposed to. So, I think I can say in all confidence that to be truly successful in the grocery business or any business, you must first have basic training, know your business from A to Z, and then give your undivided focus to the customer.

I learned at a very young age that the customer is the sole ingredient to a successful business. Sure, you can build state-of-the-art stores and hire really good people to run them, but without the acceptance of the customer, all your efforts are futile. This sounds pretty drastic, but if you think it through, it is the stone cold truth.

At Smitty's, we built our business model around focusing on the customer. It was the philosophy that supported all we did as a company. Focusing on the customer drove our staffing, guided how we operated our stores, and fueled our desire to be number one. I learned that being number one was not really about us, it was about bringing a better shopping experience to the customer. The better the shopping experience we brought to the customer, the closer to being "number one" we got. You have seen me emphasizing this throughout the book, but it bears repeating.

Our entire staff was immersed in a customer-focused culture from the first day they set foot on the job. Focusing on the customer was outlined prominently in our employee manual and was a central theme in most of our training sessions. We were never to question the customer at Smitty's, even to the point of allowing the return of a $10,000 diamond ring in one of our superstores that I am sure had been worn a few times.

As I have outlined before, I would often grab a cart and try to shop our stores through the eyes of the customer. Was the store clean and easy to navigate? Did the merchandising entice me to buy? How did the staff look? Well-groomed and energetic? Were we creating value for the customer? These are things that I knew were important to our customers and if we excelled, the numbers and rest would take care of themselves.

Focusing on the customer became our passion at Smitty's. It was the one thing that never changed about our business. While we experienced a great deal of change going from one store in Phoenix to twenty, focusing on the customer remained a constant for us. It was the single most valuable factor in our many years of success.

Worth Thinking About

- Focusing on the customer is the single most valuable factor in any retailer's success.

- I learned that being number one was not really about us, it was about bringing a better shopping experience to the customer.

- Ten more key management thoughts:
    1. Stop waste; supervise, supervise, supervise.
    2. Strive for efficiency from yourself and your staff.
    3. Get work done through people.
    4. Insist on good workmanship and quality.
    5. Be punctual.
    6. Set goals.
    7. Provide tight controls.
    8. Hold meetings to keep everyone informed.
    9. Teamwork is a must.
    10. Money—any fool can spend it or waste it. It takes effort, common sense, and management to make it.

24

Development of a Corporate Structure

"It didn't take me long to learn that the best
way to build consensus was through straight talk
and communication with my staff."

—Clyde B. Smith

Growing from one store in Phoenix to twenty stores probably took more hard work and struggles than I can remember. Life is funny that way when you look back on something you truly loved. We were challenged multiple times and faced obstacles that seemed insurmountable, but our team always prevailed. What I do remember is that relentlessly adhering to the four simple principles I outlined kept us growing and our customers coming back.

By the time we got to six stores, we began to develop more of a corporate structure. My brother Doug became our first supervisor and soon was a vital link to our store managers. It was his job to be in the stores and to act as a resource to the staff for merchandising, product mix, and staffing. Doug was a great resource to the stores, given his talent for the business and his many years of experience. This allowed me to continue to work on the vendor and merchandising side of the business, which was getting quite substantial. I also continued to scout for future locations, as I wanted Smitty's to be ahead of the growth curve in the expanding Phoenix Metropolitan Statistical Area (MSA).

The Tuesday Morning Meeting Ritual

At some point as we started adding stores, I began to bring in the store managers to our central office each Tuesday morning for what became an important ritual at Smitty's. Every Tuesday morning we would gather the store managers and our head buyers together at the warehouse to check on their special buys and to help plan the advertising for the week. Our head buyer would tell us of any special buys they made that we might want to feature in our ads.

I took great pride in including all managers in this process and genuinely wanted them to offer their ideas about what weekly specials we should run and what the ad should look like. These were lively and spirited meetings given that there were no wallflowers in our group.

To the layman, a few managers working on a weekly newspaper ad for a supermarket might seem a bit unimportant, but to a grocer, it was our lifeblood. The weekly advertisement was the primary tool we used to compete for market share, and it had to be right. Having our managers involved not only brought a frontline perspective to this process, but it also ensured that the stores would be ready and waiting for our customers when the ad broke. To this day, it gets on my nerves when I go into a store for the ad special and they are unprepared or never got the advertised item at all. Having our managers involved in the ad planning meant that Smitty's stores were always prepared with signs and that the product was on hand and properly priced.

Once the ad for the week was done, we would then go over our previous weekly sales reports, which recapped our sales in each store. These reports were in detail and included our fixed operating expenses and labor costs for each department, along with the sales for the week that had just passed. The reports were shared with all the managers, which made the successes and shortcomings of each store transparent.

I always liked the openness of this process, as it slapped the winners on the back and lit a fire under those who were behind. It also promoted a bit of competitiveness within the group. If you were a manager who was lagging in one or two areas in a given week, you did not want to come back the next week and be in the same shape. It wasn't that they were afraid of looking me in the eye; the peer pressure got under their skin.

Most of our managers had worked their way up through the ranks and knew each other quite well. Even with twenty stores and six thousand employees, they were like a big, extended family and needled each other like siblings. This worked to the customer's advantage because each one wanted to operate the best store in the system. The Tuesday meeting was their chance to show the group what they were made of and how their store stacked up against the rest. As I said, these were lively and spirited meetings punctuated with a playful jab to the ribs now and then over a manager's performance — good or bad.

The result of our managers needling each other like siblings was that they really thought of each other as family. If a recap report showed that a given manager was struggling with a certain department or area, the other managers would all pitch in and try to help solve the problem. If one or more of the managers had a particular strength in the problem area, he would go out to the troubled store and offer "hands-on" help. If the situation called for it, they would work extra hours in the problem store on top of their grueling 50–70 hour schedule in their own store. While each wanted to be the best operator in the system, they still wanted everyone to succeed.

Besides wanting every store and its manager to succeed, there was a monetary component that quietly drove this "no-store-left-behind" attitude. As I have previously said, I learned early in my career that if you were going to get work done through people, you had to reward them financially. As we grew our business into multiple stores, this basic principle became ever more important.

Our stores were set up on a performance bonus system that allowed all managers to share in the monetary success of the organization. This started with the department managers who received 10 percent of the net profit of their respective departments. Store managers received a 10 percent bonus based on the performance of their store and also received an override bonus based on the performance of all the stores in the system. Supervisors like my brother Doug and later Gene Carter received their bonuses primarily on the performance of the whole organization.

While I am sure that each manager would have still gone out of his way to help a struggling teammate, our bonus system kept them on task so that no store was left behind. A poorly performing store hit them directly in the wallet. This became a powerful incentive for all managers to look out for the success of the entire organization, not just their own stores. It also strengthened our team, as we constantly learned from each other by passing on the best practices of our most successful managers.

After we reviewed the sales recap reports to dissect our previous week's performance, I would then shift gears from the past week and challenge the team to use the reports to project the coming week's sales. With the detailed information that these reports gave us, we could compare our past week's performance by department and use historical revenue and expense numbers to project a line by line budget for the coming week. With the managers' input, we could model our income statement based on these numbers and the current sales trends in each of the markets. Barring anything out of the ordinary, we could then project what our profit each week would be and therefore eliminate any big surprises at the end of the month or quarter. If the pro forma budget did not work out as planned, the following Tuesday meeting would address the shortcomings, with the entire team focused on getting things right.

As we grew, our Tuesday meeting became a great vehicle for our managers to discuss inventory levels and, if needed, to rebalance the stores. The day before the meeting, the store buyers would meet and send their overstocked and want lists to the meeting with their respective managers. Because of the diversity of the nonfood items in our superstores, it was important for our cash flow that we move overstocked items in one store to another if the probability of selling the merchandise was better. If there was an overstocked position on an item in more stores than was prudent, the managers would then discuss an ad to move the product or return the surplus items back to the warehouse.

One of my favorite things about the Tuesday meeting was that it gave me a chance to talk with the managers on a strategic level. We would discuss everything from new locations to scooping the competition on a brand-new item. It was a chance for me to share my views on the direction of the industry and how this would affect our company. The meeting gave the managers a forum to talk about their markets and for me to hear about their plans for growing market share. If there was a particular problem facing our organization, we would put our heads together and try to solve it collectively. To this day, it amazes me how much we accomplished in those Tuesday meetings.

One of the strengths of the Smitty's organization I am especially proud of was our commitment to ongoing communication. The Tuesday meeting was a great example of this. I believed it was critical that information in our company be shared openly on a consistent basis. I felt that if I kept most of the knowledge to myself, it would be counterproductive in building a dedicated and informed team. Of course, each participant in the Tuesday meeting was sworn to secrecy about the sensitive information that we shared. I am proud to say that in all the years we practiced this ritual, I know of no instance where anyone on our team betrayed my confidence.

Too many business owners try to keep their staff in the dark, particularly when it comes to finances. I learned with our stores in Iowa that if you shared this data, it was easier to get the staff to buy into your vision than if you kept them out of the loop. Sure, they got to know your strengths and weaknesses, but how else were you going to get profitable in multiple locations without them knowing these truths? It did not take me long to learn that the best way to build consensus was through straight talk and communication with my staff.

Worth Thinking About

Our once-a-week Tuesday morning meetings were a ritual our team managers anticipated. They were a key to the development of a "no-store-left-behind" corporate structure. This worked to the customer's advantage because each manager wanted his store to be the best in the system.

A critically important strength of any organization is its commitment to ongoing communication where information about the company is being shared on a consistent basis. Our once-weekly meetings provided this opportunity.

It is counterproductive for the owner to keep all information and knowledge about the corporation to himself if he wants to build a dedicated and informed team.

—Clyde B. Smith

25

Providing Financial Incentives, Picking the Right Locations for Your Stores, and Other Factors Contributing to Success

"I don't know how many times I've proved to myself that you just never go wrong in treating the other person fair and square."

—Norm Miller, CEO, Interstate Batteries
from his book *Beyond the Norm*

I would like to say a little bit more about providing financial incentives. I have found that this and good communication are critical in building a dedicated team. At Smitty's, we embraced these concepts. I am convinced that it helped us achieve a higher level of sales and profitability, which kept us at the top of our industry. Take our stock purchase plan, for example. I like and certainly subscribe to Norm Miller's philosophy.

Fair and Square: More than Just Words

When employees had worked their way up in our organization, and we had identified them as a key long-term player, I would then offer to sell them stock in our company from our corporate treasury at book value plus 10 percent. To facilitate the purchase, I would personally take team members to the bank and introduce them to our company banker. Prior to the meeting, I would have already prearranged with the banker to finance the stock purchase based on the employee's ability to repay the loan from the incentive bonuses that they were earning. Meeting with our banker formalized this process and usually made a big impression on the team member.

I always encouraged our key staff members to live off of their base salary and to save their bonus money, or even better, to use it to purchase stock in the company. The Depression had made a huge impression on me as a child, and I wanted to pass on the conservative manner of living I had learned during those lean years to our staff. I had such great faith in our company that I knew if our key people purchased company stock, and then repaid their stock loan in full from their commission money, they would build a nest egg and security for their family's future.

As things turned out, the stock purchase plan that we offered our key staff members made many of them very wealthy. It did my heart good to see so many of our team members rewarded for the long hours they spent in building our company into a regional powerhouse and leader in the supermarket industry. I know that money could not replace the time many of them spent away from their families, but at least I hoped it provided a more secure life for them and their children. I also hoped that it gave them a sense of pride and accomplishment each time they looked at their checkbook. All we achieved — the innovative stores, the exceptional financial performance, and the many industry awards — could not have been accomplished without them!

If you are in business, I strongly encourage you to consider designing a program where you can share your success monetarily with your key staff members. A well-designed program based on quantifiable performance metrics goes a long way in building a competitive advantage. It also builds a bond and a sense of perceived ownership in your firm that is worth every dollar paid. If you truly want a competitive edge in today's marketplace, you need to share your success with your staff so that they will get down and stay in the trenches with you.

After providing a trail of growth and proven success, I found that when I offered to sell some of my personal stock to the key persons in the organization, it turned out to be a home run. Instead of it being just "my stores," it became "our stores." That's when our business really began to grow and prosper. Sharing and teamwork is definitely necessary to ensure the future success of an overall business plan. This is, as the saying goes, something you can take to the bank.

It Is All about Location

God must have been looking out for me when I decided to open up our first store in Phoenix in 1961, even though at that time in my life I wasn't paying much attention to God. In the ensuing years, both Phoenix and the cities that surround it began to experience a steady growth in population. This provided our organization a wealth of opportunity to grow our business beyond our wildest dreams. After about ten years in business, there were so many opportunities to open stores that I could hardly keep up with them. Residents would routinely write us, asking when we were going to open a Smitty's in their neighborhood.

In the early 1970s, my youngest daughter, Karen, married a nice young man named Mark Medigovich. Mark had just gotten his real estate license, and I decided to take him under my wing. With our corporate staff coming together and dealing with many of the day-to-day duties, it gave me some time to scout out new locations for future expansion. Mark was a good partner in this endeavor.

I had always been very picky when it came to choosing a location for a future store. First and foremost, the site had to be in the growth path of the city. It should be in a somewhat high traffic location but have easy access. I would often pass over a high traffic corner in favor of a site that facilitated our customer with ease of access. While it is great to have thousands of cars drive by your location and see your store, it is counterproductive when your customers have trouble getting in or out of your parking lot.

Mark and I spent hours in the car scouting Phoenix and the surrounding areas for new store locations. Occasionally, we would charter a helicopter, which I felt gave us the best feel for a store site. From the air, it was much easier to discern traffic patterns and future metropolitan growth. What looked like a deserted field often became a store site for us in a few short years. I felt it was wise to get in front of the population growth curve and the inevitable price increases on the real estate that followed. There was no better way to take the guesswork out of this process than from a few hundred feet up in a low-flying helicopter.

Another way we took the guesswork out of choosing a site location was to build a relationship with key staff members of the city's planning and zoning department. These individuals routinely dealt with developers who were determining the future growth paths of the city. While we never pushed for proprietary information, we did obtain a first look at what could be discussed publically and used this information to help drive our expansion activities.

As in our stores, I was a firm believer in building genuine relationships with people. I learned early as a young man that if you are sincere in your relationships, most people will want to help you if they can. This was evident in my relationship with my mentor Keith Rushing, as with many of the people I met as I built my supermarket career. When I started looking for store locations, I found a slap on the back and some genuine conversation with the city staff people always did us good. I learned that if you showed them a little respect, they were willing to help you get ahead of the pack, especially if you added some extra tax base to their community. It was a win–win situation.

Some of the things I taught my son-in-law about selecting a supermarket site were that traffic volume was not my primary concern. Yes, I wanted a good steady flow of traffic, but as I said before, the site had to be easy to get in and out of. Shoppers who have to fight to get in or out of your location will soon go elsewhere with their business.

Likewise, I stressed to Mark that if we purchased a site, it had to be oversized in relation to the store we were going to build. It was critical that we have more than ample parking where the customer could park out in front and have a commanding view of the front door.

Mostly, I tried to share with Mark that you had to use vision if you were buying locations for stores that were two to five years out. It took real imagination to stand in a deserted field and make a judgment call about purchasing a site for a store that was a few years away. However, if you did so successfully, you could save hundreds of thousands of dollars on the site by buying it before it was surrounded by consumers. My philosophy was that if I could buy a site before the prices increased, then I could pass the savings on to our customers.

A Backward Glance

When I look back on our phenomenal growth, I realize that there were some things that definitely kept us in a leadership position in the supermarket industry. We built the right team and provided financial incentives for them, secured the right locations, and were ahead of the pack in our merchandising plan. At one point, Smitty's enjoyed a commanding 35 percent market share in the Phoenix, Arizona, Metropolitan Statistical Area. Even by today's superstore standards, this is an overwhelming statistic in a major metropolitan market.

At ninety-plus years old, I am sure that I have forgotten many of the details of our spectacular growth, including the many obstacles that we encountered. During our peak growth years, we were adding one to two stores a year and as many as five to six hundred employees. This challenged our team in multiple ways, but they always succeeded. Never once did they lose sight of our collective objective of being number one in the market and achieving this goal by treating the customer right.

Worth Thinking About

Walter Knott, founder of the world-famous tourist attraction known as Knott's Berry Farm in Buena Park, California, wrote to his employees and said, "I wish I could make you realize, as I realize, how important you and your thinking are to this business. Did you ever stop to think when you help in the management of the business with your ideas, and when you share in the profits of the business, that you are, in effect and in fact, partners in the business? You don't know how often I think of this and how proud I am of my partners."

Not only did Walter Knott reward his employees with year-end paycheck bonuses, but he started a Profit-Sharing Retirement Program that provided a "very dignified retirement program" for them. Through the years of amazing growth and progress, Mr. Knott encouraged his employees and shared with them the ideas of others. "I am awfully anxious to surprise you with a larger share of profits this fall," he wrote them. "Give me all the help you can, but above all, be good to our customers."

Of his Profit-Sharing programs, Walter Knott said, "I know of no better way to say 'thank you' to every person who has helped us during the year than to hand him a check and say, 'Here is your share of the profits for working so hard this year.'" Mr. Knott became known for always looking after the welfare of his employees in the best possible ways. Rather than spend money on himself, Mr. Knott thought, "I could sink that amount of money back in the Farm and create twenty new job opportunities! So that's what I did. What a joy it is for me to open up these new business opportunities and then watch some person find the joy of a wonderful job that can give him the pride he deserves. My greatest satisfaction in life is knowing that some widow, some young person or other human being can come here and find an honest job and win the biggest prize life has to offer—self-respect."

—Helen Kooiman Hosier
from the book *Walter Knott—Keeper of the Flame*

"The feelings Walter Knott shared are echoed by me. He was an exemplary entrepreneur and outstanding patriot."

—Clyde B. Smith

"The greatest dividends are those paid to hardworking men and women through bonuses, gifts, scholarships, and praise."

—Jon M. Huntsman
Chairman and founder of Huntsman Corporation,
from his book *Winners Never Cheat*

Contributing to Success: An Interlude

From John Trice and Helen Hosier

It seems most appropriate that, at this juncture in this wonderful story, we give some of the amazing people who contributed so much to the success of the Smitty Stores an opportunity to share their reminiscences of those years.

From Clyde B. Smith

Without this marvelous and dedicated team, Smitty's would never have become the retail success that it was. Sure, I was a pretty fair merchant, but beyond a couple of stores, I could not have achieved the many things that we did without those individuals who dedicated a great portion of their lives to seeing that we were not only successful but also a "market maker" in every sense of the word. To this day, I thank God for all these wonderful people and their countless contributions.

While this book is about my retail journey, in many ways it is also the story of these individuals and the journey that we took together. This is the reason I feel that it is important for you to hear from some of the individuals who cast their lot and future with the Smitty's stores. It is my hope that through their words and insights you might get a different perspective on the retail path we charted together so many years ago, and that it might inspire you in your present situation.

Unfortunately, many of the important people that took this retail journey are no longer with us, such as topflight managers like Everett Larson, Swede Smith, and Tony Witte. While they may have passed away, their legacy lives on in the thousands of employees they helped train who are still active and are making a difference in the supermarket industry today.

I am delighted to say that our original baker and one of our undercover retail spies, Arnold Eggers, is still alive and going strong at eighty-plus years of age. A thin man with boundless energy, Arnold donates hundreds of hours each year at Veterans Hospitals, still wanting to make a difference in others lives. Likewise, many of the people you are going to read about are still active in the business community, and yes, some of them are grocers. I hope their comments add a bit of dimension to the journey we took together.

In Their Own Words

Dave Trottier
Store Manager, Partner in the Springfield Missouri Stores, owner of ten Smitty's Supermarkets in Missouri 1977–1998; now owner of nine Summer Fresh Supermarkets throughout Southwest Missouri— Tenure: 1962–1976

I grew up in New England and first worked in a grocery store called Boston Market in Claremont, New Hampshire. I was in the seventh grade, and every day after school, including weekends, I worked in that store: stocking shelves, filling beer coolers, and emptying buckets of water in the basement. I was paid thirty-five cents an hour and was one very ambitious kid.

In 1960, I reluctantly moved to Scottsdale, Arizona, with my parents. I got a job working for A. J. Bayless Supermarkets making seventy-five cents an hour. It was my sophomore year and some of the very first classmates I met were the Kapanicas twins, Mitch and Mike. They were working for the Bashas' Supermarkets, so we had a lot in common.

At the time, the 135,000-square-foot Smitty's Big Town was under construction at 82nd and McDowell. We all decided to apply for jobs because it was going to be the biggest combination superstore in Arizona. We interviewed with Everett Larson, the general manager, and were hired at $1.25 per hour. As this was much more than we were currently making, we happily quit our jobs and went to work at Smitty's Big Town in 1962, advertised as "the place where Ma saves Pa's dough."

As a young kid working for Smitty's supermarket, I was impressed by how Clyde Smith never met a stranger. From the janitor, carryout, checker, waitress, or executive, he treated everyone like a good friend. Many of us in the grocery business believe he could have run for President of the United States and won.

I stayed with Smitty's until 1965 when I decided to go to work for the Bill McNealy Company, a food broker. My main account was calling on Smitty's. It was starting to grow, with Clyde announcing two new stores in 1966. After eighteen months at McNealy's, Smitty managers Bob Beaudrie and Ken Walters convinced me to quit the broker business and come back to Smitty's where "I could have a future in the grocery business."

I loved sports and I loved to box. I fought some pretty good fighters in the Phoenix area through the Golden Gloves program. I was headed to the Golden Gloves Nationals in Las Vegas when I was beat by a kid named Danny Downs. The fight was stopped in the third round by the referee after we knocked each other down twice. The next day, the Phoenix Gazette made it sound like the fight of the century.

On Monday morning, I went back to work at Smitty's stocking groceries on aisle three when Clyde Smith shows up. I'm stocking away with a butterfly bandage covering the bridge of my nose and two black eyes. Smitty walks up, looks at me, and starts laughing. "You look pretty bad," he said. I replied, "You should see the other guy." I was never short of a comeback. Smitty looked me square in the eye and said, "Are you going to pursue this boxing thing or work for me?" I said, "Mr. Smith, that was my last fight. I'm going to work for you, for my future, end of story." By 1968 I had worked in the meat department under Bob Beaudrie, worked in the produce department with Louie McKie, and worked closely with Ken Walters on the grocery side of the business. Swede Smith, Clyde's brother, made me the assistant manager at the Glendale store, which was doing about $68,000 per week. When Swede was transferred to a new store, I was made the manager, and within a year, we were doing $168,000 a week in sales.

In 1969, I received my first bonus check for $10,000. This was the most money I had seen at any time. Smitty believed in paying his people well and had also made stock options available to his management team. Every quarter, I would take my bonus check and buy stock. Smitty would take 20 percent of the net profit and pay it to his management team to show his appreciation for the hard work, dedication, and loyalty.

Smitty believed in training and educating his management team. Every young up-and-coming manager would have to attend Dale Carnegie and Toastmaster's classes. Each year we would go to the Food Market Institute to learn about all the new developments in the business. After every session, we would meet back at Clyde's room for a discussion on what we had learned. Yellow legal pads and 3x5 index cards were his favorite ways to take notes. When we were there, we knew that we had better be ready for a brainstorming session.

Like the training and education Smitty provided for us, he likewise taught us how to enjoy ourselves and relax. Recreational outings with other managers were times we looked forward to. Smitty's managers were treated to fishing trips in Canada and hunting trips to Texas. Smitty liked to call it "fellowshipping together," which was a chance for some R&R and the exchange of ideas.

In 1976, the company announced that there would be two new supervisors selected from the management team. I was not one of the names mentioned. Needless to say, I was very disappointed. My old friend Mitch Kapanicas was promoted, so I congratulated him and angrily left the office when the appointments were announced.

I went directly back to my store when Clyde Smith called later that afternoon. He said, "Dave, I understand you were very upset about the changes." I said, "Wouldn't you be if you were me?" Smitty asked me to dinner where he told me the vote was very close. He asked me to accept the vote and respect the new positions. I said I could do that, but if he ever wanted to grow the company, I would be willing to move or go anywhere he needed me.

Six months later, Smitty called and asked me to have lunch with him at the Stockyard Steakhouse in Phoenix. Smitty said, "There's a store in Springfield, Missouri. It's 67,000 square feet. Would you be interested if we could put a deal together?" I said, "Yes." Smitty said, "How much money can you come up with?" "I have $180,000," I replied. After a number of scenarios, we came up with a partnership: 51 percent Clyde Smith, 49 percent Dave Trottier. With that decision made, I moved to Springfield, Missouri! In those days, $180,000 was a lot of money, but I was willing to put it all on the line for my future with Clyde Smith. Clyde agreed to underwrite the entire extra amount of money needed to remodel and upgrade the entire building.

In just three months, on September 10, 1977, we opened the first Smitty's Supermarket in Springfield at 218 South Glenstone. I asked a few Smitty employees in Phoenix who were looking for a new opportunity to move with me. Among them was a young lady named Peggy Doran. Peggy became the force that kept us going through good times and bad. Peggy was always there saying, "Boss, we can make it."

By November, we were experiencing cash flow problems due to startup costs, training, advertising, and the other many bumps in the road you encounter when you open a new store. I called Smitty and told him our problem. Smitty arranged our financial needs immediately because he believed in me and my ability at the time.

Well, Jimmy Carter was President and interest rates were 22 percent. I signed a three-year note at an interest rate of 16 percent. With lots of hard work and Smitty's counsel, I am proud to say that we paid back the money in only two short years and were officially on our way.

From the opening of our store, we were picketed by two labor unions who wanted to organize our people. Union members threatened our staff, threw tacks on our parking lot, and shot out the front window of the store. When things got tough, I would call Smitty for one of his famous pep talks about the unions and keeping our spirits up.

Like a true genius, Smitty sent me a special, very creative ad layout one day he called "The Picket Sale." The ad had people walking across the page holding signs saying "Smitty's Picket Sale." There were sixteen special items in meat, produce, and grocery, all priced "to be picked." We had picked them especially for our customers.

We ran this type of ad for several weeks and our sales shot straight up. The ads created a tremendous amount of excitement with our employees and the local news media. We were never unionized, and the picketers finally gave up. The unions told us that we paid our people too well. We all were grateful that Smitty's positive influence and resolve had come through, making a "silk purse out of a sow's ear."

With our store now doing well, in 1979 I began to get the idea of adding a second store. Smitty suggested that I start selling stock in the company to my management team, just as he had done with us. In fact, he suggested that the stock I sold my team should be his and that I should completely buy him out in the future. When I said I did not have the cash to do so, he said, "Just write it on a piece of paper, an IOU, and pay me when you can." I told him that I would not do that and that he would always be part of our company. We would carry on the Smitty's name, he would always be the chairman of our board, and we would continue to go fishing in Canada every year.

In the spring of 1983, we had growing pains. Without hesitating, Smitty came to Springfield and suggested we rent a helicopter to survey the city for a new 72,000-square-foot store. We found the location, and in 1984, we added store number three, with the biggest grand opening Springfield had ever seen. We did $129,000 on the opening day. We were having the time of our lives. With the help of Smitty and Jeff Kollmeyer, my vice president and right-hand man, we planned to open one store after another.

Two or three times a year Smitty would fly or drive to Springfield to see how things were going. He would always give us a pep talk, something that he loved to do. He is the only person I have met who can give you a kick in the pants one second and a pat on the back the next, and the whole time you know he truly cares. Sometimes, it was just what the doctor ordered: controlling expenses, labor, advertising, and bottom-line profits.

In 1987, Smitty came to Springfield to tell me that he now was really ready to sell the rest of his stock. I believe that Smitty wanted us to have full ownership. He believed in sharing the wealth and giving others the opportunity to achieve great success.

Ten years later, we had grown to ten stores and were doing over $160 million in annual sales. I called Smitty one day to tell him that Albertson's wanted to buy the stores and had made me an offer "too good to refuse." Smitty said, "Dave, be a good negotiator." Well, I had learned from the master.

Smitty strongly believed in personal development, self-confidence, and self-esteem as prerequisites for creating a successful life. He surrounded himself with good people who became his friends. He believed in us and listened to our ideas. We were never just employees; we were family, part of a team. We shared in his dreams, participating in and enjoying his successes.

I have known Smitty for more than fifty years; what a blessing it has been. The example he set for me and many others enabled us to see our dreams come true, have a successful business career, and most importantly, enjoy the opportunity to learn from the best.

John Sims
Store Manager—Tenure: 1962–1992

I started at Smitty's in 1962. I was the first carryout at store number two, the original superstore concept. I drove up on a motor scooter one day while they were building the store. I stuck my head in the door along with Jim Evans — we were on the scooter together — and I asked if they needed any help. I was not quite sixteen yet. Doug Smith, Swede Smith, and Clyde were there. Clyde asked if I could start right then. I started working for Smitty that very day.

Right off the bat, Smitty's felt like a family. Clyde and the others made me feel like a family member, not just a lowly carryout. I remember on Friday nights going to Swede and Nadine Smith's house after work. They would invite the carryouts over for cokes and chips and an occasional ice cream. We would hang out at their house for a couple of hours just like family. It made me want to work as many hours off the clock as I did on the clock. I just wanted to be there because they treated us so well.

Smitty's was "the" place to shop in the Phoenix market from the 1960s to the 1990s. It was also the number one place to work. Everyone in town recognized Smitty's, and when you went to a social event or a movie, somebody would recognize you as a Smitty's employee.

There was a sense of pride that was overwhelming as a Smitty's manager. It amazed me each day that I was in charge of something that huge. Some of my stores were over 100,000 square feet with over 300 employees. Clyde empowered us to make the most of the decisions regarding our stores at the store level. I can't ever remember calling the main office to make things right with a customer. Clyde trusted us to do the right thing.

I can recall the feeling of opening every morning. When that door opened, it was as if we were pulling the curtain back and we were on stage. It was like a theater and the customers were there to be entertained. The produce area was full, the bakery was full, and all the cans were faced the same way. That was how Clyde wanted it. The store was to be a showplace each day. Our daily routine included washing the sidewalks daily and even scraping the gum from them.

When Clyde came in the store, you knew that you were in the presence of someone really special. He was a real merchant whose eyes caught everything in your store. He wasn't afraid to tell you what he didn't like and was eager to tell you what he did like. He had a gift in the perishable area and could smell if something was not right.

Clyde had been a grocery man for a long time, and he knew what the customer wanted, and he knew how to get it to them. He knew how to merchandise it, price it, and keep it fresh. I just knew if I could make him happy, I could make the customers happy. We did that well. We were better than anyone else in town.

Jim Evans
Store Manager—Tenure: 1962–1982

I remember going to Clyde's first store on South 16th and Buckeye Road. He had a bunch of us young fellows sitting around a table, and he said, "I think we have one of the greatest opportunities you might ever have in a career, but you have to believe in me, you have to follow me, and you have to work hard. If we all do that, I think we have a concept and business plan that will really work and that will pay off for you and your families for a long time to come." That was the beginning of the Smitty complex and the superstore concept.

When he opened our number two store back in 1962, the store had it all. It was a one-stop shop with groceries and department store items. He was the innovator. When you look at the super Walmarts today, you're seeing the Smitty's back in 1962. It was a store of 135,000 square feet or better and was the forerunner of what we see today in the superstore market. This was way before anybody ever conceived that this might be the route to take. Even though he got off to a rough start, he was able to tweak it and change it. To me that was Smitty's strongest strength—his fortitude, his never-give-up attitude. When something didn't work, he would change it, change it again, and not give up until it worked!

Smitty as a manager was a technician. He was a tough guy, and he demanded and expected precision from us along with quality. He was relentless with that. It taught us some great disciplines. He took good care of us financially, but he expected a lot, which was okay with me.

The customer was the most important aspect at Smitty's. Every day, from the time we opened until the time we closed, our main objective was to take care of that customer, and it paid off. On a Friday or Saturday, we would have twenty-two cash registers running with lines backed up. That was unheard of in those days. You don't even see that today at Costco.

Smitty was a man of his word. Every promise he made to us, he kept. We, likewise, did the same. We were committed to him because he was committed to us. That mutual commitment was the strength of our team. This really set us apart from our competitors. Based on this commitment, Smitty allowed us a lot of autonomy in the stores. That was unheard of in those days.

After my time at Smitty's, I started an unrelated company using the same concepts and disciplines that Smitty taught us. It became the largest childcare company in Arizona and the tenth largest in the United States. I used the concepts he taught us of managing properly: managing the top and bottom line, being fair to employees and working with them, and providing encouragement and enthusiasm to be successful. Like Smitty, I tried to create an environment that made them want to get up and come to work each day.

Gene Carter
Supervisor of ten Smitty's stores—Tenure: 1968–1990

I kind of laugh when I hear somebody say that Walmart was the first to have the "one-stop" shopping concept; I chuckle and say that Smitty had it years before they did!

Doug Smith, Clyde's brother, belonged to the same church as we did in Scottsdale. He was always trying to get me to go to work for Smitty's. I was working for Fryes at the time, which was a competitor. Doug would say, "You need to come to work for Smitty's—we've got a better deal for you than Fryes." I told Doug that I knew he was giving me an opportunity, but that I would have to take a cut in pay and I didn't know that I wanted to do that. I eventually agreed and started my Smitty's tour as a back room manager and progressed through the ranks until I was a supervisor of ten stores. Later, I would tell people whom I hired that if you were willing to put your nose to the grindstone at Smitty's, you could do anything you wanted to. Hard work helped promote good will and would increase sales.

The culture at Smitty's was that if you worked hard and did your job as you were supposed to, you were rewarded. When people saw this, they wanted to come to work for Smitty's, no matter what the position was. Clyde did a lot for us beside the money. He took us on some great fishing trips and hunting trips and gave us some wonderful parties. You work your tail off for somebody who responds that way to you.

The Smitty's stores were special because of the way we took care of our customers. We always tried to have the right amount of help. We gave the customer the things they wanted and at a good price. We had excellent ads that would draw people in. If a customer came in with a problem, we took care of the problem instead of hassling them. We gained an awful lot of customers by doing things that way.

Clyde always wanted us to use our own ideas to merchandise and put on bigger and better displays than anybody else. This wasn't just a job; it was fun, too. We did this, and we brought in the business! He was what I would call a "hands-on boss," but his hands were not hanging on to you. He was around to see that things were done the way they should be, but he always gave you a free hand to do whatever you wanted within reason.

Smitty is creative and disciplined. He gave us an opportunity to be creative, too. He put a lot of trust in me, and I appreciated that. It was as if he turned you loose and told you to run the stores as if they were your own. The one thing I learned from

Smitty is that you can do and be anything you want to be if you put your mind to it. He changed my life, and I am sure he changed the lives of a lot of others.

Doug Smith
Area Supervisor, Store Manager, Clyde's Brother—Tenure: 1946–1983

It all came down to people. We had the best people. We had the best management. We had the best cashiers, carryouts, and department managers. You surround yourself with people who are successful, and you will be successful. We just tried to have the best people; that was the way it happened.

It was a great feeling to experience the growth of the company and see the people that grew up inside the stores. I think most of the managers were brought up from within. When we first started hiring, we would hire carryouts, and we would key in on the ones that we thought could be potential management. We would put them off in a separate little job so we could see how they produced on their own. This made them feel good, and it gave us an opportunity to see what kind of person we had—to see their inner drive. We were always looking for how they presented themselves—the way they dressed, their appearance, and the way they looked at you. We wanted them to look you in the eye. Most of all, they had to be dependable and trustworthy.

We tried to get everyone familiar with all the departments. Employees would gain a familiarity with the whole operation. They might not be proficient in every department, but they got familiar and knew the expectations. Typically, we would start in the carryout position and move them to the back room. If they worked out there, we would then get them in a department. Once they got in a department, we could keep tabs on them through their manager and the feedback we got. The message we tried to send to our managers, no matter how far up the chain, was that if they wanted to move up, they should train someone under them to take their places. This stimulated their minds and got them into the training mode. This became important to our management training.

Because we promoted mostly from within, one of the biggest problems we had was with some of the people that we hired who were older. They wanted to skip the rungs of the ladder; they wanted to jump rather than climb. Sometimes we would have a tough time keeping them in the lower jobs because they all knew what the managers were making and about their bonuses. Sometimes we could save them; sometimes we could not. Some of these individuals would leave and would eventually come back. One of my jobs was to try to save as many as I could. When we were in our growth years, we required a lot of people in management. This created a tremendous amount of responsibility but great opportunities for our staff.

We would shuffle our managers at least once a year. We would rotate the other management staff more than that. This gave the managers further growth opportunities in a new store and allowed the assistant managers and others to learn from a different style of management. If managers' styles of management made improvements, or if they had good ideas, we loved it and would let them know it. If Clyde didn't agree, we would bend a little bit. If we believed in the idea, we would discuss it in detail. We tried not to be "yes" brothers!

To recreate the success we had with the Smitty stores, you would have to have a Clyde Smith. You would need someone like Clyde who is dynamic and can motivate people. Motivating people and making them want to produce is what it is all about. That was our success story.

Back when Clyde was young, he quit school and went to work, and I thought that was the greatest. It was not that I wanted to get rid of him but that I thought that it was such a great thing that he would take off like that. We were dirt farmers, and Dad was a coal miner, but Clyde went to work for Keith Rushing in a grocery store. I always wanted to be a Clyde Smith. It never happened, but I had an awful lot of fun following him around.

Linda Barkdoll
Restaurant Waitress, Cashier, Smitty's Daughter—Tenure: 1955–1983

What made the Smitty's stores special was that everyone cared about the customer. The customer always came first. You never argued with the customer. Everything was done to please the customers. Merchandising was for the customer; pricing to make it affordable was for the customer. Our customers were primary. We would call them by name and knew about their families. That was the one thing that made the Smitty's store really different. We treated everyone with respect.

Some of the other things that made the Smitty's stores special were all the innovations and the fun promotions. And the people—oh, my!—the employees and the opportunities they had at Smitty's! The training was just incredible. Everyone had a chance to be someone in that company. It was an open door. From the sackers on up, there was an opportunity to work up to become a manager.

I was twelve when I went to work in the coffee shop in store number one in Marshalltown, Iowa. It was a wonderful experience. I went from the coffee shop to the meat market, then to the bakery, and then worked in the produce department under Tony Witte. He was a tough boss, but I learned so much from him. My sister Sandy was a cashier at the time. We were never treated like the boss's children. We were treated like employees and were actually expected to work harder than most of the other staff. We had to set the pace just like Daddy set the pace. It was just expected of us.

When Dad and Mom decided to move to Phoenix and open the stores, I was in high school. I went to work in the coffee shop in store number one there on South 16th Street as a waitress. Later I worked in the courtesy counter cashing checks under the watchful eye of Arles Larson. I worked at the store in my junior and senior year and then went off to college. In the summers, I would come back and work. That is where I met my husband, Tom, who was working highway construction while he was a college student at Arizona State University. He kept coming in, and I finally agreed to go out with him. Many years later, he would become the president of the company.

Our first store in Phoenix was very special! People were thrilled with it because it was so large. My dad picked an impoverished area to build the store, and they loved the size and the fun promotions. It was unlike any other grocery store in Phoenix. That was a very special time.

My dad was an incredible leader. He was tough, but he was kind. He did not ask you to do anything that he would not do himself. He expected his managers to be community leaders as well as store managers. He reached out to the community in a hundred ways. He was always there to do a golf tournament or help a family in need. He expected a lot out of his managers. It was great training for them.

He was an incredible trainer, too. He set the pace. The managers did not seem to mind. He caught a lot of young men who wanted a chance in life. If they worked hard, believed in the "Smitty culture," were family people and remained loyal to the community, he gave them that chance.

Another thing that made Smitty's so special was the profit sharing. The staff knew that if they went to work and worked hard by making their numbers and quotas, they would share in the profit. That made them want to work even harder. What an incentive for the employees to succeed! They made the store succeed, and then they succeeded. It made a lot of families very successful.

My dad embodies the one quality that I really admire in a leader in that he would not ask someone to do something that he would not do himself. He is a motivator and a visionary. He is hard working and has a dear heart. Most of all, he loves the Lord by the way he serves. He is always thinking of some way to help somebody or to serve Him more. I think that God was leading him the entire way while he was building the Smitty's stores.

Jim Henley
Store Manager—Tenure: 1969–1982

I grew up in the grocery business and was working as a sales manager for a bread company when Bob Beaudrie, one of Clyde's senior people, hired me. I started out as a night stocker at Smitty's, where I learned how we priced and the other nuts and bolts of the operation. I had gotten to know Clyde when I developed a private label bread program for the company. When they opened store number three and store number five, I went out and acted as a Smitty's employee on loan from the bread company for a couple of weeks. I understood what Smitty's was all about before I started to work there. I knew I had a career the day they accepted my application.

Clyde made sure that we did things right, which was a big part of our success. Number one, employees took care of the customers, and number two, Clyde took care of his employees. Clyde was a master of support. There was total support for the store manager. Clyde had a rule in the company that we all understood. There was only one person in the company that could break Clyde Smith's rules and that was the store manager. They had to make good decisions, but there were never any ramifications. When an owner supports his staff like that, the staff is willing to take that attitude to every employee that is subordinate to them!

Clyde believed we were in the people business, and we were. The whole structure was not Clyde Smith or Smitty's; it was people — employees, the vendors, the customers. We were successful because of this. People appreciated good products and good service. If you look at our economics today, you understand that the customer still wants to be served — no matter what business you are in.

I learned at Smitty's that accomplishing things, being successful, is a lot of fun. Working with your peers and your subordinates is great. At a time when most supermarkets were operating at less than 1 percent net profit pre-tax, we were operating at over 4 percent. That was part of the fun factor.

Clyde turned you loose, and each time you succeeded, you felt better about yourself and your company.

Clyde Smith does not walk on water. Clyde makes mistakes like any of us, except — and he will be the first to readily admit this — with his golf game. He won't admit anything bad about his golf game.

Dave Vandervoort
Sweet Milk Company, Vendor/Milk Supplier to the Smitty's stores.
First Sale 1962 through all the successive years

I grew up in the dairy business, and when I sold my dad's company, I knew I wanted to start my own business and sell milk in the Phoenix market. In those days, milk was fair traded for fifty cents a gallon in the Phoenix area, and I wanted to sell it for less. I just needed an outlet.

I walked into this supermarket on 16th Street and Buckeye Road in 1962, and it was the most fabulous market I had ever seen in my life. I had never seen anything that big and that wonderful! I met Everett Larson, the manager, and he introduced me to Clyde Smith. Clyde told me to go out and get some business and then come back and see him. I had no business at the time, and he wanted me to go out to the other independent markets and get some customers. A week later, I came back to see him after I had established several other accounts, and true to his word, he took me on as a vendor.

Clyde was unique in how he treated his vendors. I have dealt with a lot of managers, but I have never dealt with anybody else in any other supermarket who treated his vendors as well as he treated us. It was just not me but the other vendors too. I think his philosophy was that if he treated us right we would treat him right. That's exactly what happened. He paid quickly, we did not have to wait for our money, and he always got the best deal in town. If we had a special, who were we going to go to first? You could be sure it was Clyde Smith.

Clyde needed the vendors just as we needed him. I dealt with competitors of his who would squeeze every drop of blood out of you. It made you not want to go into their store. It was quite different from the relationship we had with Clyde and his stores. He was very honest and ethical in everything he did. In turn, we took good care of Smitty's.

What I saw about Clyde's stores and their corporate philosophy was that they were fair and treated people right. He was a good merchant from day one. He had good merchandise and at the right price. He knew how to merchandise to make the product interesting so that people would buy the product. Clyde had good displays, and the stores were clean. I thought he had a great management team, guys like Clim Gonzales and Dave Trottier, who started at the bottom in the dairy department and worked their way up. I always thought that made the difference.

I was amazed at the talent he developed. He was able to motivate his people to do what they needed to do to grow their business. Clyde has a unique personality that motivates people by just how he talks to you. He was able to convey his ideas effectively and motivate his people. I've known so many others who have to drive people; he did not. Clyde could lead them, and that's a big difference. That made him really successful.

Dan Stevens
Store Manager—Tenure: 1965–1990

I started off as a stocker at store number two in 1965. After leaving for a stint in the Army, I came back to Smitty's and began to work my way up. I became a dairy manager, then a third man, then an assistant manager, and finally got my own store in 1976.

What kept me at the Smitty Stores all those years was that the company always demonstrated a positive attitude. One of the most important parts of this was the respect that people had for each other. When I was working my way up, Clyde and his management people treated me with respect and listened to my opinions on things. As I progressed up the company ladder and became a manager, this became even better. They gave you a job and expected that you could do it. They taught you what you needed to know and then they let you do your job. They did not tell you how to do it or micromanage you. That was by far the most important thing—the respect they had for us and our decisions.

This respect was evident in the managers' meetings that we attended each week. We were close enough to the decision-making process that they would ask us questions. If we had a reason why we felt that something would or would not work, they listened. As managers, we helped to change a number of things over the years because they listened to and respected us.

We had the best employees that any company ever had. They were well taken care of, they were treated very well, and they responded in kind. The employees wanted the company to succeed as well as the managers. That is something that you do not see today.

The Smitty managers were entrepreneurs. As I worked my way up, I learned what Clyde wanted. When I was promoted to store manager, they just gave me the keys and said, "Manage well and stay on top of your store operations. You know the rules and the framework." That was so empowering. There wasn't a moment of hesitation on my part. It was just a thrill to have the opportunity to show what I could do, the success I could become, and how I could help the company become more successful.

Clyde believed in his people. He was not regimented. There was no one right way. There were a lot of right ways. He let his people be creative. He let his people try things. He had faith in them. I think that faith paid off for all of us.

Arnold Eggers
Bakery Manager—Tenure: 1955–1990

I came with Clyde in the original group from Iowa as the bakery manager of the first store. When you became a manager,

Clyde left you alone and let you run your department. He let you do the hiring, firing, ordering, and set your own prices. I was held accountable for the bottom line. As a boss, he never criticized you.

Years ago, there was a sugar shortage. Sugar was hard to come by. If you used more sugar than just a household, you were required to get on the list with the government and report your usage. I got a chance to buy 10,000 pounds of raw sugar. All I did was have to tell Clyde, and he said to order what I needed. It was a lot of sugar, but he let me do my job. I appreciated that.

In my opinion, the ads that Clyde ran made the stores special. Like one day we gave them a loaf of bread and a ten-pound bag of sugar for a ten-dollar order. It was a hot special! We also did promotions on cakes that were very successful. Sometimes we would work with Kraft or General Mills. We were the first one in our market to offer packaged bake goods in our specials.

I knew from the way Clyde worked back in Iowa that he was going to be successful. When we had about four or five stores in Phoenix, we were in a meeting in Tucson, and Clyde said, "Let's build twenty stores in twenty years!" Well, we did!

Mitch Kapanicas
Store Manager—Tenure: 1962–1979

From a merchandising standpoint, Clyde was very innovative. He liked doing things in a big way. When we had a sale on something, we did it bigger and better than any other competitor in the market. If we brought in a truckload of watermelons, there would be watermelons all over the place. If it was an anniversary sale, we would have a huge cake and events on the sidewalk outside. We would order several hundred cases of something and make a massive display on an end cap with a big price sign. Our customers would empty out those end displays like there was no tomorrow.

When I went to work for Clyde, I was just seventeen years old. To his credit, he allowed the young people to grow with the company. When we had grown to four stores, he sent forty of us to Dale Carnegie at the same time so that we would be able to handle ourselves in front of a group of people and not be afraid. I was twenty-four years old at the time and had just become a store manager. I was managing a store that was 110,000 square feet, and I had department heads who were older than my parents. I had to speak with these individuals and ask them to do things daily while gaining their respect. Because Clyde decided to invest in us through programs such as Dale Carnegie and Toastmasters, I was able to live up to the task.

Clyde was always trying to educate us. He took the young people in our company and brought us along. Our management team back in the 1970s was a group of very young people, whom he took and groomed. He was our mentor. Every one of us wanted to be like Clyde Smith.

Clyde taught us how to set goals to accomplish things. We were shown how to write down our goals and put them on the mirror in our bathroom, or on the mirror of our car. He told us that if you look at them all the time, you remember what you want to achieve. It becomes an inner drive that allows you to achieve your goals if you want them badly enough.

Early in my career, I was an assistant manager for Clyde's brother, Swede, at store number two. I decided to rearrange and merchandise a bunch of aisles. Clyde saw what I was doing and called me up to his office to ask about it. I proceeded to tell him how "I" had done this and that "I" had done that. I had stressed the "I" so much that he gave me a lesson I will never forget.

Clyde told me that *he* could say "I" and "mine" because in reality it was his company and everything was his. But he told me, he really liked for all of us, including himself, to think of the company as "we" and "ours." In his mind, this made for a team effort because he really thought of the business as not just his but "ours." To this day, I still think in terms of "we."

Nadine Smith
Courtesy Counter Staff; Married to Swede Smith, Clyde's brother—Tenure: 1962–1971

I went to work at the South Sixteenth Street store in the fall of 1962. I was at the Courtesy Counter where we approved checks, took utility payments, and cashed payroll checks. One of our primary duties was to pre-approve checks prior to the customer going through the checkout line. Because of the high volume of business at the stores, we needed to get the customer's check pre-approved so there was no slowdown at the cashier stand. While the Courtesy Counter clerks and the store cashiers were mostly women, I never noticed a difference in how the company viewed men and women. They were all treated the same by Clyde.

Clyde had a great dream, and he followed it through. The way they treated the customers made people want to shop there. You cannot go into a store today and get the same type of service. We all worked together to make the customer experience the best it could be.

My husband, Swede, was a Smitty manager, and he just loved it. He managed store number three, which presented a whole new concept of merchandising groceries with a department store. In the early days, it was not uncommon for him to get a call from Clyde saying, "Hey, get over here. We have to change up this store." They kept after it until they got that superstore concept right.

What made the Smitty stores special were the personnel. They all worked together. No matter where it was, they all pitched in to help each other. It was like family. The three brothers — Clyde, Doug, and Swede — made it feel that way.

Climaco Gonzales
Store Manger, District Manager—Tenure: 1961–1981

I went to work for Smitty's when I was sixteen years old. I was hired as a carryout at the original store. When I went to my first meeting, Doug Smith told us we were going to be called "caddies" instead of "carryouts." I immediately related to Doug because of his enthusiastic personality. Growing up on the south side of the tracks, I didn't know what a "caddy" was.

I was surprised where Smitty opened the first store because it was down the street from Food City. Even though the surrounding neighborhood was poor, Food City was one of the highest grossing stores in the state. It had been the stopping point for most people in that neighborhood for years. Smitty merchandised the store a little more upscale and offered a restaurant, bakery, self-service and full-service meats and seafood, snack bar, candy shop, and a better produce section. Our store was so much cleaner and a lot friendlier. We were taught that the customer was king and we were there to serve them. This was really different thinking considering the neighborhood. We took on Food City, one of the busiest stores in the state, and we succeeded!

We were taught to greet everyone who came into the store. This really made our customers a part of us and extremely loyal. We were trained that they were the key to everything. Clyde used to tell us that he was not the reason we had a job, it was the customer. The customer was the most important thing we had. This was so successful that the customers got to the point where they knew us all by name and knew that there wasn't anything that we would not do for them. Several years later, when I became the manager of that first store, it made our customers proud because I was from the neighborhood. Many of our customers had known me since I was a carryout and had worked my way up.

We all worked lots of hours, but we did whatever it took to get the job done. Hours did not matter. Smitty always made it feel like it was *our* store. What would *we* do to make it better? So we ran it as if it were our store, and we protected it and our customers. I can remember opening and closing, and then staying up until the next morning to get the job done. Nobody made us do it; we did because it was something we wanted to do. Clyde knew how to create an ownership attitude in us. He let us do our job.

Clyde always tried to educate us so we would know more about our business. He sent us to Dale Carnegie and Toastmasters to learn to be more confident in our role with the customers and our staff. He would tell us to continue to learn always, to read whatever we could, and to check out our competition and learn how to be a better store manager.

Smitty took us to stores all over the country. He taught us to shop our competition to learn from them. We were not there to critique them. We went there to learn what they were doing right, so we could come back and change what we were doing. Sometimes you put blinders on in your own store, and you don't see the whole picture until you go out and see what others are doing—both good and bad. Smitty taught us to learn from those occasions.

Smitty was always enthusiastic, and he created this attitude in his people. He was a great leader, and people followed him and believed in him. If he said you could do it, you did it. He led us to such unbelievable growth that at times we did not believe it. I always wanted to be just like him. I am still trying!

Steve Weiskettle
Store Manager—Tenure: 1968–1981

There was a high degree of expectation at Smitty's for both the staff and the stores. The expectations were set high, but you had plenty of help getting there. They knew we were all pretty basic individuals, so there was a high degree of reasonability in achieving these expectations. We had great role models in Clyde, Swede, Doug, and Bob Beaudrie, who showed us the way.

I went to work for Smitty's on August 28, 1968. I went into store number two looking for a job, and Doug Smith put me to work as a clerk the same day. A year later, when I graduated from Arizona State University, Clyde Smith called me into his office and inquired about my plans after graduation. When I told him I had a few interviews lined up, Clyde told me, "Stay with us. We have a future for you here." By this time, I had fallen in love with Smitty's, so that sounded good to me.

One of the strengths of Smitty's was that as you moved up the ranks, you got a wealth of training. By the time I became a manager, most of my contemporaries and I had been subjected to the same training experiences. We had all bagged, pulled cardboard, cashiered, built displays, and stocked the shelves. It was a common mutual experience that gave us a great foundation for learning the business and relating to one another.

Anybody worth their salt in those days wanted to be a store manager at Smitty's and run their own store. The way Smitty had set the organization up, he expected you to help take the role of ownership. For many of us, that was a wonderful challenge. It was an amazing thing. I was only twenty-seven years old, operating a store that I was to consider my own business and doing $100,000 – $150,000 per week! It was scary, but the theme of the company at the time was "make it happen." You had to step up to the plate.

I thought the Smitty stores were far more than a retail outlet. For a very long time, I thought that the stores were community centers. They became places where people went to not only buy groceries or department store items but also to see their friends, eat a great meal, get their hair done, or do their banking. It wasn't like what you see today, a grocery store where you run in and out. It took time for this concept to evolve, but Smitty's was much more than just a retail outlet to the communities it served.

Most every guy and gal at Smitty's modeled themselves after the executive managers, who were great people, outstanding citizens, and nice people to work for. While Smitty's might have seemed like a "total guy thing," in reality, we were one of the first businesses in the Valley to hire women managers. You did not have better role models. To this day, I claim that what we all look back on is what we learned at Smitty's: philosophically, operationally, how to stay in touch with our business on a day–to-day basis, and how to keep promises. It was an exciting place to work.

The accolades Clyde Smith received through the years could be put into more than a chapter in one book; however, Clyde wouldn't allow that! There is more to Clyde's story that must be told, and since he is a great storyteller himself, we'll let him do that.

26

Golf and a Cast of Characters

"Golf provided a physical release for me and kept me
sharp for the mental demands of the business."

—Clyde B. Smith

Since I opened my first store in 1946, I had two primary focuses in life. These were growing our grocery business and providing for my family. Unfortunately at times, growing the business must have seemed my only focus to my family, who learned to live with my absence. I spent long hours in the stores, six days a week. Until the early 1970s, I lived and breathed the supermarket business exclusively, which required huge blocks of my time due to the phenomenal growth we experienced.

Helen and I had a traditional marriage. I provided for the family through our business, and she raised our three girls. Helen did work in the number two store in Scottsdale for a couple of years to help get it in a positive position. However, for the most part she was a stay-at-home mom, with her life centered around being a good wife, mother, and homemaker. As I was working some sixty to seventy hours a week, she provided a consistent home life for the girls and did a wonderful job in raising them. Of course, I would participate whenever I could, but the stores kept me really busy during those years when we were growing our company.

Looking back, I do regret the time I spent away from my family both in Iowa and Arizona and probably would try to do things somewhat differently if given another opportunity. One of the hardest things a business person faces is to balance a career and a family. It has become even more complex for working women in today's culture and economy who try to fulfill their role at home and in the workplace. I am eternally grateful that God has generously tacked so many years on to my life, allowing me to spend more time with my precious girls and their families, hoping to make up for the time I was so involved in the business.

By the early 1970s, we had built the framework of a top-notch management team for the stores, and I no longer had to be so totally focused on the business. This allowed me to spend more time with my family and even to play golf on a more consistent basis. Golf was a game that suited my personality and busy schedule really well. It also appealed to my competitive streak and allowed me to play and practice when time permitted. In those days, I would go into the office early and spend a full day tending to business, then after dinner at home, I would often go practice at the driving range.

I loved to push myself on the practice range by trying to improve each drive, chip, or putt. My practice sessions became real physical workouts and were a great relief from the mental strain of growing our supermarkets. Even though I still did some physical work at the stores, I now was mostly an administrator and supervisor, which required more brain than brawn. Golf provided a physical release for me and kept me sharp for the mental demands of the stores.

Over time, I became a pretty fair golfer and began to play golf as regularly as possible on Wednesday afternoons at the Paradise Valley and other country clubs in Phoenix. At first, this was with friends and business associates and even an occasional member of our management team. As my brother

Doug loved to play golf also, we tried to schedule Wednesday afternoons as our time to play.

I enjoyed the competition golf offered, and I especially enjoyed the tournaments. This was great fun for me because it allowed the necessary time to improve my game and to meet and make friends with many people. As in the supermarket business, I assessed the best practices of my competitors and used these opportunities to improve my own game. Soon I began to play in regional tournaments.

Good for Business

The one thing I learned about golf was that it was good for business. I would routinely play with our vendors, which gave me another opportunity to strengthen our relationships with them. Spending time with our vendors in this casual format allowed me to reinforce how much I valued them as suppliers. It also gave me a chance to thank them for keeping Smitty's at the top of their list for the merchandise specials we needed in order to be competitive. I played a lot of golf with vendors, like our milk supplier, Dave Vandervoort, for this very purpose. In fact, Dave and I started a Phoenix food industry golf association to promote both fun and communication within our industry.

I had this business philosophy that I developed early that both the retailer and vendor should prosper in a transaction. I felt that not allowing your vendor to make a profit in the end hurts both parties. Sure, once in a while I would buy a truckload of merchandise a vendor needed to sell, but I always tried to create another opportunity for the vendor so he could also benefit from the sale. Being one on one with a vendor in a golf cart was a good way to communicate my business philosophy in hopes of building the vendor's trust and loyalty, and it provided great opportunities to develop friendships.

Because of my business contacts, I would routinely get invited to play golf in various charity events held at country clubs. Many of the events were celebrity tournaments where I met pro golfers and entertainers alike. Being the guy with the growing supermarket chain, I was invited to spend time with the hosts of these events and forged many lasting friendships.

Through the years, my love of golf and my competitive nature saw me cross paths with the likes of Lee Trevino, Billy Johnston, Joe Garagiola, Yogi Berra, Glenn Campbell, Charlie Pride, and my friend Jimmy Dean. In those days, these folks were major celebrities in their respective fields, and it was an honor getting to know them. For a Depression-era kid who started life with nothing, it was fun to pal around with these unique individuals and rub elbows with their stardom. To this day, many of them remain good friends.

"Jimmy Dean Sausage"

I first met Jimmy Dean at a convention held by the Supermarket Institute in Chicago. Jimmy had a booth where he was showing and selling his popular product, "Jimmy Dean Sausage." We selected Jimmy's sausage as the brand to feature in our supermarkets, and Jimmy and I became good friends. Whenever he was in the Phoenix area, he would call on our stores and do product demonstrations. Jimmy was a legendary country star at the time and television's favorite down-home, soft-spoken "sausage king," so we were always glad to see him. Having an entertainer of his stature in our stores fit really well into our business philosophy of creating a unique shopping experience for our customers. Jimmy Dean had a warm, larger-than-life personality that made you comfortable whenever he was around. Whether it was singing a ballad like "Big John," telling a tall tale, or reciting one of his famous poems, Jimmy was a talented individual with a very big heart.

Besides being a great entertainer, in those days Jimmy was an avid golfer. This fit nicely into my love of the game, and we shared many rounds on the golf course together. Later, when Smitty's began to sponsor its own charity golf tournament, I could always count on Jimmy to show up and do whatever he could to make the event a success. I have a copy of a poem he gave at an awards dinner we had at the Tapatio Springs Country Club, September 16, 1987, and it goes like this:

"Drinking from My Saucer"

I've never made a fortune, and it's probably too late now,
But I don't worry about that much. I'm happy anyhow.
And as I go along life's journey, I'm reaping better than I sowed,
And I'm drinking from my saucer, 'cause my cup has overflowed.
I ain't got a lot of riches, and sometimes the goin's tough,
I've got three kids that love me. That makes me rich enough.
I just thank God for His blessings and the mercies He's bestowed.
I'm drinking from my saucer, 'cause my cup has overflowed.
I remember times when things went wrong,
And my faith got a little thin,
But then all at once, the clouds broke,
And the old sun peeked through again.
So, Lord, help me not to gripe about the tough rows that I've hoed.
I'm drinking from my saucer, 'cause my cup is overflowed.
And if God gives me strength and courage
When the way grows steep and rough,
I'll not ask for other blessings. I'm already blessed enough.
And may I never be too busy to help another bear his load.
Then I'll keep drinking from my saucer,
'Cause my cup has overflowed.

That was Jimmy Dean! To this day, I'll never forget the many kindnesses he extended to me and our stores.

Joe Garagiola, Star Power Athlete-Turned Television Commentator

The same is true with Joe Garagiola. Joe and I have been friends since I first played in his charity golf tournaments in Tucson, Arizona. Like Jimmy, he supported our charity golf tournament and was a guy I could always count on. Joe had been a renowned athlete-turned television commentator and had real star power in those days. As Joe always insisted that I play with his friends when they showed up for a charity golf event, I got to meet many talented athletes. In fact, I was deeply honored when Joe asked me to play a round of golf with his special guest, President Gerald Ford. This is also how I met Yogi Berra, who was as funny in person as he was on TV.

To this day, I am still very fond of Joe. Whenever I am in Phoenix, I try to stop by and see him. The last time I saw Joe, my brother Doug was with me when we stopped by his house. Always the wise guy, Doug shouted out to the gardener that we were there to see Mr. Garagiola. Of course, Doug knew the guy digging in the dirt was Joe, so we all had a good laugh.

A Way to Give Back to the Community

With my love of golf and my exposure to thousands of people, customers and friends, I decided that Smitty's should sponsor our own charity golf event in Phoenix. This fit well into our corporate philosophy of "giving back to the community." I believed it was important that our stores were good corporate citizens. We stressed this to our managers and our store employees as well. We had been so blessed with the reception of our stores in the greater Phoenix community that I thought that giving back to the people was an appropriate gesture to a city that had been very good to us.

By this time in my golf career, I had played in enough charity golf tournaments to know a bit about the format most tournaments used. This experience convinced me that if we did a tournament, it should be done as we had approached retailing all those years. The tournament had to be first class and different from the ordinary, leaving participants and spectators in awe when it was over. If Smitty's was going to put its name on the event, it had to be as distinctive and first class as our stores.

We decided that the Smitty's golf tournament would be a Pro/Am, giving the participants a chance to play with some seasoned regional and local pros. Through my contacts with golfers like Jimmy Dean and Joe Garagiola, I felt good about building a roster of celebrities that would give the event some real excitement. Since I had played in many of these celebrity events over the years, I thought that some of the celebrities I had met would join us and make it a really special event.

When you hold a charity event, the primary focus is to raise money for the charity. If you are doing a good job, you are controlling costs wherever you can to keep every dollar raised available for donation. Some of the biggest costs in any tournament are the food and entertainment, followed by marketing, club fees, manpower, and prize money for the pros. These can be excessive, and many tournaments run in the red because of them.

I had never been afraid of failure, especially when it came to promoting our business. I had built some really good relationships with our vendors and felt sure that I could count on them to help defer some of our costs. When we started making calls, several of them jumped on board, and the Smitty's Southwest Open was born.

We held our first charity golf tournament in May of 1976. The event was a huge success, with both Jimmy and Joe attending every tournament. We had a host of regional PGA professionals and many celebrities in attendance. Billy Johnston, who was not only a good pro but a topflight golf course designer, helped us put on the entire tournament. He worked endless hours instructing and inviting his many pro friends to participate. Billy was extremely helpful, and we were grateful for the role he played in our tournament.

We had chosen the Valley of the Sun School as our charity. In that first year, we raised over $20,000 to put towards the good work that the school was doing with handicapped children. When we had our tournament dinner program and prize awards at the close of the event, the school brought a few of the children to thank us. This made me more determined to make the next event bigger and better the following year.

What made our golf tournament so special that first year, and the years that followed, was the whole-hearted participation of our vendors, guests, and customers. Our vendors went all out to provide their products in total support. On each tee box, there was an assortment of products that included sandwiches, cold drinks, ice cream, candy, and more for the amateurs, pros, and guests to enjoy. Everyone seemed stunned at the amount and diversity of products that our vendors provided. Over the years, as the event grew, this presentation would become a hallmark of the Smitty's Southwest Open, and it soon became a "must have" ticket among the local and regional golfers. Joe Garagiola and Jimmy Dean were always speakers at the awards dinner, which added a special touch to the event. I will always be grateful to them because they never missed one of our five Smitty's tournaments.

By year two of the tournament, I put my brother Doug in charge of the event, which was experiencing success. Each year it took Doug approximately two months to orchestrate the event. After that first success, the event grew tremendously, and it took Doug's undivided attention to keep up with it.

The final year in 1980, our golf tournament raised over $50,000 for the handicapped children of the Valley of the Sun School. This was a sizeable amount of money in those days, and I am sure that the administrators put the money to good use. Each year, we would try to top the last year's donation. I remember one year when Jimmy Dean, our master of ceremonies, peeled off his golf shirt to the astonishment of the crowd and auctioned it off to raise some extra money for the kids. Not to be outdone, Joe Garagiola jumped up on the stage and did the same. Besides being hilarious, this was a great and heartwarming gesture by my friends in support of a really worthy cause.

Because Smitty's Southwest Open was a golf Pro/Am, we had worked with the PGA throughout the years we sponsored the event. This was a lot of fun for me as I got to meet several people who were involved in the association. One of those persons was Dean Beaman, who was the president of the PGA at the time. After the second tournament, Mr. Beaman and Billy Johnston presented me with a lifetime honorary membership to the PGA for putting on our big event. Being somewhat naive, I thought that this honor was just symbolic. Sometime later, I presented the membership to a country club where I was not a member and they rolled out the "red carpet." What a treat for a coal miner's son from Numa, Iowa!

We sponsored the Smitty's Southwest Open Pro/Am for five consecutive years. I felt that the event met our corporate philosophy of "giving back" to the community, while meeting our objective of having a unique and distinctive format just like our stores. From the first event, Smitty's was blessed with huge crowds that attended the tournaments, which was probably the real reason that the PGA had been so impressed with us and had given me the honorary Southwest lifetime membership. From a business perspective, the event added to the momentum we had generated in the marketplace and strengthened our goodwill with our vendors. Plus, it allowed me to build lasting friendships with some really good people like Jimmy Dean, Joe Garagiola, and many others. It also provided me with a basketful of memories that are priceless, especially when viewed at a time when I thought I had finally figured out what was really important in one's life.

Worth Thinking About

"With the fearful strain that is upon me night and day, if I did not laugh I should die."

—Abraham Lincoln

"Employ thy time well, if thou meanest to gain leisure."

—Ben Franklin

"Enjoy yourself; it's later than you think."

—Ancient Adage

"The better part of one's life consists of his friendships."

—Abraham Lincoln

"While I have always recognized that the object of business is to make money in an honorable manner, I have endeavored to remember that the object of life is to do good."

—Peter Cooper

27

Moving to the Next Level

"I knew that I could always learn something from others,
which required me to tone down my ego from time to
time while keeping an open mind. We all have our limitations,
and you just hobble your company if you close your
mind to the contribution others can make."

—Clyde B. Smith

At Smitty's, 1976 was an exciting year. Not only had we planned and executed a wildly successful golf tournament, but we now had thirteen big and beautiful stores occupying over 1.2 million square feet of prime retail space in the greater Phoenix Metropolitan Statistical Area. Our "super complex" stores which we struggled so much with in the beginning, now comprised over 50 percent of our store footprints and were very popular with the consumer. It had taken time, but these superstores were now the signature of our company, offering the public everything from a can of corn to high-end electronics and jewelry under one roof. I was pleased that our stores were setting the retail pace not only in our market but also throughout the state and our country.

For me, 1976 was an important year because that was the year I accepted my first president into our company. From our humble beginnings in Iowa, I had personally done most every job there is in the supermarket business, which included a diversity of disciplines such as butchering our own meat, stocking thousands of cases of product, and merchandising countless displays of merchandise. At this point in my career I felt good about my hands-on knowledge of the supermarket business but realized that if we were going to continue to grow, I would have to delegate many of my daily tasks in order to focus on the future.

Smitty's now had thousands of employees who were generating millions of dollars a week in sales. Long gone were the days where I could huddle with a few key staff members at the front of the store and affect a consistent way of thinking and doing business. The company was now a large corporation; I needed to spend a portion of my time in the field working with our key managers and showing them the many opportunities that were before them if they performed in a consistent manner. I also needed to help them groom and promote other staff members to meet the leadership needs of our expanding company.

Of equal importance, I needed to help our management staff never lose sight of the simple principles that had brought us so far. Focusing on the customer, merchandising their products in an unusual and exciting manner, and training people to be the best they could be were fundamentals that needed to be passed on to each generation of Smitty's grocers. It was hard for me to communicate these in an effective manner when I was deskbound, doing tasks that could be done by another competent executive.

I also needed to work on developing and planning new store concepts and locations. This would continue to build on our sales momentum and the excitement we had built in the market. I was convinced that it was vital to our ongoing success that we strategically add new stores so as not to lose the growth momentum we had developed over the past ten years. Smitty's had three new stores scheduled to open in 1977, but I knew that we had to look beyond these if we were to continue our leadership in the marketplace. Years later, I would witness firsthand the problems a supermarket chain has when it loses its growth momentum by not adding new stores.

Bill Nichols, Our First President

I was very fortunate in 1976 that I had the opportunity to hire Bill Nichols, who was the president of a food supplier called Associated Grocers in Arizona. Bill was a seasoned veteran of the supermarket industry who had a wonderful background in management. Bill was a "fifty-something" executive who loved to work as much as I did. Because of the big job he had at Associated Grocers, I had confidence in his ability to execute the role of president from his first day on the job. His years of industry-specific experience mitigated any concern that we might have had because he was coming to us from outside our Smitty family. Up to this point, we had tried to fill our key management roles from within.

After a ninety-day "get acquainted" period, I was more than happy to turn over many of my daily tasks to Bill. I had been on the front lines for so long that it was good to get a little breathing room. I no longer had to be at the office at the crack of dawn and was free to pursue more strategic initiatives and growth opportunities for the company. If a golf tournament with a vendor happened to come my way now and then, I felt good about participating, given the competent leadership I had in Mr. Nichols.

I am sure that many of our longtime staff members were waiting to see how things worked out when I passed the reins of the company to Bill. Since 1961, the buck in our Phoenix operation had always landed on my desk, and I was the person who broke the tie in the end. More than a few of our managers might have considered me a "strong personality," so there must have been a few wagers on how long Mr. Nichols would last.

There is no doubt that I have been and will always be a strong personality. You cannot survive working in an Iowan coal mine at seventeen years old, or face the perils of fighting in a world war, and not be. However, all through my business career, I knew that I could always learn something from others, which required me to tone my ego down from time to time while keeping an open mind. This started with my relationship with my mentor Keith Rushing and continued through my years with the Supermarket Institute board of directors.

When I hired Bill Nichols, I made up my mind that I was going to get out of his way and let him run the daily operations of the company. While I did look over his shoulder occasionally, I tried to give Bill a free hand and not limit the many things I felt he could bring to our organization. Bill had a big job at Associated Grocers, and I wanted him to help us integrate those business techniques we might be lacking. As most of our management team had learned the business on the job, I was anxious to let Bill spread his wings while I set about my role as the chief executive officer of the company.

As it turned out, Bill Nichols was no "yes man," and that suited me just fine. While he did not radically make over our company, he did fine-tune several things that ultimately made us better and a more disciplined organization. As I had hoped and envisioned, Bill freed me up to plan the future of our company while he looked after the details. This was timely because the Phoenix area was experiencing explosive growth, and I was determined that Smitty's was going to be at the forefront of it.

Brute Force versus Leading by Building Consensus from the Input of Others

I have learned in my business career that there is a fine line between leading a company through brute force and leading it by building consensus from the input of others. Too many executives who have built a family business continue to try to lead the company in later growth stages by the same methods they built the company with in the beginning. While they may hire and develop good people, often they pay lip service to their ideas and continue to run the company as they see fit. This is often a huge mistake. We all have our limitations, and a leader just hobbles his company if he closes his mind to the contributions others can make. I was determined that this was not going to happen with our first president, Bill Nichols. I knew even a self-made man like me could still learn a lot from others if I kept my mind open.

While Bill Nichols was occupying the role as president of our company, my son-in-law, Tom Hickey, was working his way up through the ranks. Tom had joined our company a few years before Bill took over, and we all knew he was destined for great things. Tom was married to my daughter Linda, and they actually met in one of our stores while Linda was working the courtesy counter on her summer break from college. Both graduated with teaching degrees, with Tom becoming a coach and an assistant principal.

Given that Smitty's was really a family business, I had always hoped that one of my girls would join the company and make retailing a career. I first offered this opportunity to my eldest daughter, Sandy, but she chose to go to college in Cedar Rapids, Iowa. Following in her big sister's footsteps, my second daughter, Linda, graduated with a teaching degree and passed on the retail opportunity. It was strike three when my youngest daughter, Karen, decided retailing was not for her; she wanted to choose her own profession.

Not one to take no for an answer, I later tried to get Sandy's husband, Gary Sojka, to join our company. Gary also turned me down for a career as a college professor. Looking back, this was probably a good decision on Gary's part. He has had a great academic career, ultimately rising to become president of Bucknell University for eleven years. He now serves on many nationally recognized boards and is one of the most intelligent and well-educated individuals I know.

Tom Hickey: Son-in-law, but Businessman Par Excellence

You can imagine how excited I was when Linda's husband, Tom, decided to join our company. Tom was a very bright and disciplined person. Tom had a mental toughness that had served him well as a coach and school principal. He was an extremely hard worker and had a great capacity for getting the job done. I knew when he joined our organization that he would excel, but I knew first he had to get some much-needed hands-on experience and earn the respect of his peers if he was going to be president of the company one day.

In 1972, Tom started at the bottom of the ladder with our company. It was our objective to give him experience in all the various departments. Our entire management team knew that Tom had the mental capacity that he needed to do well in the business, but we also knew that there was a great deal of experience he had to get in a supermarket. Also, because Tom was my son-in-law, he needed to earn his stripes, department by department.

At the time Bill Nichols came to our company, Tom was getting accustomed to our management requirements and was maturing as a superior manager. He was also earning the respect of his peers, which is so very important. Some time later when Bill had to leave due to health reasons, Tom was elevated to the role of president. Tom would preside over the final chapter of our family-owned business much later and would continue as president of Smitty's Supermarkets after our chain was sold.

The Dave Trottier Story

Dave Trottier has been like a son to me. He joined our company in 1962 as a stocker/carryout boy and went on to have a great career at Smitty's. Dave was an integral part of our Arizona team and became one of our best store managers. Dave had a great capacity to get the job done, and this was evident in every task he undertook.

I always saw a bit of myself in Dave. Both of us were mavericks, not shy about our opinions, and are happiest when we put in a ten- to twelve-hour day. Dave was a golden glove boxer in his youth and was never afraid of a challenge. This paralleled with my hardscrabble, Depression upbringing and my fearless approach to life. Both of us have a competitive streak as big as one of our superstores, and we hate to lose at anything we try. While being so much alike might have driven us apart, those traits we shared in common somehow brought us closer together.

What is so important about Dave's story is that it illustrates some important business and life skills that each of us needs to learn. His story demonstrates that it's not just hard work, ethics, and brains that get you over the finish line but also graciously accepting fate and ultimately keeping your ego in check.

Dave's story really began when Bill Nichols became president of our company. Bill decided to reorganize our management team and create two senior positions. As it turned out, when the promotions were announced in one of our management meetings, Dave was passed over for promotion. Dave has shared his story in the Interlude section of this book, but I am relating it from my perspective as owner of Smitty's stores.

Not getting promoted to one of the newly created positions must have been very hurtful for Dave. I am sure that from his vantage point, he thought he deserved one of the promotions because of his excellent on-the-job performance. Because this was such a public pass over in front of his peers, it must have really stung, given Dave's competitive nature.

To his credit, Dave congratulated the new senior managers and left the meeting to lick his wounds. Sometime later that day, I called Dave at his store to console him and tell him that the promotions were a close decision and he almost got the nod. Dave thanked me and ended the call saying that he would respect the decisions we had made, but if there was ever an opportunity to grow the company, no matter where, I would keep him in mind.

A few months later, I got a call from Lou Fox, president of Associated Wholesale Grocers Company in Kansas City, Missouri. Lou told me about a grocery store that had closed that Associated Grocers was on the lease for. He wanted me to meet him in Springfield, Missouri, to consider buying it because the shuttered store could prove to be a platform for us to grow the Smitty's company in another state. The store was 67,000 square feet, about average-sized by our standards. The previous owner had gone broke, and Associated Grocers was motivated to get an operator in place who would assume their long-term lease.

I told Mr. Fox that I might be interested in the store and would give it serious consideration. I decided to call Dave and see if he would consider moving to Missouri and becoming a partner in the new venture if the opportunity presented itself. I met him at the Stockyard Steakhouse in Phoenix and unfolded my idea of going to Missouri. I asked Dave how much money he had saved from his bonus checks and Smitty's stock, and he replied, "$180,000." In 1977, that was a whole lot of money, and it was to Dave's credit that he had listened to our corporate philosophy about living on his base salary and banking the rest.

Dave and I agreed to go to Missouri the very next week. After looking the store over in fine detail, we both agreed that it had good possibilities and could be an opportunity for us to team up and start a new company. I knew that Dave was the right person for the job. To start a new company from scratch would take a tremendous amount of energy, and Dave was bountiful in that department. He also had a well-rounded knowledge of the supermarket business and was a topflight manager. While he might have been passed over for the promotion in Phoenix where our corporate philosophy was years old, he was just the guy to mold the Missouri operation. I knew he could positively imprint the Smitty's name with this new venture and his unique personality and operational skills. He also had the talent to make a complete overhaul on the existing store to bring it up to our strict standards prior to opening.

On September 10, 1977, Dave, his crew, and I opened our first store in Missouri, with Dave and me as partners. Dave had taken a few of our people with him to Missouri, so there was a consistency in the approach to the store and its merchandising. Dave had hired a young guy named Jeff Kollmeyer to act eventually as his right-hand man, and Jeff turned out to be a brilliant retailer. Jeff was the produce buyer of Associated Grocers and was well-experienced in the supermarket industry.

In a short time, Dave and Jeff had grown that single store into ten Smitty's Supermarkets and three Lil Smitty's super gas pumpers. By 1997, the stores were blessed with high volume and a good bottom line. This type of volume soon caught the attention of Albertson's supermarket chain, which was planning on moving into the Springfield market. As Smitty's was the dominate chain in the area, Albertson's made Dave an offer he could not refuse. During this twenty-year period, I had sold bits of my stock to the key employees, and in 1995, I sold the balance of my stock to Dave.

Even though I had sold Dave my company stock prior to the Albertson's purchase, nobody could have been happier with the sale than me. It was heartwarming to see Dave and his team take a single store operation and mold it into a successful chain of stores that commanded so much market share that a national retail chain was willing to pay serious money to get their hands on it. It was also a great compliment to Dave and his team that Albertson's said that they would rather buy them out than compete with them.

We can learn from Dave's experience that mentors can still play a large part in the business and social experience. Like Keith Rushing mentored me, I was willing to mentor Dave, provided he demonstrated those business principals I held dear like hard work, ethics, and creativity. As I have said before, there are plenty of people in this world who are willing to help you, but first they must have a desire to learn and be willing to give of themselves. Dave worked his way up through the ranks, lived his life within his means, and was willing to stick with us even though he suffered a personal defeat at what looked like the peak of his career. How could you not mentor a guy like that?

Today, Dave and his stepson Brent Brown own another chain of very successful boutique supermarkets in Southwest Missouri called Summer Fresh. The stores are managed and operated by his stepson Brent and his daughter, Summer, who came along years later. Like the gift of mentoring Keith Rushing gave to me, Dave now mentors his kids and is a great role model for them professionally and personally. When we are together fishing in Canada or out on the golf course, I still enjoy being his mentor. I am thankful each time we are together that he did not stomp out of my life that fateful day when he was passed over for the promotion he really wanted.

Worth Thinking About

What we all can take away from Dave's story is that he managed to swallow his pride in the face of a crushing disappointment. Many people would have stood up in the management meeting and quit on the spot. He also took the approach of letting me know that he was still a team player and would be interested in any other opportunity I might send his way.

Had Dave quit his job due to his disappointment and bruised ego, he would have thrown away a future that neither one of us could have conceived of at the time. Quitting might have kept his ego intact, but it would have robbed him of the brightest part of his career. Too many people today let their emotions run the major decisions in their life. We all can learn from Dave's real-life experience and how he handled himself.

—Clyde B. Smith

28

The Headlines No One Saw Coming

"We all learned from each other and had a world of
fun along the way. It was hard work, but we had developed a
corporate philosophy that bound us together like a family, not
a bunch of people who just happened to work together."

—Clyde B. Smith

The headlines on November 24, 1980, caught most of Phoenix by surprise. The headlines read, "Smitty's Tentatively OKs Selling Out to a Canadian Supermarket Firm." The article then went on to say that the sale of Smitty's was probably the largest sale of a privately-held Arizona company in the state's history. When approved by the boards of both companies, all twenty existing Smitty's stores and their distribution center would be acquired by Steinberg, Incorprated of Montreal, Canada. Steinberg's was a sixty-eight-year-old Canadian retailer that operated many grocery stores throughout Canada. While the article went into much more depth, the sale of a cornerstone of the Phoenix business community is what most people focused on that day in November 1980.

I had been a supermarket operator in the Phoenix market for twenty years, so when the article broke that day, it was sort of bittersweet for me. I had come to Phoenix with a handful of loyal employees from Iowa and, with their help and dedication, had built a life for my family, those dedicated followers, and thousands of other Smitty's employees. Together, we had opened the largest supermarket in the state in 1961 and then helped pioneer the superstore concept of today that ultimately made retail history. Smitty's was one of the first supermarkets to offer a full-scale restaurant, a real scratch bakery, and a combined supermarket and department store under one roof. I was looking forward to the enormous amount of money from the sale, and yes, I was ready for a change in my life, but I cannot tell you the emotions I felt when the sale of the Smitty's Stores became public.

As I sat there the morning the sale was announced, I could not help but think about all the wonderful people I had met and employed and the many good things that had come our way in Phoenix. God had really blessed us with how well our first store was received by the public. It was hard not to reflect on how proud we were of that first store with its new concept and wide aisles, the enthusiasm of our staff, and how Smitty's went on to redefine the shopping experience for the Phoenix consumer when it opened.

Then there were all the amazing people who had made that incredible journey with us. People like Everett Larson, Tony Witte, Doug Smith, and countless others who were really the steam engine that helped build our company into a true American success story. Through the years, I had been privileged to work side by side with some really great retailers such as my brothers Doug and Swede Smith, Dave Trottier, and Jim and Muriel Palmer, just to name a few. We all learned from each other and had a world of fun along the way. It was hard work, but we had developed a corporate philosophy that bound us together like a family, not just a bunch of people who just happened to work together.

The truth is, I never set out to sell the stores. A chance meeting with a high powered commercial realtor named Joe Tarrish set things in motion. Tarrish had a reputation for putting together some of the biggest real estate deals in Arizona. When out of the blue I mentioned to him that I might be interested in selling the stores, he seized on the opportunity.

I had been selling things since I was a kid. My brother Swede and I would catch fish in the river by our farm and take them to town, selling them for money to help our family or to purchase an occasional treat when Dad permitted it. When I got back from the war, Helen and I bought an old house that we renovated and sold it for a profit, which helped finance our first store in Roland, Iowa, two years later. Later, I sold our second store in Jefferson, Iowa, to get into a larger third store in Marshalltown, Iowa. Eleven years later, we moved our operation to Phoenix, Arizona, and the sale of a few stores in our Iowa chain provided the capital we needed to help build our Arizona stores. So by the time I bumped into Joe Tarrish, the idea of selling assets was not foreign to me if there was a potential profit to be had.

From all the sales I had conducted in my life, I had learned that selling assets is a matter of extraordinary timing. My years in business taught me that when you needed to sell an asset the most, the market generally never cooperates. Conversely, when most assets are at their peak value, you rarely think of selling them. Many of us get lulled into a sense of financial security when our assets have the most value. It is only when the market turns against us that we take a hard look at the real value of our assets and what they really are worth on the sale block. Often this is too late if you have to have the money.

By all measures of business success, there was no real need to sell the company. We had a staggering market share of 35 percent in the Phoenix MSA, a strong balance sheet, and a group of stores that were performing better on a same-store basis each year. We had built a brand in the industry that was respected for our profitability and innovation. Smitty's had a great group of vendors and were scooping the competition at every turn with our prices and merchandising. We also had a team of managers and staff that was second to none in the industry. Selling the stores made no real sense, but viewed from the classical business perspective of selling an asset at the top, it made every sense in the world.

No one was more surprised than me when Joe Tarrish returned sometime later to tell me of his chance meeting with a potential buyer for our stores. Steinberg's, a Canadian supermarket chain with many stores, was looking to move into the U.S. market, and he had gotten them interested in buying us. The company specifically wanted to be in the Sunbelt, so Smitty's would be a strategic purchase to take advantage of the Sunbelt economy where much of the growth in the U.S. was coming from at the time.

When Joe brought the deal to me with Steinberg's, he told me that he wanted a $1 million commission on the sale. After giving his request some thought, I told him any commission would need to be collected from the buyer. After all, I wasn't really that interested in selling the stores, so I decided to stick to my guns when it came to maximizing a profit, and that included any selling expenses. Seeing that this was too good a deal to pass up, he agreed to my terms.

With more than thirty years now between me and the sale of our company, I can clearly see that I was just plain ready for a change. I had been in the supermarket business since I wandered up to Keith Rushing's grocery store in Ames, Iowa, in the fall of 1937. After convincing him to hire me with my unique pay-for-performance proposition, more than half my lifetime had passed, and besides my family, the supermarket business was the most important thing in my life.

For forty years, the supermarket business had dominated my every move and most every waking thought. It was the reason I got to work at dawn and why I was often the last one to leave at night. I had faced most every challenge a grocer could face and had managed to succeed in spite of the tremendous odds that face all small businesses. When I saw Joe Tarrish that day, I just knew it was time for a change. Much like I was always making changes to our new stores, I took a hard look deep inside and decided maybe a change would be good for me too. Besides, there was an idea that kept rattling around in my brain, which could potentially be just the change I had subconsciously been looking for.

It Would Have Been a First of Its Kind

In no time, Steinberg's was in our corporate offices performing due diligence on their potential purchase. To their credit, they made it known early in the process that they would retain most of our staff if the sale was completed. I am sure that this eased a great many concerns that our staff had when the purchase was first announced. Tom Hickey, my son-in-law, was now president of the company and they wanted Tom to stay on. As president, he was responsible for many of the day to day activities of the company. His knowledge of the operation was quite valuable to them, along with providing a link to the rich corporate philosophy the company had developed.

With the Steinberg's announcement now public, and when I was not assisting in their buyout of our stores, I began flying around the country looking for that perfect piece of land to build a one-of-a-kind, first-in-America golf resort. The idea that had been rattling around in my head that day when I told Joe Tarrish about selling the stores was to build a golf resort that incorporated the participation of some of the largest corporations in America. What would make this resort so unique would be that all the companies involved catered to the supermarket industry. If I could just find the right location to build on, this unique resort might add a new dimension on how corporate America — more specifically, my buddies in the food industry — hit the links.

As you probably have figured out by now, golf was a big part of my life. I had really become involved in the sport and enjoyed competing. Smitty's had hosted a very successful tournament, and I rarely turned down a chance to play. Golf fed my competitive streak, which allowed me to experience a variety of golf courses and a host of country clubs over the years. It was through these experiences that I began to formulate a concept for a one-of-a-kind golf resort, with a unique twist.

The concept that I had been thinking about for quite some time was to get eighteen of the largest corporations in the supermarket industry involved. I wanted to convince them that they should build a corporate retreat on each one of the eighteen holes of the golf course in the resort that I wanted to build. My concept was that each company would construct an estate-type home that could accommodate management meetings, client events, and seminars. To accompany the resort homes, I would build a club house, pro shop, and restaurant as a support facility to the estate homes and their guests. If I secured the right piece of property, the project might also offer fishing, hunting, and other related outdoor activities to supplement the golf course.

The whole project would be one big cooperative with all of us sharing in the expenses of the common areas such as the golf course and central grounds. Each corporation would pay for the expenses associated with their own home and golf course, while I would maintain the clubhouse and restaurant. These would become income centers for me along with other amenities and activities I could package for sale.

I envisioned that the whole project would be a facility where some of the most important companies and individuals in the food industry would come to learn, network, and entertain. The resort would be a cost-effective way for the management teams of these companies to conduct meetings and corporate events. The resort homes could be used as an incentive to employees and reward them for their extraordinary performance. Most of these companies were spending huge amounts of money each year at resorts around the country with little to show for it but the bill. The concept I planned would allow them to "get away from the office" while building equity in the resort and ultimately having a say in controlling expenses. Just as important, it would also allow them to provide a consistent experience for their staff and guests in a manner that supported their corporate philosophy.

I knew that if I was going to make this concept work, I would have to do two things really well. First, I would have to find the perfect property that allowed for a diversity of outdoor experiences, all on the same piece of property. The property would need to be in a rural setting but have adjacent air service for ease of access. I really wanted the property to have a live running creek, beautiful lakes, an abundance of wildlife, and a good stock of trees to facilitate the outdoor experience. At that point in my career, I was too impatient for trees to grow, which ruled out many locations in the Southwest.

Once I found the location, I knew that I would have to build a "world-class" golf course that captured the imagination of each golfer as they played. To make this happen, I would have to associate with a course designer who had good experience, but also had the time to spend on the project. There were a lot of big name golfers designing courses around the country at the time, but I wanted someone who would take the time and care that was necessary to come up with a different layout for this special project.

Solving the designer problem was the easy part for me. In Phoenix, I had played lots of golf with a senior pro golfer named Billy Johnston. Besides being a really good golfer, Billy had designed a few courses, and I liked his approach. I felt he was a guy I could work with, which was very important to me, because I wanted to have some say in the final design of the course. I had spent hundreds of hours on the drawing board planning our stores, so naturally I wanted to put my two cents in and help to design and put some personal thoughts and ideas into the project to help make the project exceptional. When you think about it, a supermarket and a golf course share the common trait of creating a visual and emotional experience for the customer. This is an area in which I thought I could add some value — besides just writing the checks.

I first looked in California and then Arizona but decided that neither provided the venue I was looking for. I then began to look in the Texas Hill Country, where our management team had taken numerous hunting trips. One of the great things about being a successful chain like Smitty's was that many of our large suppliers liked to entertain us, and Texas was a favorite place to do so.

I engaged a realtor out of San Antonio, Texas, who really went out of his way to accommodate my search. This real estate guy showed me some twenty-five ranches in the Texas Hill Country. This was no easy task as Texas ranches are often off the beaten path and are not easy to access. When he finally showed me this ranch a few miles outside of San Antonio near a town called Boerne, Texas, I knew that my search was over. It was the perfect piece of property for the project I envisioned.

The ranch was called Thunder Valley Ranch, and it was owned by the Jesse Urbin family. It was 1,400 acres of majestic terrain in what they called the "Texas Hill Country." The ranch was four miles west of Boerne, Texas, which was twenty-five miles west of San Antonio on Interstate Highway 10.

The day the realtor showed me the ranch, I rode and walked most of the 1,400 acres for the entire day. To my complete satisfaction, the ranch had most everything I had been dreaming of — the terrain, the necessary water, and the proper undulation. Thunder Valley had a spring-fed stream, several nice lakes, lots of big trees, and an abundance and variety of wild game. The wild game included healthy herds of wild turkeys, quail, wild hogs, goats, and several varieties of deer. In the lakes and streams, there were large numbers of *wow* bass and catfish.

Without a doubt, I knew by the end of that day that this was the property I would build my resort on. It had all the natural attributes I had been looking for and then some. The ranch was thickly forested, with groves of trees encased in a landscape that changed elevation at every turn of the head. This remarkable terrain offered a unique venue that would accommodate not only the golf course, but the pad sites for the estate homes, a club house, and much more. It would also accommodate the outdoor activities I had envisioned that would add "experiential" value for the corporations that I wanted to bring on board.

I bought Thunder Valley Ranch for full price that very next day! I tried to negotiate with Mr. Urbin, but even an all-cash deal would not budge him from his price. Now I was a guy who hated to pay full asking price, so I had to swallow really hard to not walk away in a poker style bluff. The ranch was too perfect to risk losing in a cat-and-mouse game that I had played and won thousands of times. After all, I could not blame him for sticking to his price given the beauty and diversity of the ranch. In fact, I could relate to Mr. Urbin because this was the exact approach I had taken with Steinberg's on the sale of our stores. Both the stores and the ranch were for sale, only if you paid their price!

As I sat there thinking about the ranch I had just bought that beautiful fall day in 1980, it began to sink in that the ranch represented much more to me than just another business deal. The ranch represented a new life after the sale of our stores and a chance to start my business life over. The ranch represented a fresh start, a new direction, and a whole new set of challenges to look forward to.

I felt like that kid again walking into the bank with Mr. Rushing trying to get a loan for that first store. Only this time, I had a little more money in my pocket, a career that had experienced much success, and a wealth of knowledge to draw from. I was fortunate that even after a business career of more than forty years, at the time, I still had that eternal optimism that tells every entrepreneur that success is just around the corner. Only I had no clue that fall day as to just how many corners, and how many twists, that Thunder Valley Ranch would bring into my life.

Worth Thinking About

"That which we obtain too easily, we esteem too lightly. It is dearness only which gives everything its value. Heaven knows how to put a proper price on its good."

—Thomas Paine

"I know of no more encouraging fact than the unquestionable ability of man to elevate his life by conscious endeavor."

—Henry David Thoreau

"No one can make you feel inferior without your consent."

—Eleanor Roosevelt

"They cannot take away our self-respect if we do not give it to them."

—Gandhi

"What lies behind us and what lies before us are tiny matters compared to what lies within us."

—Oliver Wendell Holmes

"Management is doing things right; leadership is doing the right things."

—Peter Drucker and Warren Bennis

"We are more in need of a vision or destination and a compass (a set of principles or directions) and less in need of a road map. We often don't know what the terrain ahead will be like or what we will need to go through it; much will depend on our judgment at the time. But an inner compass will always give us direction."

—Stephen R. Covey
from his book *The Seven Habits of Highly Effective People*

"When you eat the labor of your hands,
    You shall be happy, and it shall be well with you."

—the Bible, Psalm 128:2

29

One Door Closes; Another One Opens

"The nicest thing about the future is that it comes one day at a time."

—Goethe

The sale of our company to Steinberg's of Canada was completed on April 1, 1980. Like all large deals, there was a good deal of "lawyering" and "drama" before we completed the transaction. One piece of drama worth mentioning was the real estate fee paid to Joe Tarrish. When Joe put the deal together, he told me he wanted $1 million for his efforts. I told him he would have to collect it from the buyer and he agreed.

Steinberg's agreed to the Tarrish fee when the initial sale documents were signed. Without fully thinking it through, they decided to make the fee a point of contention at the closing table. They tossed it out at the very last minute, saying that they were not going to pay the fee as outlined in the sales contract. Thinking that all I was seeing was a huge pile of money on the table, I am positive that the Steinberg's felt I would agree to pay Joe and they would save $1 million!

As I got up to leave the closing table without signing the documents, the Steinberg's people were in disbelief. One of them said, "You mean you would blow this deal for $1 million?"

I replied that I really did not want to sell the stores that badly anyway. Seeing that they had terribly misjudged my resolve, they quickly relented and agreed to pay Tarrish his fee. We then signed the documents and shook hands. After more than thirty-five years, I was no longer in the supermarket business.

There were many things to be proud of with our sale to Steinberg's. The financial part of the sale was breathtaking. Being bought out by a large international firm that could have spent their money elsewhere was a testament to all we had accomplished. However, one of the most flattering developments after the sale was finalized was that the only person Steinberg's sent down to Phoenix to oversee their mega-purchase was a single "in-house" lawyer. This was a great tribute to our team and the faith the new owners had in them and their ability to preserve the brand we had built.

Prior to concluding our sale, I had been going down to Texas on a frequent basis to oversee the transformation of Thunder Valley Ranch. The ranch was slowly becoming a primary business asset. During this time, I was busy coordinating the final plans for the resort, working with our architect out of California, along with interviewing local contractors to start and complete the work. This required me to stay down on the ranch for extended periods of time to get multiple things going.

As I was getting things underway in Texas, my wife, Helen, came down with me a couple of times to see the ranch. Unfortunately, being on the ranch played havoc with her allergies, which dampened her enthusiasm for the ranch and the entire project. When the sale to Steinberg's was concluded, and I was preparing to go to Texas for an extended period of time, Helen told me that she would not be coming to Texas. Our huge project did not seem to please her at all. Her voice had a tone of finality that said this would be for good.

There was no banging of pots and pans, or yelling through the night, just a silence that told us our marriage was over. Helen's refusal to go to Texas was really saying that this was the end. We had woken up the day after the sale to Steinberg's, and we were effectively strangers. I began to see that I had devoted so much of my life to building our business that our marriage had become the casualty of our time apart. During the many years of growing our market chain, I was away from home most of the time. I would leave early in the morning and work until late in the evening. I was not a good father or a good husband, always too busy. We grew apart. Helen had her friends with whom she enjoyed activities, especially in Phoenix. For the most part, she had raised our three very dear girls and made a wonderful home for us in both Iowa and Phoenix. She stayed home and accomplished this with no maid and no outside help, while I worked endless hours at the stores. She was a good person, an exceptional mother, and a faithful wife. It was one of life's unexplained mysteries that we ended up in the situation we did. None of us knows what tomorrow will bring. While one door was opening in Texas, because we had drifted apart in our marriage, another door closed. It was hard to understand at the time; what I do know is that God has a plan for each one of us, and I learned to accept that.

Our divorce was amicable, with us sharing evenly in the assets we had accumulated. We both treated each other as the other one would want to be treated with dignity, so there was no quarreling, name-calling, or long, drawn out battles or petty stunts. Helen and I signed a few papers of agreement and set out for lives on our own, hers in Phoenix and mine in Texas. We continued to be friends until her death in 2007.

Transformation of a Ranch into a Resort

After the sale of Smitty's Stores, I immediately started pursuing my second business love. The golf and country club business—designing and building my own concept, which would be new in the industry. I left our Phoenix home and my wife and family to pursue this venture with no regard to them or how this might affect our marriage. So it was that by the time of the completion of the sales transaction, work was well under way in transforming Thunder Valley Ranch into our new development as Tapatio Springs Resort.

I had visited Guadalajara, Mexico, and stayed at a hotel called "Tapatio." In Guadalajara, the locals are called "Tapatios," so I brought the name north with me for my new project. A graphic designer friend from Phoenix took the name and combined it with a silhouette of a single large Blue Heron for the new logo. At the time of construction, there were several pairs of nesting Blue Herons on the ranch, which personalized the logo for the property.

The job of turning this magnificent ranch into a first-class golf course and resort went to a dear friend of mine from Phoenix, Leo McNeal. Along with his brother Bob, he had the responsibility of interpreting Billy Johnston's designs into a working golf course and resort. This was a major task as it required moving thousands of cubic yards of dirt, while preserving as much of the original landscape and as many of the big, beautiful trees as possible. Both Leo and Bob were masters with heavy equipment, and it amazed me how good they were with a dozer or tractor.

I moved the two McNeals down to Boerne from Phoenix, and we were soon spending ten to twelve hours a day together building the golf course. I knew that building the course would be challenging, but I seriously misjudged just how difficult it really was. Besides having to understand the extensive topographic drawings that marked every inch of the proposed golf course, you then had to use huge excavating machinery to move tons of earth with skill and precision into the areas as needed. This was really challenging in the Texas Hill Country, where in some areas, the soil is rather rocky. As the McNeals discovered, and I was soon to learn, building a golf course is backbreaking work because you are constantly in the field where you are exposed to the elements from sunup to sundown. This proved taxing, even for an Iowan farm kid like me.

The ranch was blessed with an abundance of good topsoil, which was very necessary even though it was only one to three feet deep. The Hill Country soil became a problem for us because we had to work with this rocky condition under the topsoil when we discovered it was necessary to incorporate a trenching infrastructure for the Trans Glide System to travel on the golf course. This Trans Glide System was a futuristic, almost Disney-like golf cart system that moved golfers around the course in carts that were on a track like a monorail system. In order to install the tracks, we first had to provide a 3-foot deep by 6-inch wide trench down the middle of each fairway to set the steel rail on. This added to our frustrations because it was one more thing we had to accomplish in order to install this new, one-of-a-kind system.

I knew the inventor, Arnold Dahlberg of the Trans Glide System, from a bank board we served on in Phoenix. He had a proven track record as an inventor and businessman, having invented the very successful Dahlberg Hearing Aid. Dahlberg had conceived the idea for the Trans Glide System after he moved to Phoenix from the Midwest. He leased a corner on Scottsdale Road in Phoenix, where he built a working mock-up of the system to generate interest in the product.

From the first time I saw the Trans Glide System, I immediately wanted to incorporate it into our new golf course at Tapatio Springs. To me, the concept made great sense. With the Trans Glide System, the golf carts ran on a subsurface rail system that was laid straight down the middle of the fairways. The design allowed golfers to get closer to their ball, while sparing the expensive golf course grass the usual wear and tear inflicted by the wheels of traditional carts. It also allowed for play in most any weather as there was no damage to the course from maneuvering a cart over puddles of water.

Dahlberg had done a great job in his design of the Trans Glide System. The carts had a really sleek appearance and were to be equipped with a sophisticated automatic guidance system. In the cart, Dahlberg had incorporated a series of buttons that would take you to the next hole, club house, pro shop, or most anyplace on the course. The Trans Glide System incorporated a remote system that allowed the golfers to call the cart to them as they played. He designed into the system a series of switches and bypasses similar to a train track to facilitate getting around the course and other cart traffic to speed up play.

After putting the pencil to incorporating the Trans Glide System into the golf course at Tapatio Springs, I concluded that there would be at least a $100,000 per year savings related to the course. While most of this was in reduced maintenance, it would also increase revenues because the system would allow play in most any weather without damaging the course. Most of all, I was counting on the novelty of the system to attract golfers from all over the country because we would be the first course in America, or perhaps the world, to have such an unusual golf cart transportation system. Heck, I figured the free publicity would be worth a bundle to us from just the golf magazines.

I made a deal with Dahlberg, and it was official that Tapatio Springs would be the first golf course to have the Trans Glide System. I gave him a $500,000 deposit to allow him to finish the design and engineering on the project. We agreed on a delivery date and the McNeals set about preparing the subsurface trenches on the Tapatio course.

This energized me as Tapatio Springs would be making golf course history with the Trans Glide System. In my mind, the Trans Glide System would do for Tapatio Springs what our unique concepts and merchandising did for Smitty's. It would give the customer that special shopping/golfing experience that would separate us from the competition, while keeping them coming back for more.

In Over My Head

By the summer of 1981, we were going full steam ahead with the construction of Tapatio Springs and I was clearly involved in hard work and long hours. I had underestimated the amount of work that was involved in a project of this scale. Unlike our supermarkets where I grew into our business one store at a time, Tapatio Springs put me in unfamiliar territory that presented a unique set of challenges and obstacles almost overnight.

There were hundreds of details to look after on a daily basis as we built the resort. Many of these required my immediate attention, often at the same time! Besides overseeing the building of the golf course, I had to hire and supervise an army of contractors to build the club house, estate homes, and other infrastructure. This was especially difficult for me, being new to the community. Unlike my years in Phoenix, I had no knowledge of the contractor base in Boerne and whom I could trust and depend on. This would become problematic as I misjudged the integrity of some of the contractors I hired.

I had not been on my own since I had left home and hitchhiked to Ames, Iowa, when I was seventeen years old. Up to this point in my life, I always had people that I could lean on for support, guidance, and a helping hand. Suddenly there was no loyal management team or brothers like Doug or Swede to pitch in and help get the job done. Many of the people I used to count on had stayed with Smitty's where they continued on with their lives. All the things I had planned to accomplish to make Tapatio Springs a real showplace pushed my physical and mental capacities to their limits.

About this time, I had two major setbacks, which were accompanied by a number of other challenges. The first setback of significance was that two of the CEOs of the corporations that had made a commitment to be part of this new concept resort started to back out. During the early 1980s, there were a number of lawsuits on behalf of small shareholder groups that targeted management of these corporations, accusing them of reckless spending. These suits became very high profile and senior managers soon found themselves under a microscope by the press and dissident shareholders. Things like trips in corporate jets for special customers, lavish entertainment, and other corporate perks suddenly became a black mark on management.

Not wishing to invite trouble from company shareholders, the corporate executives I knew at these large food industry corporations asked me if they could possibly get out of their commitments. As most of the eight or nine I had lined up were actually accepted by only a handshake, I had no choice but to let them out of their commitment. These corporate titans were friends of mine and I certainly was not going to put them under any pressure to get involved with something their company didn't want or need.

The second piece of bad news I got was that Arnold Dahlberg notified me that he was not going to be able to deliver the Trans Glide System as promised. For numerous reasons, he could not complete the project and wanted out of the contract we signed. This was very disappointing to me because I had become such a believer in the Trans Glide System. I just knew it would be well accepted by the public. We had some real costs associated with Dahlberg's cancellation. This did cost us both time and money, and we were disappointed, to say the least, but we had to continue with our project.

Changes and a Major Turn of Events

With the major corporations now out of the picture, I had to develop a Plan B for Tapatio Springs quickly. Plan B soon evolved the need for me to build a traditional country club that would include a 90-room hotel, condominiums, and resort homes, and develop a golf course, plus lots for primary and secondary homes. This turn of events put our entire organization into overdrive, with our architects and engineers working around the clock to make the necessary changes.

One of the first things I did was stop construction on the clubhouse and pressed the architects to hurry and redesign it to a larger scale. The clubhouse had been designed to support just the eighteen estate homes and now had to be enlarged to the size of a traditional country club facility. Likewise, I instructed them to come up with a hotel design and a plan for an initial condominium project to be built adjacent to the golf course. Suddenly, my role went from organizing a corporate retreat for the food industry to actually being a real estate developer with lots of financial "skin in the game."

If I thought I was busy before my corporate buddies were forced into a change of heart, this turn of events now put my life into overdrive. This also put a much different financial requirement on me from my original business plan. Looking back, I guess I thought that when the project was completed, the eighteen corporations would end up owning this unique resort and my role would diminish over the years. I would be compensated for my development efforts but would have no long-term financial commitment to the project. Perhaps I would retain some small ownership interest with a tie to the golf course, but at no time did I figure that I would be the primary financial backstop. These are the challenges that the world of business likes to torture entrepreneurs with, forcing us to modify our business plans with each turn of events.

With these two major changes now front and center, I encountered a multitude of challenges as we continued to build the resort. In those days, Tapatio Springs was still out in the country located four miles west of Boerne, Texas, and our primary road was a two lane, farm-to-market road called "John's Road." This was a slow, winding picturesque drive but became a real problem to us as we began to build the resort. The road was not built for truck traffic, and it really slowed us down. I also knew that potential clients and owners in the resort would not put up with a slow, winding road when they might need to get to the freeway in a hurry. To me, the road was a real negative.

When I approached the County Commissioners about upgrading and improving John's Road, they agreed to do so if I would pay for the entire four-mile road improvement. I told them no deal, but I would pay for 50 percent of the cost. This didn't work either as they wanted me to negotiate with each of the ranch owners about buying the right-of-way parcels.

I knew that this would not work because I was an "outsider," and one holdout landowner could cost us dearly. I told them it would make more sense for the County Commissioners to use their rights of condemnation in the spirit of progress, leaving me, the "outsider," out of the picture. However, this being a rural setting where most everyone knew each other, the commissioners were reluctant to use their rights of condemnation. I guess they did not want to face a disgruntled constituent in church on Sunday or at the local watering hole.

It was easy to understand their reluctance with condemnation, but not upgrading the road made our job all the more difficult for real estate sales and customer access. It also was another hurdle we faced in trying to accomplish a good thing that would create jobs and a stronger economic base. However, this poor farm-to-market road did not slow down our annual property tax bite, which seemed to arrive on time every year, along with sizeable increases.

Likewise, I had a real problem hiring qualified contractors and tradesmen to build the resort. With the change of events, our building program had tripled because we had to construct a hotel, condos, and other country club amenities. This was far more construction than I had originally intended, so our contractor needs became even greater.

In Boerne, Texas, it was difficult finding qualified contractors. Unlike Phoenix, where I knew which contractor to choose, how much things cost, and what type of workmanship to expect, in Texas I had no real business contacts and virtually no experience in building on the type of terrain found on the ranch. This put me in the uncomfortable situation of having to get up to speed quickly by doing my homework on the local labor market and methods of construction.

I toured several projects in the San Antonio and Hill Country areas and chose what I believed to be the best of the local contractors to work on Tapatio Springs. Most of these contractors turned out fine, but each gave me my share of heartburn before the resort was completed. This just added to the stress of having to change my business model in midstream, along with my personal time and financial commitment.

No Easy Givens

It was interesting to learn, in what I thought was the mature cycle of my business career, that there are absolutely no easy givens in business. Even at my stage of the game, these challenges and directional changes with Tapatio Springs were teaching me that the game of business is dynamic and ever-changing. Tapatio proved to me that you still need to get up each morning and be prepared for that unexpected event, which is always lurking around the corner. It taught me that you have to be nimble and not be lulled into thinking that things with your business experience today will stay the same tomorrow.

Fortunately for me, I had the assets and the years of business experience to draw on when things with Tapatio Springs went a totally different direction than I had planned. I was also fortunate that I had developed a determination in my personality that I would do whatever work was required to see a project or a concept through to the finish. This started with my first store in Roland, Iowa, and was refined with all the challenges Smitty's faced with our number two store in Phoenix. I brought this same, single-minded drive to the challenges we faced at Tapatio Springs, thanking God that I had been given the years of "hands-on" experience in the supermarket industry before being tested again.

Worth Thinking About

"Challenges and directional changes with Tapatio Springs taught me that the game of business is dynamic and ever-changing."

"Tapatio proved to me that you still need to get up each morning and be prepared for that unexpected event, which is always lurking around the corner."

"Tapatio taught me that you have to be nimble and not be lulled into thinking that things with your business experience today will stay the same tomorrow."

"Determination in one's personality to do whatever is required to see a project or a concept through to the finish is essential to reach the realization of one's dreams."

—Clyde B. Smith

"He only is a well-made man who has a good determination."

—Ralph Waldo Emerson

"I will study and get ready, and perhaps my chance will come."

—Abraham Lincoln

"The long span of the bridge of your life is supported by countless cables called habits, attitudes, and desires. What you do in life depends how much you want it, how much you are willing to work and plan and cooperate and use your resources. The long span of this bridge of your life is supported by countless cables that you are spinning now, and that is why today is such an important day. Make the cables strong."

—L.G. Elliott

"The man without a purpose is like a ship without a rudder—a waif, a nothing, a no man. Have a purpose in life, and having it, throw such strength of mind and muscle into your work as God has given you."

—Thomas Carlyle

30

Tapatio Springs and Beyond

"The Grand Opening—this was a day I would treasure forever.
There were times when I quietly thought this day would never come."

—Clyde B. Smith

We opened Tapatio Springs Country Club and Resort on December 30, 1981. Just as I had done so many times before when we opened one of our new Smitty Stores, I used all the marketing creativity I could think of to attract as many people and media as possible to the event. Instead of tempting them with a host of discounted groceries, this time I was tempting the public with an opportunity to get in on the ground floor of a new and wonderful country club and resort. This included a chance to become a charter member of the club or perhaps purchase one of the many parcels of real estate we had for sale.

I was encouraged with the turnout that we had for our grand opening event. During the day, our golf course was full of golfers from all over experiencing Billy Johnston's amazing course for the first time. I was disappointed that we were unable to move them around the course on the Trans Glide System as planned; however, we were able to offer them one of the most unique and scenic new golf courses in Texas.

As I watched our guests enjoying themselves during our grand opening event, I found it hard to believe all that had happened over the past year and a half. During this short window of time, I had purchased the land for Tapatio Springs, sold my stores, divorced, and built a country club in a small Texas community. With the help of the McNeal brothers, Billy Johnston, and a host of great architects and engineers, we had taken my dream of a unique resort and transformed it into a reality of brick, mortar, and manicured fairways.

While not everything had worked out as originally planned, I was fortunate that in spite of numerous obstacles, we managed to move the project along to this grand opening event. I will be the first to admit that there were times I quietly thought that this day would never come. First there was the loss of our food industry partners and then the delivery problems with the Trans Glide System. These were punctuated with construction problems, roadblocks from municipal governments, and an occasional college kid with his 4x4 truck who plowed trenches in our new golf course greens and tees while it was under construction—just for fun.

I had learned in the supermarket business that to achieve success one must establish a goal, plan steps to get there, and then see these steps to conclusion. If one makes mistakes along the way, one must be agile enough to change direction, plan another strategy, and continue to work diligently towards one's goal. I also learned that one cannot change yesterday's mistakes, so why worry about them and lose focus on the day that is at hand? Had I not made these principles a big part of my life over the years, I doubt that there would ever have been a grand opening at Tapatio Springs. Looking at the grand opening crowd, I knew that this was a day I would treasure forever.

Catalyst for My Own Future

Over the next year, we continued to build additional infrastructure to complement the golf course and our extensive real estate holdings at Tapatio Springs. There were still additional roads to build, along with cart paths and infrastructure to support the development of the numerous real estate projects we hoped to sell. Now that Tapatio Springs was a traditional country club and resort, my role as developer became more important to the long-term success of the project. Any dreams I had of being a golfing buddy and ambassador for the supermarket industry went by the wayside when the food industry partners exited the picture. I was now the catalyst for my own future.

I knew we had to continue to add infrastructure to attract the public if we were going to be successful in both real estate sales and resort memberships. Just like in the supermarket business, I had to keep "merchandising" the project to keep it new and exciting. This was an expensive undertaking as there is no comparison between building a condominium project and purchasing a truckload of soda pop for a big sale.

With all we had accomplished in a short time with Tapatio Springs, you would think that the construction process would have gotten much easier. But as I learned, just like the expense side of Tapatio Springs, the construction process did not get much better. I still had difficulty finding the right contractors and getting them to stick to their word. Unless there was total supervision of each project, I would find deficiencies in the workmanship and sometimes outright misrepresentation. Since I had no "first-class" management team to whom I could delegate as I did in the stores, I frantically ran around the project most days trying to supervise and provide leadership wherever I could. I guess this is the reason so much of 1982 is a blur to me.

In addition to the big job of building out the project, I also had to learn the hotel business from the ground up. We had built a ninety-room hotel close to the clubhouse with a strategy of attracting both corporate and leisure guests. This required that I become familiar with the basics of being an innkeeper, even though I did hire a manager to look after the hotel. Nevertheless, I felt it was my responsibility to our people to know at least the basics of every aspect of the business we were in, and this was no different. Doing so would allow me to provide a level of leadership to the staff, while knowing when things were out of order.

I made a real mistake with the hotel when I decided to go it alone instead of franchising with a "flagged" brand such as Holiday Inn or Ramada. The fees associated with a "flag" seemed expensive at the time. I was to learn later, after several operational problems and inconsistencies in occupancy, that I really should have paid the price.

Our hotel blew both hot and cold with regards to occupancy most of the time. A recognized brand would have leveled this out by giving us access to a national reservation system, with a wider promotional capacity. We were still remote to San Antonio, Texas, in 1982, and a national hotel brand would have greatly supplemented our own promotional efforts. We had a great product with Tapatio Springs; we just needed to get the word out.

Not branding the hotel became a costly mistake. It taught me a valuable lesson: not all expenses are created equal. Had I done a little more due diligence on branding the hotel, it might have been more successful sooner and actually saved money in the long run. Unfortunately, the decision not to brand was made at a time when I was as busy as I had ever been in my career. I was also writing checks for Tapatio Springs as quickly as I could get my checkbook open. This made for a tough decision because the money was going out much faster than it was coming in. I simply chose the wrong area to cut.

The Seminar that Changed My Life

In January of 1983, Leo McNeal and I, along with several others active in our real estate department at Tapatio Springs, attended a real estate seminar and dinner in San Antonio, Texas. At the end of the event, the participants were invited to hear music and dance, capping off the end of a long day. I remember eyeing a beautiful woman at a table across the room, so I thought I would ask her to dance. Actually, I had been admiring her most of the evening, so the festivities provided me a proper excuse to introduce myself and meet her.

When I approached her table, she was getting up to leave. I overheard her saying good-bye to her friends just as I asked her to dance. I could see by the look in her eyes that there was hesitation as she glanced toward her girlfriend for support. Fortunately for me, there must have been a sign of encouragement in her girlfriend's eyes, so she agreed to the dance. With the song "Elvira" already started, I guess she figured that this minor interruption from the man in a red sweater-vest would be short-lived.

When we got on the dance floor, it was like we had danced together forever. Every step we took felt as though it had been coordinated and rehearsed a thousand times. I had always loved to dance, but at no time in my life had I ever experienced a dance that was so meant to be. It was like the sale of the stores, the purchase of Thunder Valley Ranch, the birth of Tapatio Springs, and all the countless challenges I had been through over the past two years were perfectly orchestrated in my life to lead me to this dance with this amazing, attractive woman.

Her name was Peggy, and she had the most beautiful eyes I had ever seen. She was petite with golden blonde hair and a confidence that was built into her every move. Peggy had come to the seminar to further her life experiences in real estate. The dance we shared was proof that it was no accident that we both had chosen the same date to be in the same room.

When the dance finished, I walked her back to her table and managed to tell her that I would like to have her visit my development and meet our real estate broker. I asked her for her phone number so I could invite her to Tapatio Springs in the near future possibly to take a position in our real estate department. It was then that she decided to give me her number. While she was gathering her things, I managed to sneak in that I owned this country club and resort, hoping to impress her with my worldly side. She just looked at me with that skeptical look only a woman can give a man and, as she headed to the door, responded, "Yes, and I'm Nancy Reagan." When I tried to convince her to stop by the club on her way back to her home, which was about thirty minutes from Boerne, she politely declined. She was far too smart to be duped by a guy who, in reality, was probably the night manager at the hotel.

No More Backseats for Me

Since my divorce, I had a few lady friends, but no serious relationships. I had been extremely busy with the construction of Tapatio Springs, which left me with little time for socializing. I guess that I had so much of my pride and money on the line with Tapatio Springs that dating took a backseat to the determination I had to make the resort a success. This sort of melted away after that "game changing" dance with Peggy.

If there is one thing I had learned in the supermarket business, it was that if there is no action, there can be no reaction. I kept telling myself this as I dialed Peggy's number a few days later. When a sweet voice on the other end of the line told me she was not there, I politely said I would return the call at a later date.

I was to go through this ritual a half dozen times before I finally got Peggy on the phone. Her daughter Cindy had been screening the calls because Peggy was unsure that she wanted to see or talk to me or anyone else at that point in her life. She was moving to the Texas Gulf Coast and had already accepted what she felt would be an unbelievable opportunity to move into a career in the coastal real estate market. I guess Cindy finally felt the desperation in my voice that last time I called and insisted that her mom take the call.

I have never been a pickup-line kind of guy, even in my high school days. As an Iowan farm kid, I was raised more as a hard worker than a spooner. It must have been fate when Peggy came to the phone, and I started our conversation with the best creative words of my life. "I just wanted to make sure you are real," I told the voice on the other end of the line. I was alluding to Cinderella, given our dance, her running off, and the multiple calls to find her.

The remark must have worked because she agreed to have lunch with me a few days later. It was getting close to Valentine's Day, so I arrived at her ladies' boutique with a cute little card and a plant wrapped in a red bow. After meeting her daughter Cindy, we headed to a popular restaurant in town that business people like to frequent. This venue gave both of us what we needed—Peggy the security of being in public, and me the simple pleasure of being with Peggy. Was it fate? Or was this a God-thing? Peggy and I were to come into an understanding that there are no coincidences with God, there are God-incidences or events perfectly orchestrated by Him in accord with His perfect timing.

The Little Girl from South Texas—Peggy!

Peggy was eighteen years my junior—a fact that probably gave her a little more concern on our first date than it did me. I had always kept myself in tip-top shape and could outwork many guys half my age. At that point in my life, age never came into the picture when it came to pursuing my athletic lifestyle. Still, at sixty-four years of age, I am sure her imagination was running wild with just where all of this might go as we went through the ritual of getting acquainted.

Peggy was the mother of three wonderful children. Her oldest daughter, Debbie, was married and had a life of her own. Her middle child, Cindy, lived with Peggy and worked in the dress shop but was planning to get married in the near future. Her son, Chuck, had just completed high school.

Peggy had always been entrepreneurial and had owned several businesses in her lifetime. Life's circumstances had thrown her into the workforce at an early age, where she thrived due to her business acumen. Like all self-starters, Peggy was always looking to better herself and the circumstances of her family.

I was disappointed to learn at lunch that Peggy had decided to move to Rockport, Texas. Her plans were to get into the booming coastal real estate market as an agent. She was in the process of selling her dress shop and would be leaving the Hill Country of Texas. In Peggy's words, she was "on her way out." She had been offered a fabulous job managing and selling new resort condo sites; she would also be given a beautiful condo for herself. Getting into this line of work held the promise of astronomical rewards because at that time there was what you call in Texas "a booming market." All this she explained to me over lunch that day, and our time together was as comfortable as the dance we shared a week earlier. We soon learned that we had lots of things in common, such as our love of business, traditional values, sports, and, of course, dancing. When our lunch ended, I invited her out to Tapatio Springs, still hoping to impress her with my material self, in addition to my charm and dancing skills.

I was to learn that beneath that poised exterior, Peggy was really a little girl from South Texas. She had a tough, austere childhood—sharing time between her parents and her two grandmothers. This unique arrangement helped mold her personality, as she became the sum of those very different experiences. Her Christian grandmother nurtured a constant stability in her life.

When her parents were separated for long periods of time, Peggy would spend extended periods with each grandmother. These experiences were quite different and left distinct footprints on her life. One grandmother was grounded in life's more worldly endeavors, while the other, a devout Southern Baptist, read to her young granddaughter verse after verse from the Bible. She also made sure that she attended Sunday school and church each time the doors were opened. This was a critical part of her upbringing as they cultivated both her "street smarts" and her soul. All this made for an amazing woman who was about to walk out of my life just as my life was beginning to get interesting again.

Worth Thinking About

I learned in the supermarket business that to achieve success you must establish a goal, plan steps to get there, and then see these steps to conclusion. If you make mistakes along the way, you must be agile enough to change direction, plan another strategy, and continue to work diligently towards your goal. I also learned that you cannot change yesterday's mistakes, so why worry about them and lose focus on the day that is at hand? Had I not made these principles a big part of my life over the years, I doubt that there would ever have been a grand opening at Tapatio Springs. Looking at the grand opening crowd, I knew that this was a day I would treasure forever.

Not all business expenses are created equal. Had I done a little more due diligence, the hotel might have been more successful sooner and actually saved money in the long run. Let my experience be a learning lesson for you.

In a business venture, you have to keep "merchandising" a project to keep it new and exciting.

There are no coincidences with God; I prefer to look upon them as God-incidences, orchestrated by Him in accord with His perfect timing.

—Clyde B. Smith

31

The Whisper Silenced:
Lonely No More

*"There had been this constant sense of loneliness,
a gaping hole in my life that whispered to me at every turn."*
—Clyde B. Smith

After seeing Peggy a few times, I knew I would do whatever it took to put an end to her plans of moving to the coast. It had been a long time since I felt such moving feelings for a woman, and I was not going to let her go. Even though my time in Texas had been extremely busy, filled with distractions and challenges, there had been this constant sense of loneliness, a gaping hole in my life, that whispered to me at every turn. My time with Peggy seemed to silence that whisper.

Our courtship was one of the best times in my life. Peggy and I shared so many things in common. Like me, she was a workaholic and did not mind the time I devoted to Tapatio Springs. Peggy and I shared good common values, the kind you get from an Iowan farm and a small South Texas town. We both loved to laugh and embraced life with a passion every day. After a few dates, we started to go to church together at Castle Hills Baptist Church on Military Drive in San Antonio. These Sunday services set in motion a series of events that are still unfolding in my life now, more than twenty-six years later.

Peggy accepted Jesus Christ into her heart at the tender age of seven by the hands of an evangelical preacher in a dusty South Texas town. This salvation experience was the result of the love of her Christian grandmother. Peggy would be the first to tell you that she didn't always walk with the Lord from the date of her salvation, but in her own words, "There were several years when I made many, many mistakes after wandering around in the wilderness, but I never strayed very far from the path." As she says, "Thank God He does take us back and forgive us." Even after the death of her husband when he was still a young man, she and her children lived through the hard times with a peace knowing they were always in God's hands. Having Christ in her life gave her a constant in a life that had its ups and downs and its share of heartaches.

As we started to attend church together, Peggy began to talk to me about Jesus. Recounting her own experiences, those challenges and victories she had seen in her life, and the way Jesus became her compass, Peggy displayed a peace and conviction about her salvation that seemed in direct contrast to my own life.

The Contrast

When we were growing up, our family never went to church. Working to keep food on the table was our most important activity during the Great Depression. My mom had an old Bible that she would read to us, but we never understood the real meaning of salvation or heaven and hell. This did not mean we were estranged from God, but as times were so tough for us, a Sunday church service was just not a part of our life.

When I was seventeen years old, I walked the aisle with my grandfather, without the knowledge of really knowing why, while I was living in Ames, Iowa. My grandfather was a Sunday school teacher and encouraged me to accept Jesus into my heart. I did so at his urging but lost my way in the frenzy that was to become my life. Helen and I did take the girls to church each Sunday over the years, but I was 100 percent focused on building my business and effectively missed out on the building blocks of Christianity. I never took enough time for God or for prayer, no time for anything except my work and my own plans and thoughts. It was a very selfish thing on my part. I still regret being an absentee father and husband during the many years I committed to the supermarket industry. Success does not come without sacrifice of some sort.

Like many individuals, I thought that being a good person — ethical, compassionate, and generous — would some-how get you into heaven. Starting in my early adult years, I ran my business on these principals and gravitated towards people who shared these values. In my military years, my best friend was our platoon chaplain. Later when I made a life in Phoenix, Dr. Richard Jackson of the North Phoenix Baptist Church was among my closest friends. Being around these individuals reinforced my belief of being a good person as a way to serve the Lord. These fine individuals looked at life in a similar manner as I did, refrained from immoral acts, and were good, honorable people. In my mind, they conducted themselves much as I did, so I rationalized that I was surely walking on their same path.

Because I never dedicated the time to understand what they were really teaching in church, it took being around Peggy to help me understand that although I shared many of the same characteristics with these fine individuals, they had a critical distinction in their life that separated them from me. They had truly accepted Jesus Christ into their lives, living each day wrapped in His promises. Yes, on the surface we looked the same, but the more I dated Peggy, the more I realized that it was not like looking into a mirror.

Worth Thinking About

Success does not come without sacrifice of some sort.

God is the One who provides stabilizing strength in one's life.

Jesus became Peggy's compass. He enabled her to display peace and conviction about her salvation that was a witness to me and was in direct contrast to what had been taking place in my own life.

—Clyde B. Smith

32

A New Man in the Mirror

"It took my courtship with Peggy, the love of my life,
to bring into focus that, without accepting Jesus Christ into my life,
I really was a poor, penniless man. I might have had lots of
material things, but my soul was effectively bankrupt."

—Clyde B. Smith

By every measure of a man in today's society, I thought I had it all in 1983. If you've stayed with me this far in this book, you know I left our farm in Iowa in 1937 with five dollars in my pocket and ended up a multimillionaire. I had been an innovator in the supermarket industry and had pioneered the superstore concept in 1962. I was fortunate to be recognized by my peers with a board appointment to the Supermarket Institute, where I received numerous honors for the contributions that Smitty's made to the industry.

I had three wonderful daughters and a growing bunch of grandkids. I had a wide circle of friends that included the likes of Jimmy Dean, Joe Garagiola, and Glenn Campbell. I was blessed to have spent so much of my life with my brothers Doug and Swede and to have all the memories we shared together. Then there were the wonderful Smitty's employees that became my family on our retail trip through life.

Along my way in getting to 1983, I picked up an airplane, a pile of cash, and an impressive real estate portfolio that included

Tapatio Springs. I had financial freedom that most people dream of and the time to enjoy it. I had experienced some of life's heartaches when I lost my brother Swede, my daughter Karen's first husband, and my divorce from Helen, but when my life was measured by success in America, I had it all.

It took my courtship with Peggy, the love of my life, to bring into focus that without accepting Jesus Christ into my life, I really was a poor, penniless man. I might have had lots of material things, but my soul was effectively bankrupt, mortgaged to the unknown. Just looking at Peggy, and how she conducted her life, I knew that without a real commitment to my salvation, I would never be a wealthy man in God's eyes. At some point during our life-changing courtship, I quieted my busy, sometimes frantic life, while I tried to make sense of just where I was and where I was going.

I walked the aisle with Peggy by my side in August of 1983 and accepted Jesus Christ as my Savior, knowing this time what had happened in my heart and what I was doing. I knew right then that I wanted Jesus to walk by my side for the rest of my life, along with this very special woman.

I somehow knew that everything that had happened in my life had been a series of events to get me to this church, in front of this pastor, standing shoulder to shoulder with Peggy. God molded my moral fiber as a child, kept me safe in the war, allowed me to have bountiful success in business, moved me to Texas, and put me at that seminar. These were the pieces of my life that were finally forged together on that Sunday in August when I asked Jesus to come into my heart. God had been leading me to this point in time. It was now clear — the reflection in the mirror showed a new man.

Learning to Walk the Walk

Peggy and I were married on September 28, 1983. We had a private service in the office of Pastor George Harris, with Linda Harris in attendance. Both Peggy and I were committed to being totally focused on each other as we were joined together. We decided to forego the usual commotion that comes with family and friends on such a big day. We wanted this moment to be as special as it could be. We could think of nothing more special than the quiet of looking into each other's eyes as we became man and wife.

As both Peggy and I were admitted workaholics, we also decided to forego a honeymoon in favor of going back to work at Tapatio Springs right away. I am sure that there were a few detours before we showed up back at work, but all we could think of in those days was making Tapatio Springs a success.

Peggy reminds me that at one point in my discouragement I had actually said, "I think I'll bulldoze the whole place." She said, "Clyde, we can do this together." She recognized that growing supermarkets was vastly different from building a resort, and that working together, we could make a great team. When she joined me in my efforts to make Tapatio Springs a positive venture, she agreed to handle the real estate sales at the resort and soon had things moving. She also became one of the biggest cheerleaders for the project, which helped breathe new life into my efforts. It felt good to have a champion in her, since I had been going it all alone for the past few years.

It was no secret that Tapatio Springs had challenged me from that very first day. Time and time again, things just seemed not to work out as planned. This was a very frustrating time in my life because I had achieved such a level of success with our supermarkets that I measured the resort by an unrealistic yardstick. When things went off track, which they did constantly, the buck stopped on my desk, seven days a week! It was a lonely job, and before Peggy, there was no one to share in this challenge.

Within months, Peggy and two of her children had taken management roles at the resort. Her daughter Debbie took over our clubhouse dining and catering operation, with her son Chuck working at the hotel and then becoming club manager. Peggy assumed various roles in real estate sales and became a trusted confidant to me. While neither of her children had extensive backgrounds or experience in the resort business, they had good business minds and were, most of all, trustworthy. They learned quickly and contributed greatly. Peggy and her children added a new dimension to my life. I had so many poor experiences with unscrupulous people associated with the resort that it felt good to have family looking after the best interests of the project.

Over the next few years, Tapatio Springs began to move forward, giving Peggy and me time to enjoy growing together as husband and wife. This period of our life afforded us time to travel on occasion. We enjoyed going to Las Vegas, where I introduced Peggy to the bright lights and some small time gambling. During my supermarket years, Vegas had been part of my recreational ritual a few times a year, where I enjoyed playing cards and an occasional visit to the dice table.

I had managed to miss most of life's vices over the years. I took a drink with friends occasionally and bet a little on my golf game. But when it came to card playing, I was kind of hopeless. I enjoyed a good poker game now and then, with wagering making the game that much more fun. You might remember that I won a pillowcase full of money on the ship returning home from World War II. That money became the seed money for my first store. To me, gambling was harmless fun, which was rocket fuel to my competitive nature.

In the first few years of our marriage, Peggy seemed to enjoy the vestiges of my old lifestyle. Like me, she enjoyed a good card game and our trips to Vegas. Once in a while, we would take her children and their spouses with us, which was a new and unusual experience for them. It was heartwarming for me to see her enjoy the freedom of our airplane and the perks I could afford on our trips.

My growth as a Christian during these years was slow at best. I continued to cling to my old ways in spite of the direction I was getting from the Bible and church. I knew down deep that my life had truly changed that day when I gave my life to Christ, but still I continued to take control on my own, not allowing God to lead and guide me more often than I really like to admit.

Stunted Growth

My slow growth as a Christian became a source of irritation the longer we were married. Peggy and I had much in common: our devotion to our work, good ethics, love of family, and our love of the Lord. Unfortunately, our paths started to diverge when it came to walking the walk of a Christian. For the first few years of our marriage, Peggy went along with my old lifestyle and ways at times, but I honestly now think she was just giving me time to mature. Even though I was consistently reading Scripture and attending church, I was slow to change my lifestyle as the Bible told me to do. Some four or five years after marrying Peggy, I knew that my time of stunted growth had finally run out.

Like all married couples, Peggy and I had our differences from time to time. Most of this was just our egos, as we are both headstrong individuals. Our differences were usually short-lived, with one of us sending up the white flag soon after they started.

By this time, Tapatio Springs had become a beautiful country club and resort. It continued to challenge me, though, and was not as profitable as I had hoped for. Texas had entered into a long, deep recession beginning in 1985 and was struggling from its effects. The Texas economy had been on fire for the ten years prior to the downturn, fueled by speculation in the oil business and real estate. By 1989, the whole Texas economy had collapsed from excessive optimism and easy money driven by the state's banks and savings and loans companies.

Tapatio Springs was not immune to the problems plaguing the Texas economy. Numerous real estate repossessions, along with an absence of bank credit, made selling our projects within the resort that much harder. I continued to fund our needs at the resort with a hope that the Texas economy would rebound soon. It was one more challenge, in a long string of challenges, that I had encountered since I first turned dirt at Tapatio Springs.

Tapatio Springs had matured into a beautiful resort with a first-class golf course, which was rated in the top ten best golf resorts in Texas. We had built several multifamily projects, along with sections of estate-type homes scattered around the grounds. Our clubhouse and pro shop had been well received by the members, and both businesses held their own against the tough times we were in. I was especially proud of our dining room and the excellent food served to our guests. Having extensive experience in the restaurant business because of our stores, I knew that good food was critical to our project's long-term success. Being consistent in food service is a monumental struggle, but it is vital in a project such as Tapatio Springs.

All this brings me back to the differences that Peggy and I had been having for quite some time. In spite of how wonderful Tapatio Springs had become during our years together, in reality, we owned a bar masked in the legitimacy of a country club. It became hard for us to go to church on Sunday, knowing that one of our staff members might have sent our patrons to their cars drunk on the night before. We believed so strongly in the importance of strong families, morals, and values, and we began to see alcohol as the hammer that beats on families, fidelity, and moral behavior. Both of us had seen the devastating effects that alcohol can inflict on families and individuals. Peggy and I had a drink now and then, but by the time we had been married four or five years, this became very rare. Neither of us could see what good really came from the effects that alcohol had on the mind and body.

For me, the decision to have alcohol at Tapatio Springs was purely a financial necessity. Since I could remember, alcohol had been the lifeblood of every country club I had been in. It was an institution, just like the pro shop and the dining room. It was also a huge generator of profits from both members and corporate clients, often being the line between profitability and loss. Alcohol was part of the timber of every country club in America if not the world.

For Peggy, serving alcohol had become a violation of her belief system. For her, there was not enough money or profit on Earth to separate her from God. When she was in conflict, Peggy always looked to Scripture for direction. The direction she was getting was that we could not own a bar and still set an example for Christ. My wife, in particular, was, and is, what George Barna, renowned pollster, calls a revolutionary. In his book *Revolution*, Barna says, "Revolutionaries invariably turn to God's Word, the Bible, for their guidance." I, too, discovered that I wanted to be a "no-holds-barred follower of His." Peggy reminded me that God didn't send Jesus to die so that we might be comfortable and complacent but that we were to set an example by the way we lived as representatives for the Lord. In this regard, sometimes I was a slow learner.

We both drew lines in the sand concerning the bar at Tapatio Springs. For months, this subject was to be a flashpoint in our marriage, which would test our bond as a couple. It was not that I did not share the same convictions as Peggy, but I had been a businessman most of my life and knew the financial consequences involved. The collapse of the Texas economy going on around us just reinforced my financial fears.

I continued to pray for a way out of this situation. I knew that my growth as a Christian had been slow, but I felt that I was making good progress. Since accepting Jesus Christ into my life, I had really changed in so many ways. However, I still clung to a way of thinking that often stood in my way of growing closer to God. I had spent too many years outside of God's word, and my default mechanism when confronted with adversity was to look at the world through a non-scriptural vision that had been validated over many years. This thinking kept me from seeing the obvious solution that was just beyond my reach.

God Answers My Prayers; a Simple Act of Faith; a Sense of Obedience

It was a fall day in 1989 when I knew that God had answered my prayers. Peggy and I both got up that day instinctively knowing that the wall that had been dividing us was beginning to crumble. This wall also had been a division between me and God. On this particular morning, I could feel a renewed energy as a Christian, knowing that the wall was coming down. He had finally given me the answer.

Peggy and I arrived at the Country Club shortly before 10:00 am. The usual crowd of golfers was now on the course, with the morning breakfast group gone. The club was quiet, and there was little movement from the staff. The sun shone through the large glass windows in the dining room, highlighting a perfect Hill Country day.

Before we left the house, we called two of our church friends to join us at the club. When they arrived, we walked into the bar, joined hands, and joyfully gave praise to God for this final decision. The four of us then took stock of the job at hand and began pouring the bottles of liquor down the drain, one by one.

We took several hours to pour over $70,000 worth of hard liquor down the drain. If there was any hesitation in my heart with that first bottle, it was gone a few minutes into our mission. I just knew that with each empty bottle, I felt a sense of obedience to God.

Looking back, I recall a surreal experience as we poured the liquor down the drain that day. Try as I might, I can't remember any questions from the staff or interruptions from the members. I just remember the joy Peggy and I felt as we finally established Jesus and our Christian principals as the most important things in our lives. I was a grown man who had been around the block more than a few times, so this simple act of faith was done with my eyes wide open. My trust in Jesus told me that He would deal with any consequences that came from this bold Christian step.

The End of a Very Difficult Road

When we finished with the hard liquor in the bar, I gathered up some of the staff and loaded my pickup truck with all the beer that was in the bar and storeroom. We then headed up fully loaded to our garbage site on the property. Once there, I instructed the staff to unload the beer and then start opening the cans pouring the contents on the ground. You can imagine the shocked expressions on their faces.

These guys were workers who maintained and worked on the golf course, and I could tell by the confused look on their faces that they thought I had lost it. I am sure that they could not fully understand why I had instructed them to pour all of this perfectly good beer onto the ground. In the back of their minds, they were probably wondering why I just didn't give them the beer for a big Saturday night party.

As the beer pouring celebration came to an end, the crew was laughing and joking about what had just happened before their eyes. The sound of their laughter added to the joy in my heart, lifting my spirits even higher. Seizing on the moment, I jokingly lined them up and frisked them, asking them to show me that their pockets were empty before I allowed them to get back into the truck. There would be no "one for the road" on our ride back to the club.

As I rode back to the clubhouse, I knew that I was at the end of a very difficult road. I had come to a fork in the road of my life that day, and I had chosen the road that would lead to my continued growth in Christ. I knew instinctively that the future would not be easy with this statement of Christian conviction, but I also knew that God would hold my hand from this day forward. He has.

A Real Test of My Faith

The reaction by the members and property owners at Tapatio Springs to my statement of faith was swift, emotional, and loud. As I suspected, the members and homeowners of the resort would be furious with my removing the bar with alcohol from the clubhouse and grounds. Their immediate reaction told me that this matter was not going away soon. Although I am sure that there were a few members who quietly supported my actions, the din of the vocal majority was all I heard in the weeks after removing the booze.

Ever the businessman, I did have a plan after the alcohol was gone as a fallback position. I really thought it would separate Tapatio Springs from all the other county clubs in the country. Just as I had marched to a different drummer in the supermarket business, Peggy and I prayed and had a peace with a unique plan for the club that we thought would fit in well to the changes we were seeing in America. Peggy says that deep down in her heart, she knew that we had made the right decision.

Our plan after removing the alcohol from the club was to turn Tapatio Springs into a health resort. It was our plan to enhance the facility with scenic jogging trails, state-of-the-art workout equipment, and healthy improvements to the menu in the dining room. In place of the traditional bar, we had planned a fruit and protein juice bar serving healthy concoctions to supplement the workout regimens of our guests. To us, this would put Tapatio Springs at the forefront of the fitness movement in America that was unfolding with the likes of Nike, aerobics classes, and the volume of fitness clubs opening nationwide.

I also wanted Tapatio Springs to have a true family feel to complement this move to health and fitness. I wanted a place where both young and old could come to enjoy the club's amenities in a spirit of Christian fellowship. I hoped Tapatio Springs would offer solitude to both our corporate and leisure guests where they could enjoy themselves without the earthly distractions such as alcohol, gambling, and infidelity. Peggy, being in marketing and sales, took immediate advantage of this concept contacting and booking the Fellowship of Christian Athletes. This group complimented our new concept by a week of meetings, training, and golf.

Having run a large corporation, I felt that many corporate clients would embrace the changes they experienced at Tapatio Springs. When I owned Smitty's, I was fortunate that I worked with the type of employees who went to a trade show or seminar to work and gain knowledge about the food industry. At most trade shows we attended, I saw my competitors partying and carousing their way through the shows, often plied with liquor by the suppliers. I thought that with the planned changes to Tapatio Springs, managers of large corporations would like their staff to be able to attend a seminar or event where the focus was not diluted with alcohol.

It was unfortunate that the members and residents of Tapatio Springs did not see the changes in the club as positive. From almost the first day, they made it clear that removing the alcohol was going to be a move that I would regret. They made their feelings known not only to me but also to anyone that would stand still and listen. Soon, the story of our bold change at the resort hit the San Antonio newspaper and was making the rounds of every country club, coffee group, and church in the immediate area. If I had any idea of this blowing over in a few days, I quickly learned that this was not going to happen.

Shortly after taking the bar out of the club, I invited the homeowners to a meeting in an attempt to calm the residents' emotions. I really wanted them to hear my side of the issue, including liability reasons for removing the alcohol. I had hoped they would offer me a semblance of courtesy and at least hear me out.

When I walked in the meeting, I felt like Daniel walking into the lion's den once I heard the tone of the crowd. There were several opinion makers in the group, and they were very vocal about my stance on the alcohol. One guy with a small, crying baby plopped down next to me and opened a can of beer. His rude behavior just added fuel to the crowd's emotions.

Needless to say, the meeting did not go well. The crowd accused me of destroying property values with the changes I planned for the club. They also accused me of using my position as developer to force my beliefs on them. This was not my intent. As the meeting dragged on, they did not want to hear about how family values and fitness would now be the new fundamentals of the club. They just wanted their booze and were set on destroying my reputation if I did not bring it back.

The Fallout and the Dwindling Bottom Line

It was not long before I was being served with several lawsuits by certain homeowners over taking the alcohol out of the club. The steps I had taken to honor our moral beliefs and standards were now headed to court. As a businessman, I was disappointed with the turn of legal events, but as a Christian, I was not fearful of what might come. God would protect Peggy and me, no matter what residents and members did. Nevertheless, Peggy suggested we call our knowledgeable and trusted friend, Pat Craus, to discuss the situation. We valued the counsel of Pat, a very successful developer in the Fort Worth area. Pat came to our home and counseled and prayed with us. The matter was finally resolved with the members.

As time wore on, my Christian bravado began to wane. I was human, and there was so much emotion tied to the alcohol event that I began to think, "God, is this going to work?" A friend told me that God understands about our humanness; after all, He became one of us! Like the reactions from the residents, the financial consequences were swift. We had several corporate clients cancel events, and real estate sales slowed to a trickle. We did have a pickup in business from Christian groups, along with several corporate groups such as AT&T, the Spurs Basketball team, and Valero Refining, who liked the new format and wanted this type of environment for their employees and Christian retreats.

It was difficult to get the businessman out of my head and accept the deterioration in business that was going on around me. Remember, the Texas economy was as bad as it could be at the time when we removed the bar. The problems at Tapatio

Springs were now worsening because of the poor economy and what I had done. Even though I constantly prayed to God for guidance, it was difficult to reconcile my instincts as a businessman and my newfound Christianity with a dwindling bottom line.

Soon my backsliding on the decision about removing the bar became a huge problem between Peggy and me. She saw the liquor going down the drain as a critical step in my growth as a Christian. It was the right thing to do for all the reasons I have pointed out. I had made the decision freely on my own accord, but now, unfortunately, there was doubt due to the problems that engulfed Tapatio Springs.

I was now in a battle on two fronts: the war over the booze with the homeowners and members consumed my time at the resort and the differences with my wife Peggy at home. I wanted to mature in my walk with God and honor Him by being obedient, but while I was trying to get things right in a new Christian life, I also had a ton of money on the line. A large staff depended on me for a paycheck.

After several months of disagreeing with Peggy over this issue, I knew things had finally come to a boiling point when Peggy cleaned out her desk at Tapatio Springs and went home. She instructed her daughter Debbie to cancel her appointments and to fill in for her as best she could. Peggy was done with me second-guessing the Lord. She was going home to stay.

We had built a large estate home on a hill that overlooked the resort by this time. Peggy retreated to this sanctuary, where she prayed to God for our marriage and guidance in this matter every day. There was not a day that she did not look down on the resort and cry for her life with me and those things we shared each day together. Besides being husband and wife, Peggy and I were now committed to making Tapatio Springs successful. We were a great team, and she often wept about now being on the outside looking down on a life she truly loved, but she knew God would do something.

Trust and Obey; Let Go

Peggy was to stay isolated in our home for thirty days. She would later tell me that her decision to clean out her desk and sever her ties came from God. Peggy recalls that it was a very definite experience when God laid it on her heart that if she would just get out of the way, He would take care of Clyde Smith and this resort. She would just have to trust Him by turning away and letting go.

On September 28, 1990, exactly thirty days from the time God told Peggy to leave the resort, I sold Tapatio Springs to Jack Parker and his business partner. It was our sixth wedding anniversary, and I could think of no better gift to my love than the sale of the resort. I had known Jack Parker for quite some time, and I felt that he would be a good steward to take over the project. Jack had accepted the Lord into his life in the spring of 1990. Jack was less troubled about owning a traditional resort with alcohol. The sale to Jack and his partner would liberate me from the conflicted emotions I had been feeling since the liquor went down the drain. It would also be the first step in having Peggy back by my side.

I walked away from the sale of the resort to Parker and his associate both happy and somewhat sad. I was happy that God had allowed me to experience this turn of events by being tested in His name for the past year. I admit that I backpedaled from time to time, but in the end, I was proud that I had remained firm in my Christian commitment. To show how sincere I was in my intent, the sale to Jack Parker was made at a huge financial loss; but while I was sad because Tapatio Springs was now out of my life and I had spent so much of the past ten years absorbed in the resort, I knew that I would miss it, but it was the right thing to do. Tapatio Springs represented a new start in my life, a do-over of my business career, and now it was gone. This was a turn of events I could not have imagined in a million years. It was hard to believe I sold the resort and at a staggering discount.

After the sale, Peggy and I went on an extended trip to Hawaii for a much-needed honeymoon. It was also time for me to draw closer to God without the distractions I had gone through with the resort. As God always does, he had a small Hawaiian church that was in dire straits cross our path. We were able to help them rebuild their church building, working there for three months along with several other volunteers. This hard work eventually rebuilt their membership, which is still growing to this day.

Peggy and I drew closer to each other doing God's work with that little church. It was nice to put our money and energy into something that would honor Him, while giving His children in that small Hawaiian town a place to worship. Like our marriage, the timbers of that little church are still standing today as a tribute to His miraculous ways.

Almost ten years before the sale of Tapatio Springs to Jack Parker, I had purchased Thunder Valley Ranch with a dream. I wanted to build a unique, one-of-a-kind golf course and resort that would do for the resort business what our "superstore concept" had done for the supermarket industry. I had headed to Texas with high hopes of accomplishing great things, only to be challenged with adversity at every turn. Along my journey, I met some really good people, got to play golf on a course I helped design and build, learned how to be an innkeeper and developer, met my wonderful mate for life, and found Jesus Christ. I will be the first to admit that as these steps were unfolding, I could not understand why all that had happened. Now it all seems to make perfect sense.

Eyes Opened: Transformation

It took our Lord to bring me through a series of changes in my life finally to open my eyes. It was our Father that uprooted my world, brought me to a small Texas community, barraged me with a series of business challenges, and then led me to Him. I had always done things my own way since I was a kid. The Lord just let me think that the series of interconnected events that had happened since I sold the stores were my idea. Just like our superstore concept, it was a spectacular, one-of-a-kind way to bring this Iowan farm boy to Him. The Lord knew the end result, and I praise Him daily for the many events that took place in this transformation.

I pray that God will continue blessing our families and our beautiful country, America. It is my prayer to the readers of my book that you, too, may find Jesus Christ as Savior and that God blesses you in a mighty way.

Worth Thinking About

We saw alcohol as the hammer that beats on families, fidelity, and moral behavior. We had seen the devastating effects that alcohol can inflict on families and individuals. Neither of us could see what good really came from the effects that alcohol had on the mind and body . . . . When she was in conflict, Peggy always looked to Scripture for direction. The direction she was getting was that we could not own a bar and still set an example for Christ . . . We joyfully gave praise to God . . . and poured the bottles of liquor down the drain, one by one . . . It took several hours to pour over $70,000 worth of hard liquor down the drain. If there was any hesitation in my heart with that first bottle, it was gone a few minutes into our mission. I just knew that with each empty bottle, I felt a sense of obedience to God. I knew that I was at the end of a very difficult road. I had come to a fork in the road of my life that day, and I had chosen the road that would lead to my continued growth in Christ. I knew instinctively that the future would not be easy with this statement of Christian conviction. I also knew that God would hold my hand from this day forward. He has.

—Clyde B. Smith

Epilogue

Traveling On: The Journey Takes on New Meaning

"Every generation wades through the murky waters of life's meaning. The discovery process is never easy, and the answers are often a long time coming. The eternal struggle to find meaning in life, which cannot occur without recognizing how God has designed and made us and how to apply that design to the context in which we live, is in full force today."

—George Barna
from his book *Revolution: Finding Vibrant Faith Beyond the Walls of the Sanctuary*

Smitty Notes
Just a personal word from the compilers of this material

John Trice and Helen Hosier

In going through Smitty's notes, we were deeply touched as we saw the heart of this kind, wonderful man. His love for the Lord so moved upon him day after day throughout his long career—even though earlier on in his life he didn't fully comprehend. It showed itself in the way he treated others and skillfully wove together the fabric of his life and businesses. We have chosen to put together in these final pages some of the thoughts of an extraordinary life well-lived.

About Your Talents, Abilities, Your Work, Your Investments, and the Future

Your talents and abilities are wasted if you don't plan your work and your investments. Go to prayer. Ask God to give you direction. Financial planning is life planning under God's leadership. Where your heart is, your treasure is also. Fast and pray. Ask God to show you what you need to do about your future. God will give you direction; you can trust Him—do it.

Reasons You Should Consider the Retail Business as a Career

Retailing is one of the biggest businesses in the world, and it is a vitally essential one. As long as people live, they must eat to survive.

Obviously, such a large industry can offer exceptional career opportunities. In a retail store you can learn the fundamentals of business: buying, advertising, salesmanship, accounting, and public relations — all elements of the free enterprise system.

There is direct contact with millions of consumers.

Retailing directly supports many industries and individuals, such as food technologists and processors, transportation companies, advertising agencies, fixture and equipment manufacturers, refrigeration engineers, packaging and container industries, and many, many more. Contact with such a wide variety of industries and individuals offers vast learning opportunities.

As a retail business professional, you are a vital part of your community, and you are respected because it is recognized that the highly competitive nature of retailing requires very talented management and personnel. Responsible positions in retailing earn much more for you in immediate returns and future security than is offered in many other fields.

The retailer's responsibility is to gather thousands of products from all over the world and offer them to the consumer in a clean, attractive, and inviting atmosphere at a reasonable cost.

Courteous, friendly, knowledgeable, and well-trained employees will always be needed to help merchants attain their goals. Job security, therefore, for the most part, remains stable. In working in retail, you are providing yourself with meaningful employment accompanied by excellent benefits for yourself and your family.

Being the biggest industry in the retail business makes the competition very keen, so the supermarket that does the best job in serving the customer will survive; weak or poorly run supermarkets will wilt and die. The difference between successful and unsuccessful stores is not just the price of a can of peas, or the advertising, or anyone of a number of different things. The difference is in people: the manner in which you convey to the customers that you care about them and the courteous service which you provide. You must have a real desire to be of service if you want to be a success in the retail business.

If you can't cultivate the idea of serving the needs of the American family in a pleasant and sincere manner, then you have chosen the wrong occupation and would do yourself and the company for which you work an injustice to continue in this field; however, if you do have this positive attitude toward people, then proceed with great energy and vigor because you will succeed.

If you have the talent, desire, and dedication, the opportunity to advance to nearly any position of your choosing — managerial, supervisory, buying, and merchandising, to name just a few specialized areas — awaits you.

About Prayer and Being Prepared

Don't pray just because it seems to be the thing to do. Cry out to God to hear your prayers. He is a prayer-hearing and a prayer-answering God.

If you want to be sure He is listening, make sure you are right with Him. The way to do that is to repent, to tell Him you are sorry for sinning. If you have never done so, invite Jesus into your heart. In reading the Old Testament book of Amos, who was just a shepherd and fig grower from Judah, in Israel, I heard him say, "Prepare to meet your God. . . . Seek the Lord and live" (Amos 2:12; 5:6).

Preparing to meet God is the most important thing we can do in our entire life. Get right — be right — with God. Judgment will come; one day you will stand before God to be judged. We all will die; we don't have to fear that when we are right with God. Make sure you are a child of God by accepting His Son, Jesus, into your life, and you will be saved.

About Obedience

Learn to obey — to be obedient. Life is too short to waste. Every one of us will die; make the most of every day. Resist temptation. Just realize that we are all sinners, and we need Jesus in our lives. We need to be daily obedient and devoted to Jesus, our loving Savior.

Since this is a book about the retail journey to success, you could summarize these thoughts like this:

Success Comes From
- Dreaming and having a vision.
- Commitment
- Dedication
- Determination
- Daring and trusting God
- Having faith
- Repenting
- Asking God to come into your heart.

Key Points to Success to Pursue and Recognize

- Choose your field of endeavor carefully.

- America has many business opportunities to offer. This great country needs new and better concepts to serve the consumer better; therefore, jumpstart your God-given entrepreneurial gifts with the desire to own and operate your own retail establishment. Consider starting your own company after you have acquired knowledge and some operating capital.

- It's about you and your desire, your ambition, your experience.

- There are rules and guidelines to follow. There are work ethics and leadership qualities to develop. Be positive; maintain a good attitude; and seek to have a pleasing personality.

- Business can be fun, challenging, and rewarding. Build a team and share the rewards. These help to build a road to success.

- Learn to lead, be first with the best ideas, and let competition follow. Communicate. Delegate. Share the values of honor, integrity, and good character. Understand that there is dignity in simplicity.

- Stay focused. Set goals, short-term and long-term.

- Develop a team of experts who are disciplined and filled with ambition and desire.

- Have faith; trust in God. Recognize that He is going to give you what you need, not always what you want.

- Value time.

- Persevere, but be patient.

- Grasp the power of kindness, the influence of example, the obligation of duty, the wisdom of economy, and the joy of creating.

- Pleasing the customer should always be number one on your path to success.

Twelve Ways to Work and Leadership Secrets to Success

1. What you do and what you think is everything. Always be positive and think success, not failure.
2. Decide what your dreams and goals are. Write down your short-term and long-term goals, and then develop a plan to reach them.

3. Take action; goals can be reached. Make decisions, and then move on with your plan.
4. Continue to learn all you can by reading books, attending training seminars, and acquiring skills.
5. Be persistent and work hard. The harder you work, the better you become. Never give up.
6. Do your homework. Learn to analyze details. Get the facts and the input. Learn from your mistakes.
7. Focus your time and money on each project. Stay focused.
8. Dare to be different; be innovative. Don't try to follow others.
9. Learn to deal and communicate with others in an effective way; getting work done through employees is the secret to success.
10. Be honest, dependable, take responsibility, and learn the art of negotiation. Remember: success comes in "cans," not "cannots."
11. Be thrifty; don't spend more than you make. Put your savings to work for you.
12. Dream. Hold onto your vision. Conceptualize. Be determined and committed. Above all, have faith and trust in God.

Words of Wisdom

- Control your tongue. The tongue is hard to control. No one can tame it. It's small but powerful. The tongue is restless and evil, full of poison. Many of us need a bridle and a bit to control the mouth. Your tongue reveals your heart, the way it really is. Therefore, exercise self-discipline and take responsi-bility for what you say. The book of James in the New Testament teaches us much about what they call the untamable tongue (see chapter 3). There are 104 references to the tongue in the Bible.

- God makes the rules; listen to Him.

- By His grace we have been forgiven and saved.

- In two years, one learns to talk. It takes more than fifty years to learn to keep your mouth shut.

"Take Time" epitomizes what Smitty was able to incorporate into his lifestyle through the years.

No. 1   **To work.** It is the price of success.

No. 2   **To think.** It is the source of power.

No. 3   **To play.** It is the secret of youth.

No. 4   **To read.** It is the fountain of knowledge.

No. 5   **To worship.** It washes the dust of Earth from our eyes.

No. 6   **To love.** It is the sacrament of life.

No. 7   **To enjoy friends.** It is the source of happiness.

No. 8   **To dream.** It is the road to greater vision.

No. 9   **To laugh.** It is the music of the soul.

No. 10   **To plan.** It is the secret of being able to have time, to take time for the first nine things.

And the Journey Goes On

"Righteousness exalts a nation,
but sin is a disgrace to any people."
—the Bible, Proverbs 14:34 NIV

Following the sale of Tapatio Springs, Clyde and Peggy built a home for themselves on a ranch near Boerne, Texas—a home they and their extended family enjoyed very much because it had wonderful recreational features which afforded them long, leisurely walks, and plenty of fishing. Still, Clyde, businessman that he is and always will be, and Peggy, astute business-woman, felt God's call to build a beautiful, million-dollar lodge. "We had been reading John 4:14. This moved upon our hearts, resulting in Living Water Retreat Center." The year was 1993.

"Following the sale of Living Water Ranch, we purchased Mission Valley Ranch right outside of Boerne. Later it was bought by Kendall County, Boerne, Texas. This was in 2007. A large county park is being developed there."

Friends and business people who have been around Clyde and Peggy Smith five minutes say, "They will roll out a new blueprint for some future project."

That "something new" in 2008 was Smith and Smith Ministries.

"We sensed there was something else God was calling us to do, and that's when we decided to purchase a piece of property that had a building and a 70-foot gold cross as a landmark on Interstate 10 leading into San Antonio. You can't miss it— it's huge and beautiful. The building on the property was transformed into a workable facility. We formed a non-profit corporation called Smith and Smith Ministries to fulfill our present day-to-day calling."

Peggy described Smith and Smith Ministries, the work God has entrusted to them, in these words:

No traditional organized church.

No choir.

No committees.

No politics.

We have a building. It belongs to God; we just manage it for Him.

We have Pastor Larry Williams, who preaches and teaches three Sundays each month, and guest speakers or other pastors who come in.

We have an average of eighty to a hundred people who attend each Sunday.

We have a small nursery.

We have a "Revolutionary Teen-Team" where teens connect with Christ and He becomes their best friend.

We have a little café where everybody meets and has donuts and coffee.

We have our offices here.

We have a Love Worship Center.

We publish *The Privilege*, a monthly newsletter that has an ever-growing number receiving and reading it.

> I work with the EvangeCube, a tool for
> training in evangelism.

And that sums up the nonprofit organization called Smith and Smith Ministries started in the spring of 2008. They said this ministry was started so that they "could help with God's work all over the world."

Are they just being modest in describing what takes place in a business building turned into a place where people from all walks of life can fellowship, worship, and find God? Spend even a short amount of time with Clyde Smith's dear Peggy and one soon discovers that what comes from her mouth comes from her heart. Unrestrained words revealing those deepest feelings spill from Peggy as she relates what has happened and is happening. The truth is, however, that there is no real way to measure the impact this outreach into the beautiful Hill Country of southern Texas and beyond is having. "We don't call it a church because, of course, the body of believers is the church," says Peggy. "The building itself is just something that holds the body of believers. We actually prefer to call it an Evangelism Center."

"God's Call" Explained by Miss Peggy

"When I speak of God's call, I feel it's one thing to do business in the business world, but another thing to do God's work. You need to be called, to feel deep in your heart that what you are feeling is God's will for your life. That's just my opinion, but I'm speaking from experience. Clyde and I experienced this. And with this call and what we have been doing there has come great fulfillment. That's the way God works. He rewards and blesses obedience.

"We meet on Sunday mornings in the Love Worship Center. It's filled with people who now come regularly and others who drop in. We have a unique format and have the best praise and worship music as there are talented and gifted musicians who participate. We have an in-house audio/video young man and his father, both of whom are very creative. The messages from Pastor Williams and others meet the needs and help people in their journey with God. Someone gave me George Barna's book *Revolution: Finding Vibrant Faith Beyond the Walls of the Sanctuary,* and it describes what has prompted Clyde and me to do this.

"My oldest daughter, Debbie, is the administrator of the entire operation and is awesome at what she does. Among other things, we publish a newsletter called *The Privilege* with the subtitle, 'to serve and think big.' *The Privilege* is mailed monthly to approximately a thousand families. Debbie is one busy gal who does serve and think big.

"Clyde's passion is 'Bringing America Back to Righteousness,' an outreach which he does with a great deal of enthusiasm. Each month he has a space in the newsletter called 'As I See It,' where he shares from his heart. His concern focuses on the instability of the times in which we live. Clyde has lived long enough so that he sees with clear and keen vision the difference between the days when he was a young man and he and others went off to war, and our nation as it is now. Those young men did this with a deep sense of the need to safeguard our nation. Patriotism ran deep. And Clyde knows how citizens loved their country and the ways in which they showed that love then."

Bringing America Back to Righteousness

Clyde shares some of his thoughts. "It is because of my love for God and this great country that I am earnestly concerned for the direction we, as a nation, are headed. The Word of God informs us that 'Righteousness exalts a nation, but sin is a disgrace to any people' (Proverbs 14:34 NIV). We are also told that 'He will judge the world in righteousness; he will govern the peoples with justice' (Psalm 9:8 NIV).

"Every day my desk is flooded with letters from organizations and others who share this same concern. To bring America back to righteousness will take a true love for this nation. By 'true,' I mean a commitment to our once genuine values and morals, belief in God and His laws, and passionate prayers.

"We face many issues that are extremely crucial to our future as Christians. We must not be manipulated by those who would frighten us into making any decision that would go against God's laws and our Christian beliefs and convictions. We must hold steadfast to these things and stay in fervent prayer for our leaders and for America.

"The Bible tells us to love those who disagree with us, to love them enough to pray God would change their direction and hearts to follow Him and only Him and His commandments. We are reminded about our generation in Proverbs 30, which describes in detail how they act and behave. I believe we are living in and living out that 'faithless and perverse generation' Jesus talks about in Matthew 17:17.

"The need has never been greater for Christians to join together in an all-out effort to bring America back to righteousness. Here, at Smith and Smith Ministries, we value honesty, integrity, and quality in everything we do for the Kingdom of God. Under the leadership of the Holy Spirit, we are committed to assisting Christ-followers in pursuing the heart of God.

"Americans are privileged to live in a nation which was founded and established many years ago by our great forefathers on godly principles, but our country today is in need of a spiritual renewal. We must stand firm and uphold our nation's freedoms and independence. We must remember that the freedoms we enjoy are made possible and were secured by those who fought and many who gave their lives to keep us safe. Never forget that what we have was because of what Jesus did for us on the cross at Calvary. Psalm 33 reminds us that 'Blessed is the nation whose God is the LORD, the people he chose for his inheritance' (v. 12 NIV). Are we still a Christian nation, a God-fearing and God-honoring country?

"As we came to the concluding chapter of this book, the book *Saving Freedom*, by Senator Jim DeMint, was called to our attention. He tells of a television documentary he saw that included an interview with a former Soviet official who visited the United States. This dignitary was asked what impressed him most about the U.S. during his visit.

"The interviewer was surprised by the Soviet official's answer. He didn't mention the New York skyline, the grand monuments in Washington, DC, or America's beautiful mountains, lakes, and rivers. It was the grocery stores that impressed him the most! The Soviet visitor could not believe the incredible variety of goods in such abundance that he saw in America's grocery stores, and he was amazed at the diversity of shoppers and that the 'common' people could find what they wanted at prices they could afford, while the more affluent shoppers also found what they wanted in the same store.

"'The Soviet's answer did not surprise me because I had long considered America's grocery stores to be showcases of free enterprise,' wrote Senator DeMint. He explained that he knew a little about the grocery store business from his days as a stock boy and bag boy when he worked in a grocery store as a kid. After college, he had worked for a consumer product manufacturing company that marketed their products in grocery stores and later worked in advertising agencies that developed promotion plans for grocery stores. With such a well-rounded background, it is no wonder the senator appreciates the grocery store business as he does.

"Senator DeMint explained that the reason the Soviet official was so impressed with America's grocery stores was the Soviet grocery stores were a product of socialism, that is the state controlled what products were controlled and sold, selection was limited, and prices were high. The contrast between free enterprise and socialism is markedly clear to people who have lived under socialism.

"This account demonstrated for me once again my own story of freedom in America to choose and pursue what I set out to do already as a young man, out of the military service, receiving no handouts from the government, but by working hard, earning and investing my money wisely in what I felt qualified to do, and achieving success. This is true freedom, and I really appreciate what Senator DeMint said about grocery stores being showcases of free enterprise. He has amazing information in this book, and I also appreciated his chapter on 'The History of Faith and Freedom: Remembering the Source of America's Strength.' I recommend that everyone get his book *Saving Freedom* [published by Fidelis Books, an imprint of B&H Publishing Group, Nashville, Tennessee].

Grass Roots Conservatives and the March on Washington

"Peggy and I felt that we wanted to be a part of the September 2009 March on Washington. We felt it could be one way to let our voices be heard. We consider ourselves grass roots conservatives, and we were impressed when we heard that this would be a grass roots movement. People were coming from all over who cared deeply about our nation and the outcome of things being considered in Washington that would affect our children and grandchildren. We learned that there would be people from all walks of life and that it represented God-fearing, God-loving people who have made this country great by standing up for freedom. So we went.

"I guess you could say that I was another 'Mr. Smith Going to Washington,' only I had a wife by my side whose concerns match my own. We saw Republicans, Democrats, and Independents joined together, stepping up and asking the government to regain their sight of the powers they were granted as our duly elected representatives in our great capital. It was a strong and urgent call for them to remember the individual freedoms that are rightfully ours, to maintain a strong national defense, to honor our traditional values, and to respect the Constitution of the United States of America.

"It was a deeply moving experience, the most patriotic involvement my wife said she had ever experienced. As a

WWII veteran, I had experienced those emotions before, but as I marched side by side with other veterans, doctors, lawyers, farmers, small business owners, homemakers, businesswomen, teenagers, and college students, once again, I, too, was overcome with my own emotions. Neither Peggy nor I will ever forget the elderly man marching along, bracing himself with a wooden cane as he walked.

"We witnessed approximately two million people singing 'God Bless America.' It seemed that we probably rocked heaven's pearly gates as we honored God and stood for what we knew was the right thing to do. And by the way, the secular media got it all wrong when they reported on thousands marching! What an underestimate that was! It was a peaceful march, very respectful, and we are proud to have been shoulder to shoulder with our fellow Americans in the nation's capital to let our presence and voices help make a difference before it is too late for the America we love and want to see preserved.

"There is much to do in the critical days that lie ahead. We must pray for God to get us, as Christians, back on track and that we stay under the spiritual authority of the Father and His directives to us that we find in the Bible, His Word, to us.

"In our work with 'Bringing America Back to Righteousness,' I now spend much of my time and energy in reading and assimilating the information about what's going on in this country that comes to me through the Internet, e-mails, blogs, and the mail. Then I contact and inform others, including a vast number of letters I send to our senators and congressmen in Washington, and I encourage others to do the same. Much of it may be falling on deaf ears, and it can be very discouraging. I want to see things done right, but we must keep on with our efforts. Peggy, with her big vision and big heart, thinks big, and she encourages me to do the same."

Thinking Big with Jesus at Your Side

Peggy Smith reminds herself, her husband, and others who will listen, that God searches hearts for the visionary that thinks big. "Because, remember," she says, "He is the CEO. Being available with faith in Him to guide, instruct, and sustain is the reason you can think big because He is big.

"I realized long ago that I do think big when I feel the Holy Spirit's leading to do something for the Kingdom. I have only to remember that Jesus told His disciples that if they would have faith as small as a mustard seed, they could move mountains (see Matthew 17:20). And those words are for us also.

"It is a privilege to finish the work we are called to do. He will supply all our needs, and we then can find it exhilarating and fulfilling to think big as God desires for His children to do. We must not allow the enemy, Satan, to bring fear and doubt, causing us to begin thinking something can't be done. We have God's promises to sustain us. After all, if God is the Creator of the universe, how could we doubt His equipping us to meet the challenges and follow as He directs?"

At Every Turn of the Cube

Peggy Smith found a tool that helps equip her to take the story of Jesus and His love into the world. It is a seven-picture cube of the life, death, and resurrection of Jesus Christ. At every turn of the cube in the hands of the presenter, the story of Christ's sacrifice unfolds before the eyes of the viewer. Just like the message of the Gospel, the images of the cube transcend all cultures and languages, and the EvangeCube is being used in many countries. Even in the hands of a child, the cube is a wonderful means of sharing Jesus. One of the primary visions and goals of Smith and Smith Ministries is to equip Christians who care about their lost friends, family, coworkers — anyone who needs to hear the Gospel story — and the cube is helping them do that.

"Our passion is to evangelize," Peggy says. "We can change the world with the simplicity of the Gospel using this small tool, the EvangeCube. If a church, Sunday school, or youth group wants to share the Gospel, we have a complete training program that will help in a dynamic outreach. We recognize that being confident when sharing is most important, and because the cube is equipped with pictures, it tells the story that Jesus saves. With this simple tool, we tell everyone 'You can do it!' The cube is available on our web site, www.SmithAndSmithMinisteries.org, and also by calling the Worship Center at 830-981-5344. The EvangeCube Ministries are out of Dallas, Texas. So we are motivated at Smith and Smith Ministries. For one thing, with every turn of the EvangeCube, I am hope-filled, believing that we are doing what Jesus would have us do. In this and other ways, seeking to fulfill what we, as Christians, call 'The Great Commission,' that is, Christ told us we are to go into all the world telling everyone and teaching all to obey the things He commanded (see Matthew 28:19, 20). And that's the reason this epilogue has been included at the conclusion of this book."

Worth Thinking About

"When freedom prevails, the ingenuity and inventiveness of people creates incredible wealth. This is the source of the natural improvement of the human condition."

—Brian S. Wesbury

"And now that the legislators and do-gooders have so futilely inflicted so many systems upon society, may they finally end where they should have begun: May they reject all systems, and try liberty; for liberty is an acknowledgment of faith in God and His works."

—Frederic Bastiat

"Government is not the solution to our problem; government is the problem."

—President Ronald Reagan

"It is essential, my son, in order that you may go through life with comfort to yourself, and usefulness to your fellow creatures, that you should form and adopt certain rules or principles, for the government of your own conduct and temper . . . . It is in the Bible you must learn them and from the Bible how to practice them. Those duties are to God, to your fellow-creatures, and to yourself. 'Thou shalt love the Lord thy God, with all thy heart, and with all thy soul, and with all thy mind, and with all thy strength, and thy neighbor as thyself.' On these two commands, Jesus Christ expressly says, 'hang all the law and the prophets.'"

—President John Quincy Adams

Clyde's Daughters Speak Their Hearts

" . . . children are a heritage from the Lord . . . "

—the Bible, Psalm 127:3

Children are very special and dear to a parent's heart. Mr. Smitty was father to three beautiful daughters. Clyde's youngest daughter, Karen, and husband were killed in a tragic motorcycle accident July 1, 2007.

Clyde's daughters: Sandra, Linda, Karen

These letters from Clyde's two remaining daughters reveal their love and respect for their father. Here are the letters which brought tears and joy to their father's heart.

Dear Daddy,

One of my first recollections of you is of a man that I didn't know very well, who had just come back from the army, taking a bath in our three-legged tub. When I came into the room, you asked me to leave (to give yourself a bit of privacy). I remember saying, "You can't reach me." That was probably the last time that you couldn't reach me, for you have been one of the most influential persons in my entire life. The very person that I have become is in great measure due to that influence.

Because you were busy building a company that would support and sustain us, you may not have been fully aware of just what you meant to your three girls as we were growing up. You were the daredevil that taught us how to put cherry bombs under tin cans. You were the outdoorsman who could find the fish, bait our hooks, remove our catch and put it on the stringer, all while running the motor and steering the boat. You were the successful, charming, and gregarious businessman with his picture in the paper, his jingles on the radio and his name on the stores. You were invariably the scorekeeper in any game the family ever played and the ultimate arbiter of any dispute. You may even remember being called in to calm the situation after Karen tattled on Linda and me for getting stuck in the mud in our back yard.

Though I missed much of your incredible success as you were building the Smitty's chain of supermarkets in Phoenix, I still had the benefit of working with you in the Marshalltown store. There I not only learned marketing by working at the knee of one of the most gifted marketers the American grocery industry has ever seen, I also saw firsthand the power of team building, engaging others in a common effort, and leading by example. I came to understand the necessity for commitment and hard work and unwavering resolve to be honest and fair in all dealings, whether with the rich and powerful or with a part-time sack boy.

When you gave me away to Gary, I started a new phase in my life. I was away from the direct influence of you and

Mom and my childhood home. But it was those intangible influences, imparted to me by my early home life, that guided me in making a home for my new family. Probably more than any of us knew, I wanted that family to reflect the values that you established. We wanted our children to be perfect, we wanted to be successful, and we wanted to live our lives and establish our careers in ways that would meet your standards and ultimately make you proud. We were certainly on that path when the Lord saw fit to bless us with Dirk. Somehow, that seemed to change everything. We now had to become almost full-time caregivers. Careers and success seemed less important, and the survival and development of our son had to take center stage. We have seen that situation drag down and split up many couples. We have seen families destroyed and children left confused and neglected by such circumstances. Yet that did not happen to us. We actually bonded more tightly, began to see the world in a more mature and thoughtful way and we found the strength to do what we had to do to sustain and support Dirk while making sure that Lisa received the kind of care and love in her upbringing to which she was entitled. In other words, we were especially blessed.

In the difficult years since we lost our Dirk, Gary and I have often pondered what it was that allowed us to face the challenge presented us and go on with our lives. I think it still comes back to what you, and my early life with you, gave me. It was you who taught me that toughness counts. Life won't always be easy or unfold according to our plans and desires. Adversity has to be met and overcome. I also internalized from my earliest years with you that toughness does not mean callousness or cruelty. It is possible to love, to grieve, to hurt, and still to persevere. I have always understood that others are counting on me and I don't have the luxury of wallowing in self-pity or unproductive depression.

In these, our later years, you are underscoring those lessons you taught me. You may never know how comforting *it is to me to see you still holding true to those concepts and that worldview that you passed on. In your nineties, you are still living the life you showed us by example. You care about this nation, and you are working to keep it strong and righteous. I know you are not doing this for you, but for the countless generations that will come after us to have the same opportunities and the same gifts that you and I and our loved ones received. You have clearly found the source of your strength in your total surrender to the will of our Lord. Daddy, the lessons just keep coming.*

Please know that I fully appreciate that your love, support, and example have, in large part, made me who I am today. Your continuing example gives me strength and direction in the present, and your legacy of honesty, integrity, commitment, hard work, concern for others, and unshakable faith in the power and love of Jesus Christ will sustain and mold me even after you have found your new home with our Lord.

I Love You,
Sandy

To the Reader: Sandy and Gary's son Dirk was a special-needs child. He passed away at thirty-two years of age. We loved and enjoyed him; he had a wonderful way about him which endeared him to each of us. His sweet humor was always delightful. See Photo in photo section.

An Ode to Smitty at Ninety
Well, what do you know,
It's the big nine-O.
You've got to wonder, where did the years go?
Young men have no end of choices.
They hear advice from many voices.
Some may say go east, and others west.
How would you know which was the best?
A miner, a soldier, a butcher, a baker.

It was clear you'd become a decision-maker.
But when you decided to move Smitty's out west,
It was plain to see you were truly the best.
You had to lead and make your way,
Through ups and downs, from day to day.
The challenges came from left and right;
You dodged the shadows and found the light.
The rewards were plenty and plain to see,
Family, friends, security.
Seizing every opportunity,
You became the best that you could be,
In the things that matter most in living,
Growing, striving, loving, giving.
Well, what do you know,
It's the big nine-O.
You have been through a lot,
But there is more to go.
You've found the Lord and will do His work,
What He asks of you, you will never shirk.
He's become the center of your life,
He's given you peace and calmed the strife.
Made wiser by all that has gone before,
Your efforts can be worth even more
Than those that came from a younger fellow,
Energetic and bright, but not as mellow.
Insight and perspective, the benefits of experience
Are the welcome gifts of true significance
That we hope will continue to be passed on
By our beloved, but feisty nonagenarian.
— Gary Sojka, son-in-law,
on the ninetieth anniversary of Clyde's birth.

Here is a letter also from Clyde's daughter, Linda, to honor her father.

Dear Dad,

Sandy's beautiful letter certainly captured everything that we cherish in you. The impact you had on your three girls, Sandy, Karen, and me, is incredible. You have shaped and molded us by your example. You have always "walked the walk."

Lifetime Lessons Learned from You, Dad:
- *That you must be tough but not indifferent.*
- *That when knocked down, you must pull yourself up and try again.*
- *That honor, fairness, and loyalty must be your credence in life.*
- *That giving back can be done every day, in small or large ways.*

From the time I can remember anything about you, Dad, you always gave back more than what you took from people and from your family to your community. Part of Smitty's success as a corporation was because of your belief that the employees would work hard and strive for excellence if they could share in the profits of the company; thus, profit sharing became part of Smitty's philosophy. Profit sharing not only benefited your employees but your entire family: Doug and Ann, Swede and Nadine, Mildred and Floyd, Sandy and Gary, Karen and her family, and certainly Tom and me. This, of course, filtered down to the grandchildren and great-grandchildren. We are eternally grateful to you, Dad, for your goodness and generosity.

If Karen were here today, she would thank you for all your love and support throughout the years, especially after Mark passed away. Dad, you were the only strong male role model Kristina and Steven ever had and you stepped up to the plate. Karen loved and admired you with all her heart and always truly was "Daddy's little girl."

As I close, I want to thank you for two things that have shaped the way I live my life. I want to thank you for the work ethic you instilled in me. I truly believe that work can solve the majority of our problems. Most importantly, I want to thank you for your spiritual leadership. Our ultimate goal in life is for the entire family to meet in heaven someday. Thank you for loving us enough to make sure we will all make that journey.

Dad, you are my hero, the man I look up to. God bless you always.

I Love You,
Daughter Linda

A Final Word from Smitty

"We have this hope as an anchor for the soul, firm and secure. . . . "
—the Bible, Hebrews 6:19a NIV

"As I read the scriptures describing the future, there seems to be a leader as well as a religious world system where the antichrist establishes control of the world. The last book in the Bible, the book of Revelation, tells us that Satan is the real power behind him. This is a book that many do not comprehend. Don't be so troubled by the timetable of the events or concerned with the details of the writer's imagery that you miss the main message — the love, power, and justice of the Lord Jesus Christ.

"The book of Revelation is a book of hope. John, the writer, the beloved apostle and eyewitness of Jesus, tells us that the victorious Lord will return to vindicate the righteous and judge the world, but this is also a book of warning. There are three elements of prophecy already at work, and I wish to call these to your attention:

1. The spirit of anti-Christ (Satan) is already operating in the world.

2. There will come a political, material, economic, and religious world system in the last days which is, in itself, "anti-Christ."

3. There will emerge a powerful individual who will control that system and use it for evil against God's people. Facts of prophecy stand clear as each day seems to bring us closer to this picture unfolding right before our eyes. God calls this picture the signs of Christ's return.

"So I say to the reader, listen to what the Word says; be full of hope, knowing that God is in control, Christ's victory is assured, and all who trust Him will be saved. A glorious Eternity awaits us. We know the end of the story: Jesus wins! And we get to be with Him forever and forever!"

About the Author

John Trice is a retired professional banker who has spent most of his career as marketing president of Frost National Bank, Texas. He has had many articles published in the *American Banking Journal* and the Padre Island *Business Bulletin*. He drew on his personal relationship with the Smiths to help tell this amazing American success story.

About the Author

Helen K. Hosier is well known in the field of Christian communications both as a writer and a speaker. Her forte is writing biographies. This bookstore-owner-turned-author has over sixty titles to her credit including the best-selling *Cameos: Women Fashioned by God, 100 Christian Women Who Changed the 20th Century, Living the Lois Legacy,* and *Step Up and Step Out.* Mrs. Hosier draws from her extensive background of interviewing hundreds of people, as well as from her reading and the research for her writing.

A Look Back

Photographs

Clyde and Ethel Smith, parents of Clyde B. Smith, in 1904.

The Smith children: right to left, William, Wilma,
Clyde, Ervin "Swede."

Before enlisting in the war in 1942: Clyde and Helen Smith
with their first daughter, Sandra.

Clyde Smith as Staff Sergeant, 2nd Platoon leader, Company C, 85th Regiment, 10th Mountain Division.

Smitty's first store in Roland, Iowa, 1947: left to right, Doug Smith, Amos Quam, Clyde Smith, Betty Hanson (cashier), Swede Smith.

Red Rooster Coffee "Something to Crow About" promotion, at Marshalltown store in 1949. The store was 40ft x 80ft. Notice the prices.

Marshalltown store in 1949. Iowa's biggest cake to date.

Super Valu's president and key personnel at the wholesalers and retailers meeting in Des Moines, Iowa, in 1949. My first speech on unusual promotions.

New 14,000-square-foot store in Marshalltown, Iowa, in 1955. Note: appearance and dress required of employees. See signs in window— donuts: $.39 per dozen, apples: $.05 per pound, catsup: 2 for $.29.

Big, new Marshalltown, Iowa, store. Check out the prices: 4 dozen oranges for $1.00, 2 dozen grapefruit for $1.00, 5 dozen tangerines for $1.00. This store had a scratch bakery and an on-premise restaurant, one of the first in America. Tony Witte, produce manager, on right.

Left to right, Clyde Smith and brother Swede Smith, year 1967.

AD BRINGS THANKS

Smitty's Big Town Stores with offices at 8302 E. Mc-Dowell, Scottsdale, has received wide acclaim, including a letter from aide to President Johnson, for full-page color advertisement in The Phoenix Gazette Dec. 20 that asked readers to "give thanks to our men in Vietnam this Christmas season." Clyde Smith, owner, showing copy of ad, also received "thanks" from Gen. W. C. Westmoreland, commanding general in Vietnam.

Ad in the Phoenix *Gazette* newspaper, President Johnson's aide thanking Clyde Smith after he advertised asking readers to give thanks to our men in Vietnam.

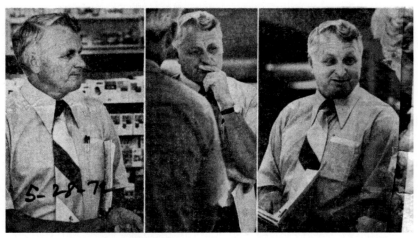

Interview with the Phoenix *Gazette* Newspaper, 1972.

Clyde Smith in Phoenix in 1973

Smitty's Iowa Palm Tree ad. Exterior of 35,000-sq.-ft. store in 1975. Note: there are corn leaves on the palm tree trunk.

Clyde Smith with Dave Trottier. Dave started working for Clyde in 1963. This picture was taken in 1978. Dave continued working for Mr. Smith and eventually became store manager and operator of the Springfield, Missouri, stores and ultimately owner.

Aerial shot of the number ten store in Tempe, Arizona.

A sample of the produce departments in Phoenix stores.

Who said it was all work and no play? Smitty's gang of key people fishing at Carroll Lake, Ontario, Canada.

A big catch! A big Walleye Pike! Clyde Smith at
Carroll Lake in Canada in 1972.

Clyde Smith and his three daughters.
Left to right: Linda, Clyde, Sandy, and Karen in Iowa in 1979.

Joe Garagiola and Clyde Smith in 1975, golf buddies and good friends.

President Ford and Clyde Smith, golf partners in 1975
at Joe Garagiola's Tucson Golf Tournament.

News article of Smitty's Third Annual Southwest Open shows Joe Garagiola, Clyde Smith, and Jimmy Dean. They were active in all five years of our tournaments.

Clyde Smith presents Valley of the Sun School for a check for $55,000 in 1980. Money raised by the annual Smitty's Golf Tournament.

T he entire resort is built around one of the most challenging 18-hole golf courses in the United States with an unsurpassed view of the Texas Hill Country. For the weekend golfer, an exciting, challenging 9-hole Executive course is also available. Country Club membership plans are available on a limited basis for both individuals as well as corporations.

A 96-room first class hotel provides the ideal setting for guests at Tapatio Springs. In addition to golf, the resort offers swimming, tennis, sauna, jacuzzi and exercise rooms.

The fine cuisine in the clubhouse restaurant is surpassed only by the spectacular view of the golf course. A perfect atmosphere of intimacy with service that isn't pushy or stuffy. Complement your meal with a fine wine from our wine list or order your favorite drink from our full service bar. Tapatio Springs has complete catering and meeting room facilities to accommodate groups up to 350. Whether you are planning a corporate conference, or simply need a weekend escape, Tapatio Springs is the truly uncommon place for you.

A new venture after the sale of Smitty's Supermarkets in 1980.
Tapatio Springs Country Club was developed and
opened for business December 1981. It is breathtaking!

September 28, 1983, may we present Mr. Clyde Smith
and wife, Peggy Smith.

Clyde and Peggy Smith, December 18, 2007, at the US Presidential
Candidate fund raiser, Dallas, Texas.

Peggy Smith's son, Chuck.

Peggy Smith's daughters, Cindy and Debbie.

Grandson Dirk Sojka who passed away July 18, 2002, at the age of
thirty-three. Dirk was a special-needs child. Dirk was the much-loved
son of our daughter Sandy and her husband, Gary, who said,
"We were so blessed to be his parents." Peggy and I were also
blessed to be Dirk's grandparents.